table of contents

pepper jack chicken pasta, pg. 114

This saucy Southwestern dish is ready in minutes due to help from packaged grocery items.

Mike Kirschbaum, Cary, North Carolina

Serve Up
home-cooked meals
in Less Time

Taste of Home Almost Homemade shows you just how easy it is to make home-style meals. The secret is to combine store-bought items such as packaged mixes, jarred sauces, precooked meats and refrigerated doughs...with fresh foods. Using these convenience items allows you to bypass time-consuming cooking steps, such as roasting peppers, simmering spaghetti sauces, mixing special seasoning blends and baking items from scratch. So much time is saved, that many of the **374** dishes in this collection require only **30 minutes** or less of hands-on prep work! Best of all, the scrumptious results are sure to please your family.

You'll be amazed at the variety of dishes you can whip up at home.

Entrees include: Three-Cheese Lasagna, Southwestern Beef Panini, Turkey Tostadas, Lemon Chicken with Rice, Upside-Down Pizza Bake, Saucy Southwestern Pork Chops and even Flounder Florentine.

Soups and side-dish choices abound: Veggie Meatball Soup, Chicken-n-Rice Soup, Sour Cream & Chive Biscuits, Green Bean & Corn Bake, Candy Bar Apple Salad and Rosemary Focaccia.

And for a fun treat, check out these dessert and snack options: Raspberry Swirl Cupcakes, Three-Fruit Shortcakes, Triple-Tier Brownies, Toffee-Almond Cookie Slices, Taco-Flavored Chicken Wings and Smackin' Good Snack Mix.

The recipes in this book were submitted by home cooks just like you. These are the ones that their familes enjoyed time and again, so you know your gang will be delighted with them, too. Every recipe was kitchen-tested and tasted by the cooking professionals at *Taste of Home*, the world's #1 cooking magazine. So, you can be assured that each and every recipe will work for you as well!

Treat your family to delicious dinners without the hassle of cooking for hours. With **Almost Homemade,** there is no "almost" about the great taste of these family-friendly recipes.

snacks & beverages

This cool, veggie-packed pizza is perfect for warm days. In an interesting "twist," breadsticks make for a fun, crispy crust idea!

Mary Ann Dell
Phoenixville, Pennsylvania

patio pizza

PREP/TOTAL TIME: 30 MIN.

1 tube (11 ounces) refrigerated breadsticks

1 teaspoon olive oil

1/2 teaspoon minced garlic

4 ounces cream cheese, softened

1/2 teaspoon dried oregano

1 can (14 ounces) water-packed artichoke hearts, rinsed, drained and chopped, divided

1 cup (4 ounces) crumbled feta cheese, divided

3/4 cup chopped tomato

1/3 cup coarsely chopped peeled cucumber

1/3 cup sliced ripe olives, drained

1/3 cup sliced onion

2 tablespoons pine nuts, toasted

1/4 cup balsamic vinaigrette

1 Unroll breadsticks. In the center of an ungreased 12-in. pizza pan, loosely wrap one breadstick around, forming a coil. Add another breadstick, pinching ends to seal and continuing to coil. Repeat with remaining breadsticks.

2 Roll or pat dough to within 1/2 in. of the edge of the pan. Brush with oil. Gently press garlic onto dough.

3 Bake at 375° for 14-16 minutes or until golden brown. Cool on a wire rack.

4 In a small bowl, combine cream cheese and oregano. Stir in 1/4 cup artichokes and half of the feta cheese; spread over crust. Arrange remaining artichokes on top. Sprinkle with tomato, cucumber, olives, onion, pine nuts and remaining feta cheese. Drizzle with vinaigrette.

YIELD: 8 SERVINGS.

warm broccoli cheese spread

PREP: 15 MIN. BAKE: 25 MIN.

I cut this spread out of a newspaper and decided to trim it down by substituting fat-free and reduced-fat ingredients. Whenever I make this for an occasion, I end up being inundated with recipe requests.

Patricia Moore, Toledo, Ohio

- 1 package (8 ounces) fat-free cream cheese, cubed
- 1 cup (8 ounces) reduced-fat sour cream
- 1 envelope Italian salad dressing mix
- 3 cups frozen chopped broccoli, thawed, drained and patted dry
- 2 cups (8 ounces) shredded reduced-fat cheddar cheese, divided

Reduced-fat wheat snack crackers

1 In a large bowl, beat the cream cheese, sour cream and salad dressing mix until blended. Fold in the broccoli and 1-1/2 cups of cheese.

2 Spoon into a shallow 1-qt. baking dish coated with cooking spray. Bake, uncovered, at 350° for 20 minutes. Sprinkle with remaining cheese. Bake 5 minutes longer or until cheese is melted. Serve warm with crackers.

YIELD: 3-1/2 CUPS.

My daughter came up with this recipe, and I'm asked for a copy of it every time I make it. It's easy to switch up the flavor by using different types of pesto.

Shirley Dickstein, Parma, Idaho

lemon-berry pitcher punch

PREP/TOTAL TIME: 5 MIN.

The tangy combination of lemonade and cranberry juice makes this drink a real thirst-quencher on a hot day.

Margaret O'Bryon, Bel Air, Maryland

- 1/4 cup sweetened lemonade drink mix
- 2 cups cold water
- 1/3 cup cranberry juice, chilled
- 3/4 cup lemon-lime soda, chilled

1 In a pitcher, combine the drink mix, water and cranberry juice. Stir in soda. Serve immediately.

YIELD: ABOUT 3 CUPS.

pesto bruschetta

PREP/TOTAL TIME: 20 MIN.

- 1 loaf (1 pound) French bread, cut into slices
- 1 jar (7 ounces) prepared pesto
- 2 medium tomatoes, seeded and finely chopped
- 1 package (4 ounces) crumbled feta cheese

1 Arrange bread slices on an ungreased baking sheet. Spread with pesto; top with tomatoes and cheese. Broil 4 in. from the heat for 3-5 minutes or until edges are lightly browned.

YIELD: 29 APPETIZERS.

smackin' good snack mix

PREP: 15 MIN. BAKE: 40 MIN. + COOLING

Tailgaters love to munch, so this crunchy snack mix is perfect for a pregame treat. Everyone likes it. I've even won a ribbon at the state fair with this recipe.

Lucile Cline, Wichita, Kansas

6 cups original Bugles
5 cups nacho cheese-flavored Bugles
4 cups miniature cheese crackers
1 package (6 ounces) miniature colored fish-shaped crackers
3 cups miniature pretzels
2 cups Crispix
2 cups lightly salted cashews
3/4 cup butter-flavored popcorn oil
2 envelopes (1 ounce each) ranch salad dressing mix

1 In a large bowl, combine the Bugles, crackers, pretzels, Crispix and cashews. Combine oil and dressing mix; pour over cracker mixture and toss to coat.

2 Transfer to three greased 15-in. x 10-in. x 1-in. baking pans. Bake at 250° for 40-45 minutes or until crisp, stirring occasionally. Cool on wire racks. Store in an airtight container.

YIELD: 6 QUARTS.

Three simple ingredients are all you need to create this fruity beverage. Light and refreshing—and so easy to make—it's bound to become a warm-weather favorite.

Krista Collins, Concord, North Carolina

strawberry spritzer

PREP/TOTAL TIME: 10 MIN.

1 package (10 ounces) frozen sweetened sliced strawberries, thawed
2 liters lemon-lime soda, chilled
1 can (12 ounces) frozen pink lemonade concentrate, thawed

1 Place the strawberries in a blender; cover and process until pureed. Pour into a pitcher; stir in the soda and lemonade concentrate. Serve immediately.

YIELD: 2-1/2 QUARTS.

TIP

To keep dips chilled, place the dip bowl in a slightly larger bowl, which is partially filled with crushed ice. Replace the ice as it melts.

black-eyed pea salsa

PREP/TOTAL TIME: 25 MIN.

My version of Texas Caviar is as flavorful as it is colorful, and works well alone or as an accompaniment.

Peg Wilson, Elm Creek, Nebraska

4 large tomatoes, seeded and chopped
1 package (16 ounces) frozen corn, thawed
1 can (15-1/2 ounces) black-eyed peas, rinsed and drained
1/2 cup chopped green pepper
3 green onions, sliced
2 tablespoons minced fresh cilantro
1 cup Italian salad dressing
Tortilla chips

1 In a large bowl, combine the vegetables and cilantro. Drizzle with dressing and toss to coat. Serve with tortilla chips. Refrigerate leftovers.

YIELD: 6 CUPS.

Salsa and apricot preserves come together as a strange combination, yet create a very tasty appetizer. Give this one a try at your next party.

Sharyl Wolter, Rosenberg, Texas

pesto chili peanuts

PREP/TOTAL TIME: 25 MIN.

Who'd ever dream of teaming pesto with peanuts? I did, and the result is a can't-stop-eating-'em snack that's salty, savory and sure to be in "hot" demand with friends and family. Just try it and see.

Dennis Dahlin, Bolingbrook, Illinois

1 envelope pesto sauce mix
3 tablespoons olive oil
1 teaspoon chili powder
1/4 teaspoon cayenne pepper
5 cups salted dry roasted peanuts

1 In a bowl, whisk the pesto mix, oil, chili powder and cayenne. Pour into a large resealable plastic bag; add peanuts. Seal bag and shake to coat. Transfer to a greased 13-in. x 9-in. baking pan.

2 Bake, uncovered, at 350° for 15-20 minutes, stirring once. Spread on waxed paper to cool. Store in an airtight container.

YIELD: 5 CUPS.

fiesta cream cheese spread

PREP/TOTAL TIME: 15 MIN.

1 package (8 ounces) cream cheese, softened
1/4 cup chunky salsa
1/4 cup apricot preserves or orange marmalade
2 tablespoons chopped avocado
1 tablespoon chopped ripe olives
1 tablespoon minced fresh cilantro
Assorted crackers

1 Place cream cheese on a serving plate. In a small bowl, combine salsa and preserves; spread over cream cheese. Sprinkle with avocado, olives and cilantro. Serve with crackers.

YIELD: 8 SERVINGS.

2 In a small saucepan, combine the preserves, chili sauce and soup mix. Cook over medium-low heat for 5 minutes. Pour over meatballs. Simmer, uncovered, for 10 minutes or until heated through.

YIELD: ABOUT 4-1/2 DOZEN.

citrus slush

PREP: 15 MIN. + FREEZING

This recipe was created years ago for church bridal and baby showers, the result of the hostess committee sharing ideas. We would use different flavored gelatins to color-coordinate with the decor of the occasion.

Joy Bruce, Welch, Oklahoma

- 2-1/2 cups sugar
- 1 package (3 ounces) lemon gelatin
- 1 package (3 ounces) pineapple gelatin
- 4 cups boiling water
- 1 can (12 ounces) frozen pineapple juice concentrate, thawed
- 1 cup lemon juice
- 1 envelope (0.23 ounce) unsweetened lemonade soft drink mix
- 10 cups cold water
- 2 liters ginger ale, chilled

1 In a large container, dissolve sugar and gelatins in boiling water. Stir in the pineapple juice concentrate, lemon juice, drink mix and cold water. If desired, place in smaller containers. Cover and freeze, stirring several times.

2 Remove from freezer at least 1 hour before serving. Stir until mixture becomes slushy. Just before serving, place 9 cups slush mixture in a punch bowl; stir in 1 liter ginger ale. Repeat with remaining slush and ginger ale.

YIELD: ABOUT 6 QUARTS (ABOUT 25 SERVINGS).

When my daughter and her husband come to visit during the holidays, we enjoy nibbling on these mouthwatering meatballs while playing games. Water chestnuts add a bit of crunch.

Christine Martin, Durham, North Carolina

peach-glazed meatballs

PREP: 25 MIN. COOK: 30 MIN.

- 2 eggs, lightly beaten
- 1 can (8 ounces) water chestnuts, drained and chopped
- 3/4 cup dry bread crumbs
- 1 tablespoon beef bouillon granules
- 1-1/2 pounds ground beef
- 1 jar (16 ounces) peach preserves
- 1 bottle (12 ounces) chili sauce
- 1 envelope onion soup mix

1 In a large bowl, combine the eggs, water chestnuts, bread crumbs and bouillon. Crumble beef over mixture and mix well. Shape into 1-in. balls. In a large skillet, cook meatballs in batches until no longer pink; drain. Return all to the skillet.

Once you try these mini-sized calzones, you may never go back to the large ones. Not only do these pretty bites take advantage of convenient refrigerator crescent rolls, but they can be made ahead and popped in the oven right before company arrives.

Lisa Smith
Bryan, Ohio

calzone pinwheels

PREP/TOTAL TIME: 30 MIN.

1/2 cup ricotta cheese
1 teaspoon Italian seasoning
1/4 teaspoon salt
1/2 cup shredded part-skim mozzarella cheese
1/2 cup diced pepperoni
1/4 cup grated Parmesan cheese
1/4 cup chopped fresh mushrooms
1/4 cup finely chopped green pepper
2 tablespoons finely chopped onion
1 package (8 ounces) refrigerated crescent rolls
1 jar (14 ounces) pizza sauce, warmed

1 In a small bowl, combine the ricotta, Italian seasoning and salt. Stir in the mozzarella cheese, pepperoni, Parmesan cheese, mushrooms, green pepper and onion. Separate crescent dough into four rectangles; seal perforations.

2 Spread cheese mixture over each rectangle to within 1/4 in. of edges. Roll up jelly-roll style, starting with a short side; pinch seams to seal. Cut each into four slices.

3 Place cut side down on greased baking sheets. Bake at 375° for 10-15 minutes or until golden brown. Serve warm with pizza sauce. Refrigerate the leftovers.

YIELD: 16 APPETIZERS.

grits & shrimp tarts

PREP/TOTAL TIME: 30 MIN.

1 cup water

1/4 cup quick-cooking grits

2 ounces cream cheese, softened

1/4 cup shredded cheddar cheese

3 tablespoons butter, divided

1/4 teaspoon garlic salt

1/8 teaspoon salt

Pepper to taste

1 pound uncooked small shrimp, peeled and deveined

3 green onions, sliced

2 packages (1.9 ounces each) frozen miniature phyllo tart shells

1 In a small saucepan, bring water to a boil. Gradually stir in grits. Reduce heat; cover and simmer for 4 minutes. Stir in the cheeses, 1 tablespoon butter, garlic salt, salt and pepper.

2 In a large skillet, saute shrimp and onions in remaining butter until shrimp turn pink. Fill tart shells with grits; top with shrimp mixture. Refrigerate leftovers.

YIELD: 2-1/2 DOZEN.

italian snack mix

PREP/TOTAL TIME: 15 MIN.

This filling no-bake medley can be put together in minutes, and it stores well in an airtight container.

Nancy Zimmerman, Cape May Court House, New Jersey

- 8 cups Crispix
- 4 cups sourdough pretzel nuggets
- 3 tablespoons canola oil
- 1/4 cup grated Parmesan cheese
- 1 tablespoon spaghetti sauce mix
- 2 teaspoons garlic powder

1 In a 2-gal. resealable plastic bag, combine cereal and pretzels. Drizzle with oil; seal bag and toss to coat. Combine remaining ingredients; sprinkle over cereal mixture. Seal bag and toss to coat.

YIELD: ABOUT 3 QUARTS.

I found this beverage recipe more than 15 years ago, when I was in high school. My husband and I also relax with a cup of it after the children go to bed.

Sally Seidel, Banner, Wyoming

sweet & salty popcorn

PREP: 10 MIN. BAKE: 25 MIN. + COOLING

This popcorn recipe is a family favorite on weekend movie nights, thanks to the classic salty and sweet flavor.

Hilary Kerr, Hawks, Michigan

- 10 cups air-popped popcorn
- 1 tablespoon butter
- 5 tablespoons instant vanilla pudding mix
- 1/3 cup light corn syrup
- 1 teaspoon vanilla extract
- Dash salt

1 Place popcorn in a large bowl. In a small microwave-safe bowl, melt butter; whisk in the pudding mix, corn syrup, vanilla and salt until smooth. Microwave, uncovered, for 45 seconds or until bubbly. Pour over popcorn; toss to coat.

2 Spread in a 15-in. x 10-in. x 1-in. baking pan coated with cooking spray. Bake at 250° for 25-30 minutes or until crisp, stirring once. Remove popcorn from pan to waxed paper to cool. Break into clusters. Store in airtight containers.

YIELD: 12 CUPS.

EDITOR'S NOTE: This recipe was tested in a 1,100-watt microwave.

winter warmer

PREP/TOTAL TIME: 10 MIN.

- 2 envelopes (1 ounce each) instant hot cocoa mix or 1/2 cup instant hot cocoa mix
- 3 cups hot brewed coffee
- 1/4 cup half-and-half cream
- 3/4 teaspoon rum extract
- 1/4 cup whipped topping
- Ground cinnamon, optional

1 In a small saucepan, whisk together the cocoa mix, coffee, cream and rum extract until heated through and cocoa is dissolved. Pour into mugs. Garnish with whipped topping; sprinkle with cinnamon if desired.

YIELD: 2 SERVINGS.

tortellini with roasted red pepper dip

PREP/TOTAL TIME: 25 MIN.

- 1 package (19 ounces) frozen cheese tortellini
- 1 jar (7 ounces) roasted sweet red peppers, drained
- 3 garlic cloves, minced
- 1/2 cup fat-free mayonnaise
- 1/2 teaspoon balsamic vinegar
- 1/4 teaspoon salt
- 1/8 teaspoon pepper
- 1 tablespoon olive oil
- 1 large zucchini, cut into strips

1 Prepare tortellini according to package directions. Meanwhile, place red peppers and garlic in a food processor; cover and process until combined. Add the mayonnaise, vinegar, salt and pepper; cover and process until blended. Transfer to a small bowl.

2 Drain tortellini; toss with oil. Serve with zucchini strips and red pepper dip.

YIELD: 10 SERVINGS.

shrimp lover squares

PREP: 20 MIN. + CHILLING

These shrimp squares are part of an hors d'oeuvre buffet I prepare for family every Christmas. During the holidays, we enjoy having a variety of appetizers as a meal while playing a board game or watching a movie together.

Ardyce Piehl, Poynette, Wisconsin

1 tube (8 ounces) refrigerated crescent rolls
1 package (8 ounces) cream cheese, softened
1/4 cup sour cream
1/2 teaspoon dill weed
1/8 teaspoon salt
1/2 cup seafood cocktail sauce
24 cooked medium shrimp, peeled and deveined
1/2 cup chopped green pepper
1/3 cup chopped onion
1 cup (4 ounces) shredded Monterey Jack cheese

1 In a greased 13-in. x 9-in. baking dish, unroll crescent dough into one long rectangle; seal seams and perforations. Bake at 375° for 10-12 minutes or until golden brown. Cool completely on a wire rack.

2 In a small bowl, beat the cream cheese, sour cream, dill and salt until smooth. Spread over crust. Top with the seafood sauce, shrimp, green pepper, onion and cheese. Cover and refrigerate for 1 hour. Cut into squares.

YIELD: 2 DOZEN.

People will rave over this super-easy cheesecake appetizer. Make it a day ahead for convenience, adding salsa just before serving.

Sandy Burkett, Galena, Ohio

mexican cheesecake

PREP: 20 MIN. BAKE: 30 MIN. + CHILLING

2 packages (8 ounces each) reduced-fat cream cheese
1-1/4 cups reduced-fat sour cream, divided
1 envelope taco seasoning
3 eggs, lightly beaten
1-1/2 cups (6 ounces) shredded sharp cheddar cheese
1 can (4 ounces) chopped green chilies
1 cup chunky salsa, drained
Tortilla chips or fresh vegetables

1 In a large bowl, beat cream cheese, 1/2 cup sour cream and taco seasoning until smooth. Add eggs; beat on low speed just until combined. Stir in cheddar cheese and chilies.

2 Transfer to a greased 9-in. springform pan. Place on a baking sheet. Bake at 350° for 25-30 minutes or until center is almost set. Spread the remaining sour cream evenly over top. Bake for 5-8 minutes or until the topping is set. Cool on a wire rack for 10 minutes. Carefully run a knife around the edge of the pan to loosen; cool 1 hour longer. Refrigerate overnight.

3 Remove sides of pan. Just before serving, spread salsa over cheesecake. Serve with the tortilla chips or vegetables.

YIELD: 24 SERVINGS.

taco-flavored chicken wings

PREP/TOTAL TIME: 20 MIN.

I dress up chicken wings with grill marks and a lively marinade to create a fantastic summertime appetizer that's always a hit. I like these wings spicy, so I often add a little extra hot sauce.

Deb Keslar, Utica, Nebraska

  1 envelope taco seasoning
  3 tablespoons canola oil
  2 tablespoons red wine vinegar
  2 teaspoons hot pepper sauce, divided
  34 fresh or frozen chicken wingettes
      (about 4 pounds)
  1 cup ranch salad dressing

1 In a large resealable plastic bag, combine the taco seasoning, oil, vinegar and 1 teaspoon hot pepper sauce; add chicken. Seal bag and turn to coat.

2 Grill chicken, covered, over medium heat for 5 minutes. Grill 10-15 minutes longer or until juices run clear, turning occasionally.

3 In a small bowl, combine ranch dressing and remaining hot pepper sauce. Serve with chicken.

YIELD: ABOUT 2-1/2 DOZEN.

This flavorful dip is addictive, so be careful! It's also delicious served with pita chips, crackers and fresh veggies.

Iola Egle, Bella Vista, Arkansas

mustard pretzel dip

PREP: 10 MIN. + CHILLING

  1 cup (8 ounces) sour cream
  1 cup mayonnaise
  1 cup prepared mustard
  1/2 cup sugar
  1/4 cup dried minced onion
  1 envelope ranch salad dressing mix
  1 tablespoon prepared horseradish
  Sourdough pretzel nuggets

1 In a large bowl, combine the sour cream, mayonnaise, mustard, sugar, onion, salad dressing mix and horseradish. Cover and refrigerate for at least 30 minutes. Serve with pretzels.

YIELD: 3-1/2 CUPS.

My family has relied on this homespun mix to make hot spiced tea and a heartwarming punch for years. My parents always served steaming mugs of this punch for Thanksgiving.

Deb McKinney
Cedar Falls, Iowa

spiced tea mix

PREP/TOTAL TIME: 10 MIN.

1 jar (21.1 ounces) orange breakfast drink mix
1 jar (6 ounces) sugar-free instant lemon iced
    tea mix
2/3 cup sweetened lemonade drink mix
2 teaspoons ground cinnamon
1 teaspoon ground cloves
ADDITIONAL INGREDIENT FOR HOT SPICED TEA:
1 cup boiling water
ADDITIONAL INGREDIENTS FOR
HOT SPICED PUNCH:
2 quarts apple juice or cider
1-1/2 cups cranberry juice
3 cinnamon sticks (3-1/2 inches)

1 In an airtight container, combine the first five
    ingredients. Store in a cool dry place for up
    to 6 months.

YIELD: ABOUT 7-1/2 CUPS TOTAL.

2 **To prepare tea:** Dissolve about 1 tablespoon
    tea mix in boiling water; stir well.

YIELD: 1 SERVING.

3 **To prepare punch:** In a 3-qt. slow cooker, combine
    the juices, 1/4 to 1/3 cup tea mix and cinnamon
    sticks. Cover and cook on low for 4 hours.

YIELD: ABOUT 12 SERVINGS (6 OUNCES EACH).

1 In a large airtight container, combine the sugars, creamer, coffee granules, cocoa and cherry soft drink mix. Store in a cool dry place for up to 2 months.

2 **For each serving:** Place 2 tablespoons cappuccino mix in the bottom of a mug. Stir in hot milk until combined; top with marshmallows.

YIELD: 48 SERVINGS (6 CUPS CAPPUCCINO MIX).

cheese meatballs

PREP: 20 MIN. BAKE: 15 MIN.

I rely on these rich, cheesy meatballs for party starters.

Rachel Frost, Tallula, Illinois

3 cups (12 ounces) finely shredded cheddar cheese
1 cup biscuit/baking mix
1/2 teaspoon salt
1/4 teaspoon pepper
1/4 teaspoon garlic powder
1 pound lean ground beef (90% lean)

1 In a bowl, combine the cheese, biscuit mix, salt, pepper and garlic powder. Crumble beef over mixture and mix well. Shape into 1-in. balls. Place meatballs on a greased rack in a shallow baking pan. Bake at 400° for 12-15 minutes or until the meat is no longer pink; drain.

YIELD: 4 DOZEN.

I wanted something that both coffee and noncoffee drinkers would enjoy, so I added cherry flavoring to a cappuccino mix. This creamy dessert coffee is extra festive when garnished with holiday sprinkles.

Jennifer Waters, Lubbock, Texas

chocolate cherry cappuccino

PREP/TOTAL TIME: 20 MIN.

3 cups sugar
2 cups confectioners' sugar
1-1/3 cups powdered nondairy creamer
1-1/3 cups instant coffee granules
1 cup baking cocoa
1 envelope (.13 ounce) unsweetened cherry soft drink mix
EACH SERVING:
1 cup hot milk
2 tablespoons miniature marshmallows

mexican fiesta platter

PREP: 15 MIN. COOK: 35 MIN.

You don't need to fuss to feed a crowd...just serve this appetizer. With generous layers of beef, rice, corn chips and cheese, it's a nacho lover's dream.

Ann Nace, Perkasie, Pennsylvania

2-1/2 pounds ground beef

2 cans (16 ounces each) kidney beans, rinsed and drained

2 cans (15 ounces each) tomato sauce

1 envelope chili seasoning

1 package (10-1/2 ounces) corn chips

3 cups hot cooked rice

2 large onions, chopped

2 cups (8 ounces) shredded Monterey Jack cheese

1 medium head iceberg lettuce, shredded

4 medium tomatoes, chopped

1-1/2 cups chopped ripe olives

Hot pepper sauce, optional

1 In a Dutch oven, cook beef over medium heat until no longer pink; drain. Add the beans, tomato sauce and chili seasoning; simmer for 30 minutes, stirring occasionally.

2 On two serving platters with sides, layer the corn chips, rice, onions, meat mixture, cheese, lettuce, tomatoes and olives. Sprinkle with hot sauce if desired.

YIELD: 20-24 SERVINGS.

This yummy, island-inspired dip is bursting with pineapple and coconut flavor.

Taste of Home Test Kitchen

tropical dip

PREP: 10 MIN. + CHILLING

1 can (8 ounces) crushed pineapple, undrained

1 package (3.4 ounces) instant vanilla pudding mix

3/4 cup cold 2% milk

1/2 cup flaked coconut

1/2 cup sour cream

Toasted coconut

Assorted fresh fruit

1 In a blender, combine the pineapple, pudding mix, milk, coconut and sour cream; cover and process for 30 seconds.

2 Transfer to a serving bowl; cover and refrigerate for 30 minutes. Garnish with toasted coconut. Serve with fruit.

YIELD: 2 CUPS.

1 In a large skillet, cook the sausage, onion and peppers over medium heat until the meat is no longer pink; drain. Combine crust mixes; prepare according to package directions. With greased fingers, press onto the bottom of a greased 15-in. x 10-in. x 1-in. baking pan.

2 Combine the sausage mixture, mozzarella cheese, pepperoni and egg; spread over dough to within 1/2 in. of the edges. Sprinkle with the Parmesan cheese, oregano and garlic powder.

3 Roll up jelly-roll style, starting with a long side; pinch seams to seal. Arrange seam side down on pan and shape into a crescent. Bake at 400° for 30 minutes or until golden brown.

YIELD: 15 SERVINGS.

chilled cocoa

PREP/TOTAL TIME: 5 MIN.

Enjoy the rich taste of hot chocolate, thanks to this frosty version. It's a great summertime treat, but for those who enjoy shakes it's good any time of the year.

Mary Tallman, Arbor Vitae, Wisconsin

1-1/2 cups warm water
4 envelopes (1 ounce each) instant hot cocoa mix
2 cups vanilla ice cream
1-1/2 cups half-and-half cream

1 In a blender, combine water and cocoa mix; cover and process until dissolved. Add ice cream and cream; cover and process for 30 seconds or until smooth. Pour into chilled mugs.

YIELD: 4 SERVINGS.

Savory slices of this bread make a popular Saturday night meal for my family. Just like pizza, it can be eaten as a fun finger food. Guests can't stop nibbling when I serve it at parties. Plus, it's good served warm or cold.

Pat Coon, Ulster, Pennsylvania

sausage pizza loaf

PREP: 20 MIN. BAKE: 30 MIN.

1 pound bulk Italian sausage
1/4 cup each chopped onion, sweet red pepper and green pepper
2 packages (6-1/2 ounces each) pizza crust mix
1 cup (4 ounces) shredded part-skim mozzarella cheese
1/2 cup chopped pepperoni
1 egg, lightly beaten
2 tablespoons grated Parmesan cheese
1 teaspoon dried oregano
1/4 teaspoon garlic powder

spinach & artichoke dip

PREP: 15 MIN. BAKE: 30 MIN.

This is the perfect dip to serve to guests at your next get-together. It tastes delicious and is fabulous served with either tortilla chips or bread.

Naomi Judd, Nashville, Tennessee

- 2 packages (10 ounces each) frozen chopped spinach, thawed and squeezed dry
- 1 can (14 ounces) water-packed artichoke hearts, rinsed, drained and chopped
- 1 cup (8 ounces) sour cream
- 1 cup mayonnaise
- 1 package (1.7 ounces) vegetable soup mix
- 1/2 cup plus 2 tablespoons grated Parmesan cheese, divided
- 1/2 cup shredded cheddar cheese
- Assorted crackers

1 In a large bowl, combine the spinach, artichokes, sour cream, mayonnaise, soup mix and 1/2 cup Parmesan cheese. Transfer to a 1-1/2-qt. baking dish. Sprinkle with cheddar cheese and remaining Parmesan cheese.

2 Bake, uncovered, at 350° for 30-35 minutes or until cheese is melted. Serve warm with crackers.

YIELD: 4 CUPS.

TIP

If you are going to nibble on the Beef-Stuffed Crescents throughout the night, just bake a dozen at a time. When there are just a few remaining of the first dozen, bake the second dozen and they will be ready to enjoy fresh from the oven in just a few minutes.

I love that these handheld bundles are so easy and have so few ingredients. I've made them often...and never have any leftovers.

Jennifer Bumgarner, Topeka, Kansas

beef-stuffed crescents

PREP: 25 MIN. BAKE: 15 MIN.

- 1 pound ground beef
- 1 can (4 ounces) chopped green chilies
- 1 package (8 ounces) cream cheese, cubed
- 1/4 teaspoon ground cumin
- 1/4 teaspoon chili powder
- 3 tubes (8 ounces each) refrigerated crescent rolls

1 In a skillet, cook beef and chilies over medium heat until meat is no longer pink; drain. Add the cream cheese, cumin and chili powder. Cool slightly.

2 Separate crescent dough into 24 triangles. Place 1 tablespoon of beef mixture along the short end of each triangle; carefully roll up.

3 Place point side down 2 in. apart on ungreased baking sheets. Bake at 375° for 11-14 minutes or until golden brown. Serve warm.

YIELD: 2 DOZEN.

3 Place 1 in. apart on greased baking sheets. Bake at 375° for 12-14 minutes or until golden brown. Serve warm.

YIELD: 32 APPETIZERS.

citrus iced tea

PREP: 20 MIN. + COOLING

I think I have finally found an iced tea drink that doesn't have that artificial sweetener aftertaste.

Dawn Lowenstein, Hatboro, Pennsylvania

8 cups water, divided
6 individual tea bags
1 to 2 mint sprigs
1/2 ounce sugar-free lemonade soft drink mix
2 cups orange juice
Ice cubes

1 In a Dutch oven, bring 1 qt. of water to a boil. Add tea bags and mint. Cover and steep for 10 minutes. Strain; discard tea bags and mint.

2 In a large container, combine lemonade mix and remaining water. Stir in the tea and orange juice. Cool. Serve over ice.

YIELD: 8 SERVINGS.

EDITOR'S NOTE: This recipe was tested with one 1/2-oz. tub of Crystal Light lemonade soft drink mix.

My guests are always happy to see these wonderful treats when I'm serving snacks. The tender bites are made with hassle-free refrigerated crescent rolls and a flavorful chicken and cream-cheese filling.

Amber Kimmich, Powhatan, Virginia

champion chicken puffs

PREP/TOTAL TIME: 30 MIN.

4 ounces cream cheese, softened
1/2 teaspoon garlic powder
1/2 cup shredded cooked chicken
2 tubes (8 ounces each) refrigerated crescent rolls

1 In a small bowl, beat cream cheese and garlic powder until smooth. Stir in chicken.

2 Unroll crescent dough; separate into 16 triangles. Cut each triangle in half lengthwise, forming two triangles. Place 1 teaspoon of chicken mixture in the center of each. Fold short side over filling; press sides to seal and roll up.

TIP

To soften cream cheese quickly, remove the wrapper and discard it. Place the cream cheese on a microwave-safe plate and microwave on high for about 15 seconds. Add more time if necessary, but don't overheat it...you don't want the cream cheese to melt or cook.

Vegetables, cheese and bacon make these memorable morsels so tasty that they are bound to be requested at your house. The tarts are impressive, but they're quite easy to make.

Kendra Schertz
Nappanee, Indiana

bacon quiche tarts

PREP: 15 MIN. BAKE: 20 MIN.

2 packages (3 ounces each) cream cheese, softened

5 teaspoons 2% milk

2 eggs

1/2 cup shredded Colby cheese

2 tablespoons chopped green pepper

1 tablespoon finely chopped onion

1 tube (8 ounces) refrigerated crescent rolls

5 bacon strips, cooked and crumbled

1 In a small bowl, beat cream cheese and milk until smooth. Add the eggs, cheese, green pepper and onion; mix well.

2 Separate dough into eight triangles; press onto the bottom and up the sides of greased muffin cups. Sprinkle half of the bacon into cups. Pour egg mixture over bacon; top with remaining bacon.

3 Bake, uncovered, at 375° for 18-22 minutes or until a knife inserted near the center comes out clean. Serve warm.

YIELD: 8 SERVINGS.

cheesy pizza fondue

PREP: 10 MIN. COOK: 4 HOURS

- 1 jar (29 ounces) meatless spaghetti sauce
- 2 cups (8 ounces) shredded part-skim mozzarella cheese
- 1/4 cup shredded Parmesan cheese
- 2 teaspoons dried oregano
- 1 teaspoon dried minced onion
- 1/4 teaspoon garlic powder
- 1 loaf (1 pound) unsliced Italian bread, cut into cubes

1 In a 1-1/2-qt. slow cooker, combine the spaghetti sauce, cheeses, oregano, onion and garlic powder. Cook on low for 4-6 hours or until cheese is melted and sauce is hot. Serve with bread cubes.

YIELD: 12 SERVINGS.

TIP

Other fun dippers for the Cheesy Pizza Fondue are: thin, crispy breadsticks; toasted, thin slices of French bread; tortilla chip scoops; bagel chips; and pita chips.

crab & cheese spirals

PREP: 20 MIN. BAKE: 15 MIN.

These pretty pinwheels are loaded with cheese, imitation crabmeat and black olives. Using refrigerated crescent rolls is so convenient.

Lisa Harke, Old Monroe, Missouri

- 2 packages (8 ounces each) cream cheese, softened
- 2 cups chopped imitation crabmeat
- 1 can (4-1/4 ounces) chopped ripe olives
- 1/4 cup minced chives
- 3 tubes (8 ounces each) refrigerated crescent rolls
- 3/4 cup shredded part-skim mozzarella cheese
- 3/4 cup shredded Parmesan cheese

1 In a small bowl, beat the cream cheese, crab, olives and chives.

2 Unroll one tube of crescent dough into one long rectangle; seal seams and perforations. Spread with 1 cup cream cheese mixture; sprinkle with 1/4 cup each mozzarella and Parmesan cheeses. Roll up jelly-roll style, starting with a long side; pinch seam to seal. Using a serrated knife, cut into 10 slices; place cut side down on a greased baking sheet. Repeat with remaining crescent dough, cream cheese mixture and cheeses.

3 Bake at 375° for 14-16 minutes or until golden brown. Serve warm.

YIELD: 2-1/2 DOZEN.

Enjoyed for years in our family, this was the punch my mom served when I graduated from high school. And I made it when my own kids graduated.

Deb Waggoner, Grand Island, Nebraska

graduation punch

PREP: 15 MIN. + COOLING

- 1-1/2 cups sugar
- 8 quarts water, divided
- 4 packages (.14 ounce each) unsweetened strawberry soft drink mix
- 3 cans (6 ounces each) frozen orange juice concentrate, thawed
- 2-1/4 cups thawed lemonade concentrate
- 2 cans (46 ounces each) unsweetened pineapple juice
- 2 liters ginger ale, chilled

1 In a large saucepan, combine sugar and 2 qts. water. Cook and stir over medium heat until sugar is dissolved. Remove from the heat; stir in soft drink mix. Cool completely.

2 Just before serving, divide the syrup between two large containers or punch bowls; add the concentrates, pineapple juice and remaining water to each. Stir in ginger ale.

YIELD: 3-3/4 GALLONS.

garlic-onion appetizer rounds

PREP: 30 MIN. + COOLING BAKE: 15 MIN.

2 large sweet onions, chopped (about 4 cups)
2 tablespoons butter
2 garlic cloves, minced
1 sheet frozen puff pastry, thawed
1 egg
1 tablespoon water
1/3 cup shredded Swiss cheese
1/4 cup grated Parmesan cheese
2 tablespoons minced fresh basil

1 In a large skillet over medium-low heat, cook onions in butter until golden brown, stirring frequently. Add garlic; cook 1 minute longer. Remove from the heat; cool to room temperature.

2 Unfold puff pastry. In a small bowl, whisk egg and water; brush over pastry. Spread onion mixture to within 1/2 in. of edges. Sprinkle with cheeses and basil; roll up jelly-roll style. Cut into 16 slices. Place 2 in. apart on greased baking sheets.

3 Bake at 425° for 12-14 minutes or until puffed and golden brown. Serve warm.

YIELD: **16 APPETIZERS.**

brunch

Served with butter and maple syrup, these waffles go great with bacon or sausage on the side. Sometimes I put them together with scrambled eggs and bacon for a terrific breakfast sandwich.

Ruth Harrow
Alexandria, New Hampshire

orange pecan waffles

PREP/TOTAL TIME: 20 MIN.

1 cup biscuit/baking mix
1 egg, lightly beaten
3 tablespoons canola oil
1 tablespoon sugar
1/2 teaspoon vanilla extract
1/4 teaspoon grated orange peel
1/2 cup club soda
3 tablespoons finely chopped pecans, toasted
Maple syrup, optional

1 In a small bowl, combine the biscuit mix, egg, oil, sugar, vanilla and orange peel. Stir in club soda until smooth. Gently fold in pecans.

2 Bake in a preheated 7-in. waffle iron according to manufacturer's directions until golden brown. Serve with syrup if desired.

YIELD: 3 WAFFLES.

blueberry syrup

PREP/TOTAL TIME: 15 MIN.

Blueberries and blueberry preserves make this syrup burst with flavor. Try it over your favorite pancakes, French toast or waffles.

Lorrie McCurdy, Farmington, New Mexico

- 1 cup packed brown sugar
- 1 cup sugar
- 1/2 cup fresh or frozen blueberries
- 1/2 cup water
- 1/2 cup blueberry preserves
- 1 teaspoon maple flavoring

1 In a small saucepan, combine sugars, blueberries and water. Bring to a boil; cook and stir for 2 minutes. Remove from heat; stir in the preserves and maple flavoring. Refrigerate leftovers.

YIELD: ABOUT 2 CUPS.

baked apple french toast

PREP: 20 MIN. + CHILLING BAKE: 35 MIN.

- 20 slices French bread (1 inch thick)
- 1 can (21 ounces) apple pie filling
- 8 eggs
- 2 cups 2% milk
- 2 teaspoons vanilla extract
- 1/2 teaspoon ground cinnamon
- 1/2 teaspoon ground nutmeg
- TOPPING:
- 1 cup packed brown sugar
- 1/2 cup cold butter, cubed
- 1 cup chopped pecans
- 2 tablespoons corn syrup

This is a simply wonderful brunch recipe that tastes special and will have your guests asking for seconds. I serve it with whipped topping, maple syrup and additional nuts. Some people say it tastes good enough to be dessert!

Beverly Johnston, Rubicon, Wisconsin

1 Arrange 10 slices of bread in a greased 13-in. x 9-in. baking dish. Spread with pie filling; top with remaining bread. In a large bowl, combine the eggs, milk, vanilla, cinnamon and nutmeg. Pour over bread. Cover and refrigerate overnight.

2 Remove from the refrigerator 30 minutes before baking. Meanwhile, place brown sugar in a small bowl. Cut in butter until mixture resembles coarse crumbs. Stir in pecans and corn syrup. Sprinkle over French toast.

3 Bake, uncovered, at 350° for 35-40 minutes or until a knife inserted near the center comes out clean.

YIELD: 10 SERVINGS.

2 Bake in a preheated waffle iron according to manufacturer's directions until golden brown.

YIELD: 12 WAFFLES.

frozen fruit cups

PREP: 30 MIN. + FREEZING

Add some sparkle to your next brunch, get-together or church supper with these sunny citrus treats. The refreshing cups burst with color and flavor, plus they look so cute served in shiny foil containers.

Sue Ross, Casa Grande, Arizona

- 1 package (3 ounces) lemon gelatin
- 2 cups boiling water
- 1 can (20 ounces) unsweetened pineapple tidbits, undrained
- 1 can (11 ounces) mandarin oranges, drained
- 1 can (6 ounces) frozen orange juice concentrate, partially thawed
- 1 large firm banana, sliced

1 In a bowl, dissolve gelatin in boiling water; cool for 10 minutes. Stir in the remaining ingredients.

2 Spoon into foil cups. Place on a baking pan. Freeze until firm. Remove from the freezer 30 minutes before serving.

YIELD: ABOUT 2 DOZEN.

These waffles are cozy and comforting anytime—morning or evening. The smell of toasty waffles with apples is sure to warm you up even on the most blustery of winter days.

Jane Sims, De Leon, Texas

apple spice waffles

PREP/TOTAL TIME: 30 MIN.

- 2 cups biscuit/baking mix
- 2 teaspoons ground cinnamon
- 1 teaspoon ground nutmeg
- 2 eggs
- 1-1/2 cups milk
- 6 tablespoons butter, melted
- 1 cup chopped peeled apple

1 In a large bowl, combine the biscuit mix, cinnamon and nutmeg. In another bowl, combine the eggs, milk and butter; stir into dry ingredients just until moistened. Stir in apple.

cheddar hash brown omelet

PREP/TOTAL TIME: 20 MIN.

My husband loves it when I make crescent rolls to go with this easy family favorite.

Betty Kleberger, Florissant, Missouri

2 cups frozen shredded hash brown
  potatoes, thawed
1/2 cup chopped onion
1/2 cup chopped green pepper
2 tablespoons butter
1 cup diced fully cooked ham or Polish sausage
6 eggs
1/4 cup milk
1/4 teaspoon pepper
1/8 teaspoon salt
1/2 cup shredded cheddar cheese

1 In a 10-in. nonstick skillet, saute potatoes, onion and green pepper in butter until tender. Sprinkle with ham. In a large bowl, whisk the eggs, milk, pepper and salt; add to the skillet.

2 As the eggs set, lift edges, letting uncooked portion flow underneath. When eggs are set, remove from the heat. Sprinkle with cheddar cheese; fold omelet in half. Cover and cook for 1-2 minutes or until cheese is melted.

YIELD: 4 SERVINGS.

This breakfast bake is a snap to prepare. It's perfect when out-of-town guests stay the night. Full of bacon, cheese, hash browns and eggs, the all-in-one dish is a hearty crowd-pleaser.

Margaret Edmondson, Red Oak, Iowa

cheesy o'brien egg scramble

PREP: 20 MIN. BAKE: 20 MIN.

1 package (28 ounces) frozen O'Brien potatoes
1/2 teaspoon garlic salt
1/4 teaspoon pepper
1 can (10-3/4 ounces) condensed cheddar
  cheese soup, undiluted
1 pound sliced bacon, cooked and crumbled
12 eggs, lightly beaten
2 tablespoons butter
2 cups (8 ounces) shredded cheddar cheese

1 In a large skillet, prepare hash browns according to package directions. Sprinkle with garlic salt and pepper. Transfer to a greased 2-1/2-qt. baking dish. Top with soup. Set aside 1/2 cup of bacon; sprinkle remaining bacon over soup.

2 In a bowl, whisk the eggs. In another large skillet, heat butter until hot. Add eggs; cook and stir over medium heat until eggs are nearly set. Spoon over bacon. Sprinkle with cheese and reserved bacon.

3 Bake, uncovered, at 350° for 20-25 minutes or until cheese is melted.

YIELD: 12 SERVINGS.

and onion in drippings until potatoes are golden brown, stirring occasionally.

2 In a large bowl, whisk eggs and sour cream. Stir in 1/4 cup cheese, taco sauce and hot pepper sauce. Pour over potato mixture; add bacon. Cook and stir over medium heat until eggs are completely set.

3 Spoon about 3/4 cup down the center of each tortilla; sprinkle with remaining cheese. Fold bottom and sides of tortilla over filling. Serve immediately with sour cream and tomatoes if desired.

YIELD: 4 SERVINGS.

banana nut pancakes

PREP/TOTAL TIME: 20 MIN.

I like these versatile pancakes since they're a satisfying breakfast and can be a deliciously different dessert.

Diane Hixon, Niceville, Florida

1 package (3 ounces) cream cheese, softened
1/2 cup whipped topping
1 cup pancake mix
1 tablespoon sugar
1 egg
3/4 cup 2% milk
2 teaspoons canola oil
1 medium ripe banana, mashed
1/2 cup chopped pecans

1 In a small bowl, beat cream cheese until smooth. Mix in whipped topping (mixture will be stiff); set aside.

2 In a large bowl, combine pancake mix and sugar. Beat the egg, milk and oil; add to pancake mix and mix well. Fold in banana and pecans.

3 Pour batter by 1/4 cupfuls onto a lightly greased hot griddle; turn when bubbles form on top of pancakes. Cook until second side is golden brown. Serve with cream cheese topping.

YIELD: 8-10 PANCAKES.

My husband and I discovered these delicious burritos when we drove a truck as a team in the Southwestern states. Jason created this version that our guests enjoy as much as we do.

Robyn Larabee, Lucknow, Ontario

bacon & egg burritos

PREP/TOTAL TIME: 25 MIN.

6 bacon strips, diced
1 cup frozen cubed hash brown potatoes
2 tablespoons chopped onion
6 eggs
1/4 cup sour cream
3/4 cup shredded cheddar cheese, divided
2 tablespoons taco sauce
1/2 to 1 teaspoon hot pepper sauce
4 flour tortillas (10 inches), warmed
Sour cream and chopped tomatoes, optional

1 In a large skillet, cook bacon over medium heat until crisp. Using a slotted spoon, remove to paper towels; drain, reserving 1 tablespoon drippings. Saute potatoes

Corn bread mix gives this fluffy quiche a slightly sweet flavor you're sure to savor. This is one of my favorite recipes. I serve it with fresh veggies, fruit or slices of zucchini cooked in the microwave until tender.

Melissa Loupe
Thibodaux, Louisiana

zucchini quiche

PREP: 10 MIN. BAKE: 40 MIN. + STANDING

1/2 cup corn bread/muffin mix
1/4 cup grated Parmesan cheese
1/4 teaspoon salt
1/8 teaspoon pepper
2 eggs, lightly beaten
1/2 cup half-and-half cream
1 tablespoon canola oil
1 cup sliced zucchini

1 In a small bowl, combine the muffin mix, cheese, salt and pepper. Stir in the eggs, cream and oil until blended. Fold in zucchini.

2 Pour into a 7-in. pie plate coated with cooking spray. Bake at 375° for 40-45 minutes or until a knife inserted near the center comes out clean. Let stand for 10 minutes before cutting.

YIELD: 3 SERVINGS.

honey wheat pancakes

PREP: 10 MIN. COOK: 5 MIN./BATCH

1-1/2 cups reduced-fat biscuit/baking mix
1/2 cup whole wheat flour
1/4 cup wheat germ
1 teaspoon baking powder
1 teaspoon ground cinnamon
2 eggs, lightly beaten
1-1/2 cups buttermilk
1 medium ripe banana, mashed
2 tablespoons honey
Assorted fresh fruit and/or maple syrup, optional

1 In a small bowl, combine the biscuit mix, flour, wheat germ, baking powder and cinnamon. Combine the eggs, buttermilk, banana and honey; add to dry ingredients just until moistened.

2 Pour batter by 1/4 cupfuls onto a hot griddle coated with cooking spray; turn when bubbles form on top. Cook until the second side is golden brown. Serve with fruit and/or syrup if desired.

YIELD: 12 PANCAKES.

special brunch bake

PREP: 10 MIN. BAKE: 30 MIN.

This eye-opener features buttermilk biscuits. If you don't have Canadian bacon, try it with turkey bacon or ham.

Nicki Woods, Springfield, Missouri

- 2 tubes (4 ounces each) refrigerated buttermilk biscuits
- 3 cartons (8 ounces each) egg substitute
- 7 ounces Canadian bacon, chopped
- 1 cup (4 ounces) shredded reduced-fat cheddar cheese
- 1 cup (4 ounces) shredded part-skim mozzarella cheese
- 1/2 cup chopped fresh mushrooms
- 1/2 cup finely chopped onion
- 1/4 teaspoon pepper

1 Arrange biscuits in a 13-in. x 9-in. baking dish coated with cooking spray. In a large bowl, combine all the remaining ingredients; pour over biscuits.

2 Bake, uncovered, at 350° for 30-35 minutes or until a knife inserted near the center comes out clean.

YIELD: 12 SERVINGS.

I like to start my family's day with this luscious French toast breakfast that tastes like dessert. It's ready in a flash and disappears even faster.

Taryn Kuebelbeck, Plymouth, Minnesota

strawberries & cream french toast sticks

PREP/TOTAL TIME: 15 MIN.

- 1 container (16 ounces) frozen sweetened sliced strawberries, thawed
- 1/4 to 1/2 teaspoon ground cinnamon
- 1 teaspoon cornstarch
- 2 teaspoons water
- 1 package (12.7 ounces) frozen French toaster sticks
- 2 ounces cream cheese, softened
- 1-1/2 teaspoons brown sugar
- 1 ounce white baking chocolate, melted and cooled

1 In a small saucepan, combine strawberries and cinnamon. Combine cornstarch and water until smooth; stir into berries. Bring to a boil; cook and stir for 2 minutes or until thickened.

2 Prepare French toast sticks according to package directions. Meanwhile, in a small bowl, beat cream cheese and brown sugar until light and fluffy. Stir in chocolate. Serve berry mixture over French toast; dollop with cream cheese topping.

YIELD: 4 SERVINGS.

EDITOR'S NOTE: This recipe was tested with Eggo French Toaster Sticks.

2 Spread 1/2 cup Alfredo sauce in a greased 10-in. square or 13-in. x 9-in. baking dish. Layer with four lasagna noodles (trim noodles if necessary to fit dish), ham, green pepper and onions.

3 Top with half of the remaining Alfredo sauce and the remaining noodles. Layer with scrambled eggs, cheddar cheese and remaining Alfredo sauce. Sprinkle with Parmesan cheese.

4 Bake, uncovered, at 375° for 45-50 minutes or until heated through and bubbly. Let stand for 10 minutes before cutting.

YIELD: **10-12 SERVINGS.**

sausage egg squares

PREP: 15 MIN. BAKE: 35 MIN. + COOLING

Chock-full of sausage and cheesy flavor, this fluffy egg bake is an absolute winner for breakfast, lunch or anytime. Our children and grandkids request it when they visit.

Myrna Duke, Chelan, Washington

1 pound turkey Italian sausage links, casings removed
1 medium green pepper, chopped
1 small onion, chopped
2 cups (16 ounces) 1% cottage cheese
2 cups (8 ounces) shredded reduced-fat cheddar cheese
1-1/2 cups egg substitute
1 cup fat-free milk
1 cup reduced-fat biscuit/baking mix
1 can (4 ounces) chopped green chilies

1 In a large nonstick skillet, cook sausage, green pepper and onion over medium heat until meat is no longer pink; drain. Stir in all the remaining ingredients. Pour into a 13-in. x 9-in. baking dish coated with cooking spray.

2 Bake at 350° for 35-40 minutes or until a knife inserted near the center comes out clean. Let stand for 10 minutes before cutting.

YIELD: **12 SERVINGS.**

Everyone can appreciate make-ahead dishes like this one. Pop it into the oven before guests arrive—add fresh fruit and muffins—and you have an instant brunch. You can serve it as a hearty supper, too, drizzled with a little salsa.

Judy Munger, Warren, Minnesota

brunch lasagna

PREP: 25 MIN. BAKE: 45 MIN. + STANDING

8 uncooked lasagna noodles
8 eggs
1/2 cup milk
Butter-flavored cooking spray
2 jars (16 ounces each) Alfredo sauce
3 cups diced fully cooked ham
1/2 cup chopped green pepper
1/4 cup chopped green onions
1 cup (4 ounces) shredded cheddar cheese
1/4 cup grated Parmesan cheese

1 Cook noodles according to package directions. Meanwhile, in a large bowl, beat eggs and milk. In a large nonstick skillet coated with butter-flavored cooking spray, cook eggs over medium-low heat until set but moist. Remove from the heat. Drain noodles.

This is a springtime
Sunday brunch item
at our house.

Mark Morgan
Waterford, Wisconsin

asparagus eggs benedict

PREP/TOTAL TIME: 15 MIN.

12 fresh asparagus spears, trimmed
   and cut in half
1 envelope hollandaise sauce mix
6 eggs
3 English muffins, split and toasted
1/2 cup shredded Swiss cheese
Paprika

1 Place asparagus in a steamer basket. Place in a large saucepan over 1 in. of water; bring to a boil. Cover and steam for 3-4 minutes or until crisp-tender. Set aside.

2 Prepare hollandaise sauce according to package directions. Meanwhile, in a large skillet, bring 2-3 in. water to a boil. Reduce heat; simmer gently.

3 Break cold eggs, one at a time, into a custard cup or saucer. Holding the dish close to the surface of the water, slip the eggs, one at a time, into the water. Cook, uncovered, for 3-5 minutes or until the whites are completely set and the yolks begin to thicken. With a slotted spoon, lift each egg out of the water.

4 To assemble, place 4 pieces of asparagus on each muffin half. Top with a poached egg; sprinkle with cheese. Top each with about 3 tablespoons of hollandaise sauce and garnish with a dash of paprika. Serve immediately.

YIELD: 6 SERVINGS.

breakfast pizza

PREP/TOTAL TIME: 25 MIN.

- 1 tube (13.8 ounces) refrigerated pizza crust
- 2 tablespoons olive oil, divided
- 6 eggs
- 2 tablespoons water
- 1 package (3 ounces) real bacon bits
- 1 cup (4 ounces) shredded Monterey Jack cheese
- 1 cup (4 ounces) shredded cheddar cheese

1 Unroll crust into a greased 15-in. x 10-in. x 1-in. baking pan; flatten dough and build up edges slightly. Brush with 1 tablespoon oil. Prick dough thoroughly with a fork. Bake at 400° for 7-8 minutes or until lightly browned.

2 Meanwhile, in a small bowl, whisk eggs and water. In a small skillet, heat remaining oil until hot. Add eggs; cook and stir over medium heat until completely set.

3 Spoon eggs over crust. Sprinkle with bacon and cheeses. Bake 5-7 minutes longer or until cheese is melted.

YIELD: 8 SLICES.

mallow fruit salad

PREP: 10 MIN. + CHILLING

A handful of ingredients is all you'll need for this sweet and fluffy salad. Your gang will love the combination of canned fruit, mini marshmallows and whipped topping, and you'll love how simple it is to assemble.

Sandy Ward, Madisonville, Texas

1-1/3 cups cold buttermilk

1 package (5.1 ounces) instant vanilla pudding mix

1 can (30 ounces) fruit cocktail, drained

2 cans (11 ounces each) mandarin oranges, drained

1 cup pastel miniature marshmallows

1 carton (8 ounces) frozen whipped topping, thawed

1 In a large bowl, whisk buttermilk and pudding mix for 2 minutes. Let stand for 2 minutes or until soft set. Fold in the fruit cocktail, oranges, marshmallows and whipped topping. Refrigerate until serving.

YIELD: 8-10 SERVINGS.

I wanted to make a quiche but didn't want the usual flavors, so I used items I had in my pantry and refrigerator to come up with this recipe. I was surprised at the great taste and how well the flavors came together.

Tamie Bradford, Grand Forks AFB, North Dakota

chicken taco quiche

PREP: 20 MIN. BAKE: 35 MIN. + STANDING

2 unbaked pastry shells (9 inches)

2 cups cubed cooked chicken

2 envelopes taco seasoning, divided

2/3 cup salsa

2 cups (8 ounces) shredded cheddar cheese

8 eggs

2 cups half-and-half cream

2 tablespoons butter, melted

1 can (4 ounces) chopped green chilies

1/2 cup sliced ripe olives

1 Line unpricked pastry shells with a double thickness of heavy-duty foil. Bake at 400° for 4 minutes. Remove foil; bake 4 minutes longer.

2 In a small bowl, combine chicken and one envelope taco seasoning; spoon into pastry shells. Top with salsa and cheese. In a bowl, whisk the eggs, cream, butter and remaining taco seasoning. Stir in chilies and olives. Pour over cheese.

3 Cover and freeze one quiche for up to 3 months. Cover edges of remaining quiche loosely with foil; place on a baking sheet. Bake at 400° for 33-35 minutes or until a knife inserted near the center comes out clean. Let stand for 10 minutes before cutting.

4 **To use frozen quiche:** Remove from the freezer 30 minutes before baking (do not thaw). Cover edges of crust loosely with foil; place on a baking sheet. Bake at 400° for 70-75 minutes or until a knife inserted near the center comes out clean. Let stand for 10 minutes before cutting.

YIELD: 2 QUICHES (6 SERVINGS EACH).

1. Unroll crescent dough into a greased 13-in. x 9-in. baking dish; seal seams and perforations. Bake at 375° for 6 minutes or until golden brown.

2. Meanwhile, in a skillet, cook sausage and onion over medium heat until meat is no longer pink; drain. In a small bowl, combine the eggs, milk, green pepper, oregano, pepper and garlic salt; pour over crust. Sprinkle with sausage mixture.

3. Bake for 15-20 minutes. Sprinkle with cheese; bake 5 minutes longer or until cheese is melted.

YIELD: 12 SERVINGS.

Whenever I want to serve something special for a family brunch, this is usually what I prepare. I get the ingredients together the night before, so it's a snap to bake the next morning.

Miriam Yoder, Houstonia, Missouri

speedy sausage squares

PREP: 15 MIN. BAKE: 30 MIN.

1 tube (8 ounces) refrigerated crescent rolls
1 pound bulk pork sausage
1/4 cup chopped onion
6 eggs, lightly beaten
3/4 cup 2% milk
2 tablespoons chopped green pepper
1/2 teaspoon dried oregano
1/2 teaspoon pepper
1/4 teaspoon garlic salt
1 cup (4 ounces) part-skim shredded mozzarella cheese

onion brunch squares

PREP: 15 MIN. BAKE: 25 MIN.

I found this recipe years ago but have modified it to my gang's liking. I make it with ham instead of bacon or without meat and have added various veggies to keep everyone happy.

Danna Givot, San Diego, California

2 large onions, chopped
2 tablespoons butter
1 tablespoon all-purpose flour
1/2 cup sour cream
1/2 teaspoon salt
1/2 teaspoon caraway seeds, optional
3 eggs, lightly beaten
3 bacon strips, cooked and crumbled
1 tube (8 ounces) refrigerated crescent rolls

1. In a small skillet, saute onions in butter until tender; cool. Meanwhile, in a large bowl, combine the flour, sour cream, salt and caraway seeds if desired until blended. Add eggs and mix well. Stir in bacon and reserved onions.

2. Unroll crescent roll dough into an ungreased 9-in. square baking pan. Press seams together to seal; press dough 1 in. up the sides of pan. Pour onion mixture into crust.

3. Bake at 375° for 25-30 minutes or until a knife inserted near the center comes out clean.

YIELD: 9 SERVINGS.

ham & egg pockets

PREP/TOTAL TIME: 20 MIN.

Refrigerated crescent roll dough makes these savory breakfast pockets a snap to prepare. For a delicious variation, substitute shredded Swiss cheese for the cheddar cheese.

Taste of Home Test Kitchen

1 egg
2 teaspoons 2% milk
2 teaspoons butter
1 ounce thinly sliced deli ham, chopped
2 tablespoons shredded cheddar cheese
1 tube (4 ounces) refrigerated crescent rolls

1 In a small bowl, combine egg and milk. In a small skillet, heat butter until hot. Add egg mixture; cook and stir over medium heat until eggs are completely set. Remove from the heat. Fold in the ham and cheese.

2 On a greased baking sheet, separate crescent dough into two rectangles. Seal perforations; spoon half of the filling down the center of each rectangle. Fold in ends and sides; pinch to seal. Bake at 375° for 10-14 minutes or until golden brown.

YIELD: 2 SERVINGS.

The tantalizing aroma of cinnamon and brown sugar helps wake my brood. Convenient toast sticks topped with granola, banana and syrup carry them through busy days.

Terri McKitrick, Delafield, Wisconsin

cherry-granola french toast sticks

PREP/TOTAL TIME: 20 MIN.

1/4 cup heavy whipping cream
3 tablespoons brown sugar
2 tablespoons butter
1 tablespoon dried cherries
1/4 teaspoon ground cinnamon
1/4 teaspoon vanilla extract
1 package (12.7 ounces) frozen French toast sticks
1 medium banana, sliced
1/4 cup granola without raisins

1 For syrup, in a small saucepan, combine the cream, brown sugar, butter, cherries and cinnamon. Bring to a boil over medium heat, stirring constantly. Cook and stir for 2 minutes. Remove from the heat; stir in vanilla.

2 Prepare French toast sticks according to package directions. Serve with banana, granola and syrup.

YIELD: 4 SERVINGS.

EDITOR'S NOTE: This recipe was tested with Eggo French Toaster Sticks.

1/8 teaspoon curry powder
1/8 teaspoon ground cinnamon
Dash salt and pepper
FRITTERS:
2 cups biscuit/baking mix
1 can (11 ounces) gold and white corn, drained
2 eggs, lightly beaten
1/2 cup 2% milk
1/2 cup sour cream
1/2 teaspoon salt
Oil for frying

1 In a small skillet, saute onion in oil until golden brown. Add vinegar; cook and stir for 2-3 minutes. Set aside.

2 In a small saucepan, combine the jelly, tomatoes, tomato paste, curry, cinnamon, salt and pepper. Cook over medium heat for 5-7 minutes or until heated through. Add onion mixture. Cook and stir for 3 minutes; set aside and keep warm.

3 In a small bowl, combine the baking mix, corn, eggs, milk, sour cream and salt just until combined.

4 In a deep-fat fryer or electric skillet, heat oil to 375°. Drop batter by heaping tablespoonfuls into hot oil; fry for 1-1/2 minutes on each side or until golden brown. Drain on paper towels. Serve warm with jam.

YIELD: 2 DOZEN (3/4 CUP JAM).

A friend's husband, who's a chef, came up with these light and fluffy fritters accompanied perfectly by a sweet-tart jam. I would never ask a chef to divulge his secrets, so I created my own version.

Kim Cupo, Albany, Georgia

corn fritters with caramelized onion jam

PREP: 30 MIN. COOK: 15 MIN.

1 large sweet onion, halved and thinly sliced
1 tablespoon olive oil
2 teaspoons balsamic vinegar
1/3 cup apple jelly
1/3 cup canned diced tomatoes
1 tablespoon tomato paste

TIP

A tablespoon or two of tomato paste adds richness and color to many savory dishes. Here's how to store leftover tomato paste. Line a baking sheet with waxed paper. Mound the tomato paste in 1 tablespoon portions on the waxed paper. Freeze until firm, then transfer to a resealable freezer bag.

beef

steak and rice roll-ups

PREP: 25 MIN. COOK: 1-1/4 HOURS

1 cup finely chopped fresh mushrooms
2 green onions, finely chopped
1/4 cup finely chopped green pepper
2 tablespoons butter
1-1/2 cups cooked long grain rice
2 tablespoons diced pimientos
1/4 teaspoon dried thyme
1/4 teaspoon dried marjoram
2 pounds beef top round steak (1/2 inch thick)
2 tablespoons canola oil
2 tablespoons plus 1 teaspoon onion soup mix
1 cup water

1 In a large skillet, saute the mushrooms, onions and pepper in butter until tender. Transfer to a small bowl; stir in the rice, pimientos, thyme and marjoram.

2 Cut steak into six pieces; flatten to 1/2-in. thickness. Spread evenly with mushroom mixture; roll up and secure with toothpicks.

3 In the same skillet, brown roll-ups in oil on all sides. Add soup mix and water; cover and simmer for 1 to 1-1/4 hours or until meat is tender, occasionally spooning cooking liquid over roll-ups. Thicken cooking juices if desired; serve with roll-ups. Discard toothpicks.

YIELD: 6 SERVINGS.

flavorful pot roast

PREP: 10 MIN. COOK: 7 HOURS

You can cook a pot roast to tender perfection with a slow cooker. Convenient packages of dressing and gravy combine in a delicious sauce. It makes a hearty dinner with just a few minutes of your time.

Arlene Butler, Ogden, Utah

2 boneless beef chuck roasts (2-1/2 pounds each)
1 envelope ranch salad dressing mix
1 envelope Italian salad dressing mix
1 envelope brown gravy mix
1/2 cup water

1 Place the chuck roasts in a 5-qt. slow cooker. In a small bowl, combine the salad dressing and gravy mixes; stir in water. Pour over meat. Cover and cook on low for 7-8 hours or until tender. If desired, thicken cooking juices for gravy.

YIELD: 12-15 SERVINGS.

My gang can't get enough of this savory entree. We have to have it at least once a month, or everyone goes through withdrawal. Leftovers freeze well, too.

Cori Cooper, Boise, Iowa

meatball calzones

PREP: 1-1/2 HOURS + STANDING BAKE: 25 MIN.

3 eggs, lightly beaten
1 cup seasoned bread crumbs
1 cup grated Parmesan cheese
3 teaspoons Italian seasoning
2 pounds ground beef
3 loaves (1 pound each) frozen bread dough, thawed
3 cups (12 ounces) shredded part-skim mozzarella cheese
1 egg white, lightly beaten
Additional Italian seasoning
1 jar (14 ounces) spaghetti sauce, warmed

1 In a large bowl, combine the eggs, bread crumbs, Parmesan cheese and Italian seasoning. Crumble beef over mixture and mix well. Shape into 1-in. balls.

2 Place meatballs on a rack in a shallow baking pan. Bake, uncovered, at 400° for 10-15 minutes or until no longer pink. Drain on paper towels. Reduce heat to 350°.

3 On a floured surface, roll each portion of dough into an 18-in. x 12-in. rectangle. Spoon a third of the meatballs and mozzarella cheese down the center of each rectangle. Fold dough over filling; press edges firmly to seal.

4 Place seam side down on greased baking sheets. Brush tops with egg white; sprinkle with Italian seasoning. Let stand for 15-30 minutes. Bake for 25-30 minutes or until golden brown. Serve with spaghetti sauce.

YIELD: 3 CALZONES (4 SERVINGS EACH).

EDITOR'S NOTE: The meatballs can be made a day in advance and refrigerated. Reheat in the microwave before assembling the calzone.

2 In a large skillet, saute crab in butter for 3-4 minutes or until heated through. Add garlic; cook 1 minute longer. Stir in lemon juice; keep warm.

3 Grill steaks, covered, over medium heat or broil 4 in. from the heat for 6-8 minutes on each side or until meat reaches desired doneness (for medium-rare, a meat thermometer should read 145°; medium, 160°; well-done, 170°). Top with crab mixture, asparagus and bearnaise sauce. Sprinkle with paprika.

YIELD: 4 SERVINGS.

chili pockets

PREP/TOTAL TIME: 25 MIN.

Bring some fun to the table with this scrumptious twist on chili. These are just awesome. Made with only a few basic items, these pockets make a meal in no time.

Diane Angell, Rockford, Illinois

1 can (15 ounces) chili with beans
1/2 cup shredded cheddar cheese
2 tablespoons minced fresh cilantro
1 can (13.8 ounces) refrigerated pizza crust
4-1/2 teaspoons cornmeal, divided
Sour cream and salsa

1 In a small bowl, combine the chili, cheese and cilantro. Roll pizza dough into a 12-in. square; cut into four 6-in. squares. Spoon 1/2 cup chili mixture onto the center of each square; brush edges of dough with water. Fold one corner of each square over filling to the opposite corner, forming a triangle. Using a fork, crimp edges to seal.

2 Sprinkle 1-1/2 teaspoons cornmeal over a greased 15-in. x 10-in. x 1-in. baking pan. Place pockets in the pan; prick tops with a fork. Sprinkle with the remaining cornmeal.

3 Bake at 425° for 10-12 minutes or until golden brown. Serve with sour cream and salsa.

YIELD: 4 SERVINGS.

You can create this elegant dish by using fantastic ingredients such as beef tenderloin, crabmeat and fresh asparagus.

Cindy Dorsett, Lubbock, Texas

asparagus steak oscar

PREP/TOTAL TIME: 30 MIN.

1 envelope bearnaise sauce
1 pound fresh asparagus, trimmed
1/4 pound fresh crabmeat
2 tablespoons butter
1/2 teaspoon minced garlic
1 tablespoon lemon juice
4 beef tenderloin steaks (1 inch thick and 3 ounces each)
1/8 teaspoon paprika

1 Prepare bearnaise sauce according to package directions. Meanwhile, place asparagus in a steamer basket; place in a large saucepan over 1 in. of water. Bring to a boil; cover and steam for 8-10 minutes or until crisp-tender.

simple shepherd's pie

PREP: 20 MIN. BAKE: 30 MIN.

My son fixes this entree when we have leftover mashed potatoes. It's a great dinner with a green salad.

Lera Joe Bayer, Wirtz, Virginia

- 1 pound ground beef
- 2 cans (10-3/4 ounces each) condensed cream of potato soup, undiluted
- 1-1/2 cups frozen peas, thawed
- 1-1/2 cups frozen sliced carrots, thawed
- 4 cups mashed potatoes (with added milk and butter)

1 In a large skillet, cook beef over medium heat until no longer pink; drain. Add the soup, peas and carrots. Pour into a greased 11-in. x 7-in. baking dish. Top with potatoes. Bake, uncovered, at 350° for 30-40 minutes or until heated through.

YIELD: 4 SERVINGS.

I love this recipe because it makes a lot—two hearty casseroles.

Debra Butcher, Decatur, Indiana

meaty pasta casseroles

PREP: 45 MIN. BAKE: 35 MIN.

- 1 package (16 ounces) penne pasta
- 1 pound ground beef
- 1 pound bulk Italian pork sausage
- 1-3/4 cups sliced fresh mushrooms
- 1 medium onion, chopped
- 1 medium green pepper, chopped
- 2 cans (14-1/2 ounces each) Italian diced tomatoes
- 1 jar (25.6 ounces) Italian sausage and garlic spaghetti sauce
- 1 jar (16 ounces) chunky mild salsa
- 1 package (8 ounces) sliced pepperoni, chopped
- 1 cup (4 ounces) shredded Swiss cheese, divided
- 4 cups (16 ounces) shredded part-skim mozzarella cheese, divided
- 1-1/2 cups shredded Parmesan cheese, divided
- 1 jar (26 ounces) three-cheese spaghetti sauce

1 Cook pasta according to package directions. Meanwhile, in a Dutch oven, cook the beef, sausage, mushrooms, onion and green pepper over medium heat until meat is no longer pink; drain.

2 Drain pasta; add to meat mixture. Stir in the tomatoes, sausage and garlic spaghetti sauce, salsa and pepperoni.

3 Divide half of pasta mixture between two greased 13-in. x 9-in. baking dishes. Sprinkle each with 1/4 cup Swiss cheese, 1 cup mozzarella cheese and 1/3 cup Parmesan cheese. Spread 3/4 cup of three-cheese spaghetti sauce over each. Top with remaining pasta mixture and three-cheese spaghetti sauce. Sprinkle with remaining cheeses.

4 Cover and freeze one casserole for up to 3 months. Cover and bake remaining casserole at 350° for 25 minutes. Uncover; bake 10 minutes longer or until cheese is melted.

5 **To use frozen casserole:** Thaw in the refrigerator overnight. Remove from the refrigerator 30 minutes before baking. Cover and bake at 350° for 45 minutes. Uncover; bake 10 minutes longer or until cheese is melted.

YIELD: 2 CASSEROLES (6 SERVINGS EACH).

A jar of chipotle salsa makes it easy to spice up beef sirloin for my mouthwatering sandwiches. Keep this no-stress recipe in mind the next time you have to feed a hungry crowd.

Jessica Ring, Madison, Wisconsin

meatball stroganoff

PREP/TOTAL TIME: 25 MIN.

This is a quick-and-easy way to make a comfort-food dinner for your family. To save time, you can defrost the meatballs in the microwave.

Sarita Powers, Madison, Virginia

- 1 jar (12 ounces) home-style beef gravy
- 1/2 cup sour cream
- 1 package (12 ounces) frozen fully cooked homestyle meatballs, thawed
- Hot cooked egg noodles

1 In a large saucepan, combine gravy and sour cream. Bring to a gentle boil over medium heat; stir in meatballs. Reduce heat; cook, uncovered, for 15-20 minutes or until heated through, stirring occasionally. Serve with noodles.

YIELD: 4 SERVINGS.

loaded flank steak

PREP/TOTAL TIME: 25 MIN.

For a delicious steak entree, try this recipe. The tasty stuffing will make this elegant enough to serve to guests.

Tammy Thomas, Mustang, Oklahoma

- 1/2 cup butter, softened
- 6 bacon strips, cooked and crumbled
- 3 green onions, chopped
- 2 tablespoons ranch salad dressing mix
- 1/2 teaspoon pepper
- 1 beef flank steak (1 inch thick and 1-1/2 to 2 pounds)

1 In a bowl, combine the butter, bacon, onions, salad dressing mix and pepper. Cut a deep slit in steak, forming a pocket. Stuff butter mixture into slit.

2 Grill steak, covered, over medium heat or broil 4-6 in. from the heat for 5-7 minutes on each side or until meat reaches desired doneness (for medium-rare, a meat thermometer should read 145°; medium, 160°; well-done, 170°). To serve, thinly slice across the grain.

YIELD: 6-8 SERVINGS.

chipotle beef sandwiches

PREP: 25 MIN. COOK: 7 HOURS

- 1 large sweet onion, halved and thinly sliced
- 1 beef sirloin tip roast (3 pounds)
- 1 jar (16 ounces) chipotle salsa
- 1/2 cup beer or nonalcoholic beer
- 1 envelope beefy onion soup mix
- 10 kaiser rolls, split

1 Place onion in a 5-qt. slow cooker. Cut roast in half; place over onion. Combine salsa, beer and soup mix. Pour over top. Cover and cook on low for 7-8 hours or until meat is tender.

2 Remove roast. Shred the meat with two forks and return to the slow cooker; heat through. Using a slotted spoon, spoon shredded meat onto each roll.

YIELD: 10 SERVINGS.

On chilly days, it's a pleasure coming home to this savory pot roast bubbling in the slow cooker. The tender beef, vegetables and tasty gravy are wonderful over a bed of noodles.

Lora Snyder
Columbus, Massachusetts

burgundy beef

PREP: 20 MIN. COOK: 8 HOURS

1/2 pound sliced fresh mushrooms

1/2 pound fresh baby carrots

1 medium green pepper, julienned

1 boneless beef chuck roast (2-1/2 pounds)

1 can (10-3/4 ounces) condensed golden mushroom soup, undiluted

1/4 cup Burgundy wine or beef broth

1 tablespoon Worcestershire sauce

1 envelope onion soup mix

1/4 teaspoon pepper

2 to 3 tablespoons cornstarch

2 tablespoons cold water

Hot cooked wide egg noodles

1 In a 5-qt. slow cooker, combine the mushrooms, carrots and green pepper; place roast on top. In a large bowl, combine the soup, wine, Worcestershire sauce, soup mix and pepper; pour over roast. Cover and cook on low for 8-9 hours or until meat is tender.

2 Transfer roast and vegetables to a serving platter; keep warm. Strain cooking juices and skim fat; place in a large saucepan.

3 Combine cornstarch and cold water until smooth; gradually stir into cooking juices. Bring to a boil; cook and stir for 2 minutes or until thickened. Serve with the beef, vegetables and noodles.

YIELD: 6-8 SERVINGS.

baked spaghetti

PREP: 20 MIN. BAKE: 40 MIN.

- 1 package (16 ounces) spaghetti
- 1-1/2 pounds ground beef
- 1 medium onion, chopped
- 1/2 cup chopped green pepper
- 1 can (10-3/4 ounces) condensed cream of mushroom soup, undiluted
- 1 can (10-3/4 ounces) condensed tomato soup, undiluted
- 1 can (8 ounces) tomato sauce
- 1 cup water
- 2 tablespoons brown sugar
- 1 teaspoon salt
- 1 teaspoon dried basil
- 1 teaspoon dried oregano
- 1/2 teaspoon dried marjoram
- 1/2 teaspoon dried rosemary, crushed
- 1/8 teaspoon garlic salt
- 1 cup (4 ounces) shredded part-skim mozzarella cheese, divided

1 Break spaghetti in half; cook according to package directions. Meanwhile, in a Dutch oven, cook the beef, onion and green pepper over medium heat until meat is no longer pink; drain. Stir in the soups, tomato sauce, water, brown sugar and seasonings.

2 Drain spaghetti; stir into meat sauce. Add 1/2 cup cheese. Transfer to a greased 13-in. x 9-in. baking dish.

3 Cover and bake at 350° for 30 minutes. Uncover; sprinkle with remaining cheese. Bake 10-15 minutes longer or until cheese is melted.

YIELD: 12 SERVINGS.

taco bundles

PREP: 25 MIN. BAKE: 15 MIN.

I took a gourmet Mexican cooking class, and I had so much fun in class that I came up with many of my own recipes. These spicy bundles are just one of the dishes that class inspired. Kids especially love them.

GaleLynn Peterson, Long Beach, California

3/4 pound ground beef
1/3 cup chopped onion
2 tablespoons taco seasoning
2 tablespoons sliced ripe olives, drained
2 tablespoons taco sauce
2 tubes (8 ounces each) refrigerated crescent rolls
1 cup (4 ounces) shredded Colby cheese
1 cup (4 ounces) shredded Monterey Jack cheese
Shredded lettuce, chopped tomatoes, guacamole and sour cream

1 In a large skillet, cook the beef and onion over medium heat until meat is no longer pink; drain. Stir in the taco seasoning, olives and taco sauce.

2 Unroll crescent dough; separate into eight rectangles. Seal seams and perforations. Place meat mixture in the center of each rectangle; sprinkle with cheeses. Fold dough over filling and pinch to seal. Place seam side down on an ungreased baking sheet.

3 Bake at 375° for 15-20 minutes or until golden brown. Layer with lettuce, tomatoes, guacamole and sour cream on four serving plates; top each with two bundles.

YIELD: 4 SERVINGS.

This recipe is a big hit with my husband and two children. We like it so much that I fix it twice a month and never have any leftovers.

Barbara Spohn, Broken Arrow, Oklahoma

beef fettuccine dinner

PREP/TOTAL TIME: 20 MIN.

1 pound ground beef
1-1/2 cups water
1 package (4.3 ounces) fettuccine and beef-flavored sauce mix
1 can (8 ounces) tomato sauce
2 teaspoons chili powder
1 can (11 ounces) whole kernel corn, drained
1 cup (4 ounces) shredded cheddar cheese, divided

1 In a large skillet, cook beef over medium heat until no longer pink; drain. Add water; bring to a boil. Stir in the fettuccine mix, tomato sauce and chili powder. Return to a boil. Reduce heat; simmer, uncovered, for 7 minutes or until thickened.

2 Stir in corn and 2/3 cup cheese; heat through. Sprinkle with remaining cheese.

YIELD: 4 SERVINGS.

1 In a 3-qt. slow cooker, combine all the ingredients. Cover and cook on low for 3-1/2 to 4-1/2 hours or until meat is tender.

YIELD: 6 SERVINGS.

beef tips on potatoes

PREP/TOTAL TIME: 15 MIN.

Dressing up store-bought convenience items makes this satisfying supper a snap to put on the table. It's hot, delicious and ready to eat in minutes.

Taste of Home Test Kitchen

2 packages (17 ounces each) refrigerated beef tips with gravy
1 package (24 ounces) refrigerated mashed potatoes
3/4 cup fresh broccoli florets, finely chopped
1 tablespoon water
3/4 cup shredded cheddar cheese, divided

1 Prepare beef tips and mashed potatoes according to package directions. Place broccoli and water in a microwave-safe dish; cover and microwave on high for 3 minutes or until crisp-tender.

2 Stir the broccoli and 1/2 cup cheese into potatoes. Serve beef tips with potatoes; sprinkle with the remaining cheese.

YIELD: 4 SERVINGS.

EDITOR'S NOTE: This recipe was tested in a 1,100-watt microwave.

Preparation couldn't be simpler for this hearty no-fuss stew! I created this recipe when I didn't have some of my usual ingredients for vegetable beef soup. My husband says it's the best I ever made!

Margaret Turza, South Bend, Indiana

zesty beef stew

PREP: 10 MIN. COOK: 3-1/2 HOURS

1 pound beef stew meat, cut into 1-inch cubes
1 package (16 ounces) frozen mixed vegetables, thawed
1 can (15 ounces) pinto beans, rinsed and drained
1-1/2 cups water
1 can (8 ounces) pizza sauce
2 tablespoons medium pearl barley
1 tablespoon dried minced onion
2 teaspoons beef bouillon granules
1/4 teaspoon crushed red pepper flakes

steak fajita pasta

PREP/TOTAL TIME: 30 MIN.

This steak and pasta supper combines foods my gang craves with the convenience I need.

Veronica Callaghan, Glastonbury, Connecticut

1 pound beef flank steak or beef top sirloin steak

1 small onion, thinly sliced

2 tablespoons butter

1 can (14-1/2 ounces) diced tomatoes, drained

1 jar (7 ounces) roasted sweet red peppers, drained and coarsely chopped

1-1/3 cups water

1/4 teaspoon hot pepper sauce

1 package (4.8 ounces) angel hair pasta with herbs

2/3 cup half-and-half cream

1 Place steak on a broiler pan. Broil 4 in. from the heat for 5-7 minutes on each side or until meat reaches desired doneness (for medium-rare, a meat thermometer should read 145°; medium, 160°; well-done, 170°).

2 In a skillet, saute onion in butter until tender. Add tomatoes and peppers; saute 1 minute longer. Add water and pepper sauce. Bring to a boil; stir in pasta with contents of seasoning packet. Return to a boil. Reduce heat to medium; cook, uncovered, for 5-6 minutes or until pasta is tender, stirring frequently. Stir in cream; heat through. Thinly slice beef; serve over pasta.

YIELD: 4 SERVINGS.

EDITOR'S NOTE: This recipe was tested with Pasta Roni.

pizza casserole

PREP: 20 MIN. BAKE: 30 MIN.

3 cups uncooked spiral pasta

2 pounds ground beef

1 medium onion, chopped

2 cans (8 ounces each) mushroom stems and pieces, drained

1 can (15 ounces) tomato sauce

1 jar (14 ounces) pizza sauce

1 can (6 ounces) tomato paste

Friends and family love my new spin on pizza. Packed with cheeses, meats and tomatoes, this hearty pasta dinner will go fast!

Nancy Foust, Stoneboro, Pennsylvania

1/2 teaspoon sugar

1/2 teaspoon garlic powder

1/2 teaspoon onion powder

1/2 teaspoon dried oregano

4 cups (16 ounces) shredded part-skim mozzarella cheese, divided

1 package (3-1/2 ounces) sliced pepperoni

1/2 cup grated Parmesan cheese

1 Cook pasta according to package directions. Meanwhile, in a Dutch oven, cook beef and onion over medium heat until meat is no longer pink; drain. Stir in the mushrooms, tomato sauce, pizza sauce, tomato paste, sugar and seasonings. Drain pasta; stir into meat sauce.

2 Divide half of the mixture between two greased 11-in. x 7-in. baking dishes; sprinkle each with 1 cup mozzarella cheese. Repeat layers. Top each with pepperoni and Parmesan cheese. Cover and bake at 350° for 20 minutes. Uncover; bake 10-15 minutes longer or until heated through.

YIELD: 2 CASSEROLES (8 SERVINGS EACH).

To have supper on the table in no time, cook all four quesadillas on a large nonstick griddle.

Taste of Home Test Kitchen

barbecued beef quesadillas

PREP/TOTAL TIME: 20 MIN.

1/2 cup sour cream
1/3 cup minced fresh cilantro
1 teaspoon lime juice
1 carton (18 ounces) refrigerated fully cooked barbecued shredded beef
8 flour tortillas (8 inches)
1/2 cup refried beans
1 cup (4 ounces) shredded Mexican cheese blend
1-1/2 cups shredded lettuce
Chopped fresh tomatoes, optional

1 In a small bowl, combine the sour cream, cilantro and lime juice; set aside. Heat barbecued beef according to package directions. Spread four tortillas with refried beans; top each with 1/2 cup beef and 1/4 cup cheese. Top with remaining tortillas.

2 In a large skillet coated with cooking spray, heat quesadillas over medium heat for 1-2 minutes on each side or until lightly browned. Cut each into four wedges. Serve with shredded lettuce, sour cream sauce and tomatoes if desired.

YIELD: 4 SERVINGS.

italian beef sandwiches

PREP: 20 MIN. COOK: 5 HOURS

With a little kick and plenty of tender meat and juices, these hearty sandwiches are a meal. If you'd like, add a slice of provolone for a real treat.

Troy Parkos, Verona, Wisconsin

1 boneless beef chuck roast (3 pounds)
1 teaspoon Italian seasoning
1/4 teaspoon cayenne pepper
1/4 teaspoon pepper
1/4 cup water
1 jar (16 ounces) sliced pepperoncinis, undrained
1 medium sweet red pepper, julienned
1 medium green pepper, julienned
1 garlic clove, minced
1 envelope reduced-sodium onion soup mix
2 tablespoons Worcestershire sauce
2 loaves (1 pound each) Italian bread, halved lengthwise

1 Cut roast in half; place in a 5-qt. slow cooker. Sprinkle with the Italian seasoning, cayenne and pepper. Add water. Cover and cook on high for 4 hours or until meat is tender.

2 Remove roast; shred meat with two forks and return to the slow cooker. In a large bowl, combine the pepperoncinis, peppers, garlic, soup mix and Worcestershire sauce; pour over meat. Cover and cook on high for 1 hour longer or until peppers are tender.

3 Spoon beef mixture over the bottom halves of bread; replace bread tops. Cut each loaf into six sandwiches.

YIELD: 12 SERVINGS.

This flavorful stir-fry is easy and relatively inexpensive. It's served over ramen noodles, which is a nice change from rice we usually have. To simplify preparation, I use store-bought garlic infused olive oil instead of minced garlic and olive oil.

Dottie Wanat
Modesto, California

asparagus beef lo mein

PREP/TOTAL TIME: 20 MIN.

1 beef top sirloin steak (1 pound), thinly sliced

2 tablespoons olive oil

1 pound fresh asparagus, trimmed and cut into 2-1/2-inch pieces

1/4 teaspoon minced garlic

2-1/4 cups water, divided

2 packages (3 ounces each) beef ramen noodles

2/3 cup hoisin sauce

1 In a large skillet or wok, stir-fry beef in oil for 5 minutes or until meat is no longer pink.

Add the asparagus and garlic; stir-fry for 2 minutes or until asparagus is crisp-tender.

2 In a bowl, combine 1/4 cup water and 1/2 teaspoon seasoning from one ramen noodle seasoning packet; stir until dissolved. Add hoisin sauce; stir into the beef mixture. Bring to a boil; cook and stir for 2 minutes or until thickened. (Discard remaining seasoning from opened packet.)

3 In a large saucepan, bring remaining water to a boil; add ramen noodles and contents of remaining seasoning packet. Cook for 3 minutes. Remove from the heat; cover and let stand until noodles are tender. Serve with beef mixture.

YIELD: 4 SERVINGS.

meatball pizza

PREP/TOTAL TIME: 25 MIN.

I always keep meatballs and bread shell crusts in the freezer to make this pizza at the spur of the moment. Add a tossed salad and you have a delicious dinner.

Mary Humeniuk-Smith, Perry Hall, Maryland

1 prebaked 12-inch pizza crust
1 can (8 ounces) pizza sauce
1 teaspoon garlic powder
1 teaspoon Italian seasoning
1/4 cup grated Parmesan cheese
1 small onion, halved and sliced
12 frozen fully cooked homestyle meatballs (1/2 ounce each), thawed and halved
1 cup (4 ounces) shredded part-skim mozzarella cheese
1 cup (4 ounces) shredded cheddar cheese

1 Place the crust on an ungreased 12-in. pizza pan. Spread with pizza sauce; top with garlic powder, Italian seasoning, Parmesan cheese and onion. Arrange the meatball halves over top; sprinkle with cheeses.

2 Bake at 350° for 12-17 minutes or until heated through and cheese is melted.

YIELD: 6-8 SLICES.

I adapted this recipe to suit our love of spicy food. The ravioli taste like mini enchiladas. I serve them with a Mexican-inspired salad and pineapple sherbet for dessert.

Debbie Purdue, Westland, Michigan

fiesta ravioli

PREP/TOTAL TIME: 20 MIN.

1 package (25 ounces) frozen beef ravioli
1 can (10 ounces) enchilada sauce
1 cup salsa
2 cups (8 ounces) shredded Monterey Jack cheese
1 can (2-1/4 ounces) sliced ripe olives, drained

1 Cook ravioli according to package directions. In a skillet, combine enchilada sauce and salsa. Cook and stir over medium heat until heated through. Drain ravioli; add to sauce and gently toss to coat. Top with cheese and olives. Cover and cook over low heat for 3-4 minutes or until cheese is melted.

YIELD: 4-6 SERVINGS.

presto stew & garlic mashed potatoes

PREP/TOTAL TIME: 30 MIN.

To lighten up this recipe, I use ground turkey breast and fat-free gravy. This hearty stew is also good served over your favorite pasta, biscuits or leftover mashed potatoes.

Mary Tallman, Arbor Vitae, Wisconsin

1 pound lean ground beef (90% lean)
1/4 cup chopped onion
1 can (14-1/2 ounces) diced tomatoes, drained
1 jar (12 ounces) fat-free beef gravy
1 cup frozen mixed vegetables
1/2 teaspoon dried marjoram
1/2 teaspoon pepper
POTATOES:
1 cup water
1/2 cup fat-free milk
1 tablespoon butter
1/2 teaspoon garlic powder
1/4 teaspoon pepper
1-1/3 cups mashed potato flakes
1 tablespoon minced fresh parsley

1 In a large nonstick skillet, cook beef and onion over medium heat until meat is no longer pink; drain. Stir in the tomatoes, gravy, vegetables, marjoram and pepper. Bring to a boil. Reduce heat; cover and simmer for 5-8 minutes or until vegetables are tender.

2 Meanwhile, in a small saucepan, bring the water, milk, butter, garlic powder and pepper just to a boil. Remove from the heat; stir in potato flakes and parsley. Cover and let stand for 5 minutes. Fluff with a fork. Serve with stew.

YIELD: 4 SERVINGS.

taco macaroni

PREP/TOTAL TIME: 30 MIN.

1 package (16 ounces) elbow macaroni
1 pound ground beef

This dish uses tomatoes three different ways. And it's a hearty way to warm up, and fill up, this winter!

Marissa Undercofler, Howard, Pennsylvania

3/4 cup chopped onion
1 can (14-1/2 ounces) diced tomatoes, undrained
1 can (10-3/4 ounces) condensed tomato soup, undiluted
1 can (8 ounces) tomato sauce
1 envelope taco seasoning
Shredded cheddar cheese

1 Cook macaroni according to package directions.

2 Meanwhile, in a Dutch oven, cook beef and onion over medium heat until meat is no longer pink; drain. Stir in the tomatoes, soup, tomato sauce and taco seasoning. Bring to a boil. Reduce heat; simmer, uncovered, for 8-10 minutes or until thickened.

3 Drain macaroni; stir into meat mixture and heat through. Sprinkle with cheese.

YIELD: 6 SERVINGS.

The secret to these pretty flank steak pinwheels lies in their butterfly treatment. Because the steaks are flattened, marinade isn't needed. Instead, they're filled with a colorful stuffing of red pepper and spinach and draped with a flavorful, homemade blue cheese sauce.

Taste of Home
Test Kitchen

flank steak pinwheels

PREP: 30 MIN. GRILL: 10 MIN.

8 bacon strips
1 beef flank steak (1-1/2 pounds)
4 cups fresh baby spinach
1 jar (7 ounces) roasted sweet red peppers, drained

CREAM CHEESE SAUCE:

1 package (3 ounces) cream cheese, softened
1/4 cup 2% milk
1 tablespoon butter
1/4 teaspoon pepper
1/2 cup crumbled blue cheese

1 Place bacon strips on a microwave-safe plate lined with microwave-safe paper towels. Cover with another paper towel; microwave on high for 2-3 minutes or until partially cooked.

2 Meanwhile, cut steak horizontally from a long side to within 1/2 in. of opposite side. Open meat so it lies flat; cover with plastic wrap. Flatten to 1/4-in. thickness. Remove plastic. Place spinach over steak to within 1 in. of edges; top with red peppers.

3 With the grain of the meat going from left to right, roll up jelly-roll style. Wrap bacon strips around beef; secure with toothpicks. Slice beef across the grain into eight slices.

4 Grill, covered, over medium heat for 5-7 minutes on each side or until meat reaches desired doneness (for medium-rare, a meat thermometer should read 145°; medium, 160°; well-done, 170°). Discard toothpicks.

5 In a small saucepan, combine the cream cheese, milk, butter and pepper. Cook and stir over low heat just until smooth (do not boil). Stir in blue cheese. Serve with pinwheels.

YIELD: 4 SERVINGS.

EDITOR'S NOTE: This recipe was tested in a 1,100-watt microwave.

texts tamale pie

PREP/TOTAL TIME: 25 MIN.

My aunt shared this great South Texas dish with me. With just four ingredients, the spicy casserole can be served swiftly...and will undoubtedly disappear quickly. When I take it to church dinners, there aren't any leftovers.

Billy Boyd, Houston, Texas

- 1 package (6.8 ounces) Spanish rice and pasta mix
- 1 can (15 ounces) chili with beans
- 1 can (15 ounces) beef tamales, drained and cut into 1-inch pieces
- 1 cup (4 ounces) shredded cheddar cheese

1 Prepare rice mix according to package directions. Meanwhile, spoon chili into a greased 8-in. square baking dish. Top with tamales.

2 Bake, uncovered, at 350° for 10 minutes. Top with cooked rice; sprinkle with cheese. Bake 5 minutes longer or until cheese is melted.

YIELD: 6 SERVINGS.

Put this zippy twist on your meat loaf dinner. It has a sweet and sour taste, which will delight your family. They will be requesting it all the time.

Deb Thompson, Lincoln, Nebraska

sweet-and-sour meat loaf

PREP/TOTAL TIME: 25 MIN.

- 1 egg, lightly beaten
- 5 tablespoons ketchup, divided
- 2 tablespoons prepared mustard
- 1/2 cup dry bread crumbs
- 2 tablespoons onion soup mix
- 1/4 teaspoon salt
- 1/4 teaspoon pepper
- 1 pound lean ground beef (90% lean)
- 1/4 cup sugar
- 2 tablespoons brown sugar
- 2 tablespoons cider vinegar

1 In a large bowl, combine the egg, 2 tablespoons ketchup, mustard, bread crumbs, soup mix, salt and pepper. Crumble beef over mixture and mix well. Shape into an oval loaf.

2 Place in a shallow 1-qt. microwave-safe dish. Cover and microwave on high for 10-12 minutes or until no pink remains and a meat thermometer reads 160°; drain.

3 Meanwhile in a small bowl, combine the sugars, vinegar and remaining ketchup; drizzle over meat loaf. Cover and microwave on high for 2-3 minutes longer or until heated through. Let stand for 10 minutes before slicing.

YIELD: 4 SERVINGS.

EDITOR'S NOTE: This recipe was tested in a 1,100-watt microwave.

italian pot roast

PREP: 20 MIN. BAKE: 2 HOURS

I had so many requests for this recipe that I made up cards to hand out every time I serve it at a get-together. My husband and son think it's world-class eating!

Carolyn Wells, North Syracuse, New York

- 1 tablespoon all-purpose flour
- 1 large oven roasting bag
- 1 boneless beef chuck roast (3 pounds)
- 1-2/3 cups water
- 1 can (10-3/4 ounces) condensed tomato soup, undiluted
- 1 envelope onion soup mix
- 1-1/2 teaspoons Italian seasoning
- 1 garlic clove, minced
- 1/4 cup cornstarch
- 1/4 cup cold water

1 Sprinkle flour into oven bag; shake to coat. Place in a 13-in. x 9-in. baking pan; add roast. In a small bowl, combine the water, tomato soup, soup mix, Italian seasoning and garlic; pour into oven bag.

2 Cut six 1/2-in. slits in top of bag; close with tie provided. Bake at 325° for 2 to 2-1/2 hours or until meat is tender.

3 Remove roast to a serving platter and keep warm. Transfer cooking juices to a small saucepan; skim fat. Bring to a boil. Combine cornstarch and cold water until smooth; stir into cooking juices. Return to a boil; cook and stir for 2 minutes or until thickened. Slice roast; serve with gravy.

YIELD: 8-10 SERVINGS (3 CUPS GRAVY).

One busy weeknight, I created these quick and hearty sandwiches with frozen meatballs and canned pizza sauce. They're a snap to prepare, taste delicious and my gang thinks they're great.

Ann Nolte, Elmendorf AFB, Alaska

meatball pizza subs

PREP/TOTAL TIME: 25 MIN.

- 1-1/3 cups pizza sauce
- 4 submarine buns, split and toasted
- 1-1/3 cups shredded part-skim mozzarella cheese
- 20 slices pepperoni
- 1 package (12 ounces) frozen fully cooked Italian meatballs, thawed
- Italian seasoning to taste

1 Spread 1/3 cup pizza sauce on the bottom of each bun. Top each with 1/3 cup cheese, five slices of pepperoni and three meatballs; sprinkle with Italian seasoning. Replace tops.

2 Wrap each sandwich in foil. Bake at 400° for 10-12 minutes or until heated through.

YIELD: 4 SERVINGS.

hearty short ribs

PREP: 15 MIN. COOK: 6-1/4 HOURS

1 large onion, sliced

4 pounds bone-in beef short ribs

1/2 pound sliced fresh mushrooms

1 can (10-3/4 ounces) condensed cream of mushroom soup, undiluted

1/2 cup water

1 envelope brown gravy mix

1 teaspoon minced garlic

1/2 teaspoon dried thyme

1 tablespoon cornstarch

2 tablespoons cold water

Hot mashed potatoes

1 Place onion in a 5-qt. slow cooker; top with ribs. Combine the mushrooms, soup, 1/2 cup water, gravy mix, garlic and thyme; pour over ribs. Cover and cook on low for 6 to 6-1/2 hours or until meat is tender.

2 Remove meat to serving platter; keep warm. Skim fat from cooking juices; transfer to a small saucepan. Bring to a boil.

3 Combine cornstarch and cold water until smooth. Gradually stir into pan. Bring to a boil. Cook and stir for 2 minutes or until thickened. Serve with meat and mashed potatoes.

YIELD: 6 SERVINGS.

nacho cheese beef bake

PREP: 25 MIN. BAKE: 15 MIN.

- 2 cups uncooked egg noodles
- 1 pound ground beef
- 1 can (14-1/2 ounces) diced tomatoes
- 1 can (10-3/4 ounces) condensed nacho cheese soup, undiluted
- 1 jar (5-3/4 ounces) sliced pimiento-stuffed olives, drained
- 1 can (4 ounces) chopped green chilies
- 1-1/2 cups (6 ounces) shredded cheddar cheese
- 2 cups crushed tortilla chips
- 1/3 cup prepared ranch salad dressing
- Shredded lettuce, sour cream and/or salsa, optional

1 Cook the noodles according to the package directions; drain.

2 Meanwhile, in a large saucepan, cook beef over medium heat until no longer pink; drain. Stir in the tomatoes, soup, olives and chilies. Bring to a boil. Reduce heat; simmer, uncovered, for 10 minutes. Stir in noodles.

3 Transfer to a greased 11-in. x 7-in. baking dish. Sprinkle with cheese. Bake at 350° for 15-20 minutes or until heated through. Top with tortilla chips; drizzle with salad dressing. Serve with lettuce, sour cream and/or salsa if desired.

YIELD: 4 SERVINGS.

dressed-up beef tips

PREP/TOTAL TIME: 25 MIN.

Convenient packaged beef tips and gravy can be jazzed up for dinner by adding vegetables and a wine sauce.

Taste of Home Test Kitchen

- 2 tablespoons cornstarch
- 1 can (14-1/2 ounces) beef broth
- 1/4 cup dry red wine or additional beef broth
- 1/2 cup cut fresh green beans (1-inch pieces)
- 1/4 cup sliced fresh carrot
- 1 tablespoon finely chopped onion
- 1 tablespoon butter
- 1 package (17 ounces) refrigerated beef tips with gravy
- 1 tablespoon minced fresh parsley

1 In a small bowl, combine the cornstarch, broth and wine until smooth; set aside. In a large skillet, saute the beans, carrot and onion in butter for 3-4 minutes or until tender.

2 Add beef tips; heat through. Stir broth mixture and add to skillet. Bring to a boil; cook and stir for 2 minutes or until thickened. Stir in parsley.

YIELD: 4 CUPS.

EDITOR'S NOTE: Try these saucy beef tips over refrigerated mashed potatoes, noodles or rice for a quick weeknight meal.

A friend shared this recipe with me, and I've prepared it monthly ever since. The crust is made from refrigerated crescent roll dough. While the ground beef is browning, I simply press the dough into a baking dish. Guests always comment on the tasty crust as well as the zesty filling and crunchy topping.

Patricia Eckard, Singers Glen, Virginia

taco crescent bake

PREP: 25 MIN. BAKE: 25 MIN.

- 1 tube (8 ounces) refrigerated crescent rolls
- 2 cups crushed corn chips, divided
- 1-1/2 pounds ground beef
- 1 can (15 ounces) tomato sauce
- 1 envelope taco seasoning
- 1 cup (8 ounces) sour cream
- 1 cup (4 ounces) shredded cheddar cheese

1 Unroll crescent dough into a rectangle; press onto the bottom and 1 in. up the sides of a greased 13-in. x 9-in. baking dish. Seal seams and perforations. Sprinkle with 1 cup of chips; set aside.

2 In a large skillet, cook beef over medium heat until no longer pink; drain. Stir in tomato sauce and taco seasoning; bring to a boil. Reduce heat; simmer, uncovered, for 5 minutes. Spoon over chips. Top with sour cream, cheese and remaining chips.

3 Bake, uncovered, at 350° for 25-30 minutes or until crust is lightly browned.

YIELD: 8 SERVINGS.

1 In a 3-qt. slow cooker, combine the meat, soups, onion, mushrooms, soup mix and pepper. Cover and cook on low for 8 hours or until beef is tender. Stir in sour cream. Serve with noodles.

YIELD: 6 SERVINGS.

beef noodle casserole

PREP: 15 MIN. BAKE: 25 MIN.

This is truly an old standby that's been in my family for years. It is comfort food at its best.

Karen Mathis, Penfield, New York

4-1/2 cups uncooked yolk-free noodles
1 pound lean ground beef (90% lean)
1 small onion, chopped
1/2 cup chopped green pepper
1 can (10-3/4 ounces) reduced-fat reduced-sodium condensed cream of mushroom soup, undiluted
1/4 cup grated Parmesan cheese
1 can (4 ounces) mushroom stems and pieces, drained
1 jar (2 ounces) diced pimientos, drained
1 tablespoon butter, melted
1 teaspoon dried thyme
1/4 teaspoon salt

1 Cook noodles according to package directions; drain. Meanwhile, in a nonstick skillet, cook the beef, onion and green pepper over medium heat until meat is no longer pink; drain.

2 In a large bowl, combine the soup, cheese, mushrooms, pimientos, butter, thyme and salt. Stir in the noodles and beef mixture.

3 Transfer to a 2-qt. baking dish coated with cooking spray. Cover and bake at 350° for 25-30 minutes or until heated through.

YIELD: 6 SERVINGS.

Cream of celery soup adds rich flavor to this family-favorite Stroganoff. Besides its delicious taste, I love the ease I have preparing this recipe. Just put the ingredients in the slow cooker and dinner will be ready without any effort!

Kim Wallace, Dennison, Ohio

creamy celery beef stroganoff

PREP: 20 MIN. COOK: 8 HOURS

2 pounds beef stew meat, cut into 1-inch cubes
1 can (10-3/4 ounces) condensed cream of celery soup, undiluted
1 can (10-3/4 ounces) condensed cream of mushroom soup, undiluted
1 medium onion, chopped
1 jar (6 ounces) sliced mushrooms, drained
1 envelope onion soup mix
1/2 teaspoon pepper
1 cup (8 ounces) sour cream
Hot cooked noodles

almost homemade

spaghetti casserole

PREP: 20 MIN. BAKE: 55 MIN.

This make-ahead casserole can be refrigerated and then baked just before company arrives. Canned soup makes this dish creamy, but it still cuts well for serving.

Kim Rocker, LaGrange, Georgia

- 1 package (16 ounces) angel hair pasta
- 1-1/2 pounds ground beef
- 1 jar (26 ounces) spaghetti sauce
- 2 cans (8 ounces each) tomato sauce
- 1 can (10-3/4 ounces) condensed cream of mushroom soup, undiluted
- 1 cup (8 ounces) sour cream
- 2 cups (8 ounces) shredded Colby-Monterey Jack cheese

1 Cook pasta according to package directions. Meanwhile, in a large skillet, cook beef over medium heat until no longer pink; drain. Stir in spaghetti sauce and tomato sauce. Remove from the heat.

2 Drain pasta. Combine soup and sour cream. In two 8-in. square baking dishes, layer half of the meat sauce, pasta, soup mixture and cheese. Repeat layers.

3 Cover and freeze one casserole for up to 3 months. Cover and bake the remaining casserole at 350° for 55-65 minutes or until cheese is melted.

4 **To use frozen casserole:** Thaw in the refrigerator overnight. Remove from the refrigerator 30 minutes before baking. Bake as directed in Step 3.

YIELD: 2 CASSEROLES (6 SERVINGS EACH).

tater beef bake

PREP: 25 MIN. BAKE: 35 MIN.

- 1-1/2 pounds ground beef
- 1-1/4 cups water
- 2 envelopes sloppy joe sauce mix
- 1 can (6 ounces) tomato paste
- 3-1/2 cups frozen cut green beans
- 1 can (4 ounces) mushroom stems and pieces, drained

I combined two childhood classics—sloppy joes and Tater Tots—to create this home-style dinner that will keep your youngsters coming back for more. Serve this with salad, and dinner is ready!

Karla Wiederholt, Cuba City, Wisconsin

- 6 cups frozen Tater Tots
- 1 cup (4 ounces) shredded cheddar cheese

1 In a Dutch oven, cook beef over medium heat until no longer pink; drain. Stir in water and sauce mix. Bring to a boil. Reduce heat; simmer, uncovered, for 3-5 minutes or until thickened. Add tomato paste; stir until blended. Add green beans and mushrooms.

2 Transfer to a greased 13-in. x 9-in. baking dish. Top with Tater Tots. Bake, uncovered, at 350° for 30 minutes. Sprinkle with cheese; bake 5-10 minutes longer or until heated through and cheese is melted.

YIELD: 6-8 SERVINGS.

This fast favorite will hit the spot, particularly when you're short on time. Shredded beef, spicy Jack cheese and sauteed onion and green pepper are sandwiched between slices of hearty bread, then lightly grilled in a panini pan.

Taste of Home Cooking School

southwestern beef panini

PREP/TOTAL TIME: 30 MIN.

1 package (17 ounces) refrigerated
   fully cooked beef roast au jus
SAUCE:
1 medium onion, finely chopped
1 medium tomato, finely chopped
1 tablespoon minced jalapeno pepper
1 tablespoon minced cilantro
1 carton (8 ounces) sour cream
SANDWICHES:
1 medium green pepper, cut into strips
1 onion, cut into thin wedges
1 tablespoon canola oil
3 tablespoons butter, softened
8 slices firm Italian or sourdough bread
   (1/2 inch thick)

1 medium ripe avocado, peeled and
   thinly sliced
8 to 12 slices deli-style pepper Jack cheese

1 Prepare roast beef according to package directions; drain. Shred beef using 2 forks; set aside. Meanwhile, in a small bowl, combine all the sauce ingredients; set aside.

2 In a panini grill with lid, cook pepper and onion in oil until tender. Remove from pan and set aside.

3 Butter one side of each slice of bread. Place four slices, buttered side down, on work surface. Top each slice with 1-2 slices of cheese, one-quarter of each shredded beef, pepper and onions, avocado and about 2 tablespoons sauce.

4 Top with remaining bread, butter side up. Cover and cook over medium heat about 4 minutes or until golden brown, turning once. Serve warm.

YIELD: 4 SANDWICHES.

EDITOR'S NOTE: When cutting hot peppers, disposable gloves are recommended. Avoid touching your face.

campfire taco salad

PREP/TOTAL TIME: 25 MIN.

Served in a corn chip bag, this easy outdoor meal is flavorful and fun. My neighbor entertained Girl Scouts with this clever recipe.

Jean Komlos, Plymouth, Michigan

6 snack-size bags (1-1/2 ounces each) corn chips
1 can (15 ounces) chili without beans
3 cups (12 ounces) shredded cheddar cheese
3/4 cup sour cream
1 jar (8 ounces) mild salsa
1/2 medium head iceberg lettuce, shredded

1 Cut the top off each bag of chips; set aside. Place chili in a saucepan; cook on a grill over medium heat for 10 minutes or until heated through, stirring occasionally. Spoon about 2 tablespoons of chili into each bag of chips. Top with cheese, sour cream, salsa and lettuce.

YIELD: 6 SERVINGS.

The sweet and savory brisket is a great complement to the zesty potatoes. The rich color of the meat makes it an elegant holiday option.

Racelle Schaefer
Studio City, California

cranberry brisket with horseradish mashed potatoes

PREP: 20 MIN. BAKE: 3 HOURS

1 fresh beef brisket (3 to 4 pounds)
1 can (14 ounces) whole-berry cranberry sauce
1 can (12 ounces) ginger ale
1/2 cup dried cranberries
1 envelope onion soup mix
8 medium potatoes, peeled and quartered
1/3 cup milk
1/4 cup butter, cubed
2 tablespoons prepared horseradish

1 Place brisket in a greased 13-in. x 9-in. baking dish. Combine the cranberry sauce, ginger ale, cranberries and soup mix; pour over meat. Cover and bake at 375° for 2 hours.

2 Uncover; bake 1 hour longer or until meat is tender, basting occasionally.

3 Meanwhile, place potatoes in a Dutch oven; cover with water. Bring to a boil. Reduce heat; cover and cook for 15-20 minutes or until tender. Drain potatoes; mash with milk, butter and horseradish.

4 Let brisket stand for 5 minutes; thinly slice across the grain. Serve meat and juices with potatoes.

YIELD: 8 SERVINGS (1-2/3 CUPS GRAVY).

EDITOR'S NOTE: This is a fresh beef brisket, not corned beef.

packet from dinner mix. Add shells and water to skillet. Bring to a boil; cover and simmer for 10-12 minutes or until pasta is tender.

2 Stir in the salsa, beans, chili powder, salt and contents of cheese sauce packet. Remove from the heat; cover and let stand for 5 minutes.

YIELD: 6 SERVINGS.

beef spinach hot dish

PREP: 30 MIN. BAKE: 20 MIN.

My family, which includes my parents and six brothers and sisters, all love this recipe. I occasionally use ground turkey in place of the ground beef.

Rachel Jones, Roland, Arkansas

- 1 pound ground beef
- 1 medium onion, chopped
- 2 garlic cloves, minced
- 1 can (4 ounces) mushroom stems and pieces, drained
- 1 teaspoon salt
- 1 teaspoon dried oregano
- 1/4 teaspoon pepper
- 2 packages (10 ounces each) frozen chopped spinach, thawed and squeezed dry
- 1 can (10-3/4 ounces) condensed cream of celery soup, undiluted
- 1 cup (8 ounces) sour cream
- 2 cups (8 ounces) shredded part-skim mozzarella cheese, divided

1 In a large skillet, cook beef and onion over medium heat until the meat is no longer pink. Add garlic; cook 1 minute longer. Drain. Stir in the mushrooms, salt, oregano and pepper. Add the spinach, soup and sour cream. Stir in half of the cheese.

2 Transfer to a greased 2-qt. baking dish. Bake, uncovered, at 350° for 15 minutes. Sprinkle with the remaining cheese; bake 5 minutes longer or until cheese is melted.

YIELD: 6-8 SERVINGS.

Boxed macaroni and cheese, store-bought salsa and canned beans make this kid-pleaser a snap to fix. I add shredded Monterey Jack or cheddar cheese for extra flavor.

Louise Graybiel, Toronto, Ontario

↑ beefy shells and cheese

PREP/TOTAL TIME: 30 MIN.

- 1 pound ground beef
- 1 package (12 ounces) shells and cheese dinner mix
- 2 cups water
- 1-1/4 cups salsa
- 1 can (15 ounces) black beans, rinsed and drained
- 1 to 2 teaspoons chili powder
- 1/8 teaspoon salt

1 In a large skillet, cook beef over medium heat until no longer pink; drain. Set aside cheese sauce

salisbury steak

PREP/TOTAL TIME: 30 MIN.

Sometimes I forget about this tasty recipe, so my husband will say, "How about Salisbury Steak for dinner?" He really likes it.

Toni Martin, Byron Center, Michigan

1 egg
1/4 cup 2% milk
1/4 cup dry bread crumbs
1 envelope brown gravy mix, divided
1 teaspoon dried minced onion
1/2 pound lean ground beef (90% lean)
1/2 cup water
1 tablespoon prepared mustard

1 In a large bowl, whisk egg and milk. Add the bread crumbs, 1 tablespoon gravy mix and onion. Crumble beef over mixture and mix well. Shape into two patties, about 3/4 in. thick.

2 Broil 3-4 in. from the heat for 6-7 minutes on each side or until a meat thermometer reads 160° and juices run clear.

3 Place the remaining gravy mix in a small saucepan; stir in water and mustard. Bring to a boil; cook and stir until thickened. Serve with patties.

YIELD: 2 SERVINGS.

meaty corn bread casserole

PREP: 20 MIN. BAKE: 15 MIN.

1/2 pound ground beef
1/2 pound bulk pork sausage
1-3/4 cups frozen corn, thawed
1 cup water
1 envelope brown gravy mix
1 package (8-1/2 ounces) corn bread/muffin mix
1 tablespoon real bacon bits
1-1/2 teaspoons pepper

This casserole is as indulgent as it is delicious. It's stick-to-your-ribs down-home comfort food at its finest.

Justina Wilson, West Salem, Wisconsin

1/8 teaspoon garlic powder
1 envelope country gravy mix

1 In a large skillet, cook beef and sausage over medium heat until no longer pink; drain. Stir in the corn, water and brown gravy mix. Bring to a boil; cook and stir for 1 minute or until thickened. Spoon into a greased 8-in. square baking dish.

2 Prepare corn bread batter according to package directions; stir in the bacon bits, pepper and garlic powder. Spread over meat mixture.

3 Bake, uncovered, at 400° for 15-20 minutes or until a toothpick inserted into corn bread layer comes out clean. Meanwhile, prepare country gravy mix according to package directions; serve with casserole.

YIELD: 6 SERVINGS.

three-cheese lasagna

PREP: 25 MIN. BAKE: 15 MIN.

- 2 pounds ground beef
- 1/2 cup chopped onion
- 1 package (6.4 ounces) lasagna dinner mix
- 2-1/4 cups hot water
- 2 cans (14-1/2 ounces each) diced tomatoes, undrained
- 1 package (10 ounces) frozen chopped spinach, thawed and squeezed dry
- 1 cup sliced fresh mushrooms
- 1/2 cup chopped green onions
- 1 cup (8 ounces) 4% cottage cheese
- 1/4 cup grated Parmesan cheese
- 1-1/2 cups (6 ounces) shredded part-skim mozzarella cheese

1 In a large skillet, cook beef and onion over medium heat for 10-12 minutes or until meat is no longer pink; drain. Stir in pasta from the dinner mix, contents of seasoning mix, water, tomatoes, spinach, mushrooms and onions. Bring to a boil.

2 Reduce heat; cover and simmer for 10-13 minutes or until pasta is tender. Stir in cottage cheese and Parmesan cheese.

3 Transfer to two greased 8-in. square baking dishes. Sprinkle with mozzarella cheese. Cover and freeze one casserole for up to 3 months.

4 Cover and bake the remaining casserole at 350° for 15-20 minutes or until bubbly and cheese is melted.

5 **To use frozen casserole:** Remove from the freezer 30 minutes before baking (do not thaw). Cover and bake at 350° for 1 hour. Uncover; bake 15-20 minutes longer or until heated through.

YIELD: 2 CASSEROLES (4 SERVINGS EACH).

EDITOR'S NOTE: This recipe was tested with Hamburger Helper Lasagna Dinner Mix.

pork

cordon bleu lasagna

PREP: 25 MIN. BAKE: 50 MIN. + STANDING

2 eggs, lightly beaten

1 carton (15 ounces) ricotta cheese

1 cup (8 ounces) 4% cottage cheese

1/2 cup grated Parmesan cheese

1/4 cup plus 2 tablespoons minced fresh parsley, divided

1 jar (15 ounces) roasted garlic Alfredo sauce

2 cups cubed cooked chicken

2 cups cubed cooked ham

1/4 teaspoon garlic powder

6 lasagna noodles, cooked and drained

2 cups (8 ounces) shredded part-skim mozzarella cheese

1 cup (4 ounces) shredded Swiss cheese

1 In a large bowl, combine the eggs, ricotta, cottage cheese, Parmesan and 1/4 cup parsley; set aside. In another bowl, combine the Alfredo sauce, chicken, ham and garlic powder.

2 Spread 1/2 cup of the chicken mixture in the bottom of a greased 13-in. x 9-in. baking dish. Layer with half of the noodles and ricotta mixture. Top with half of the remaining chicken mixture and half of the mozzarella and Swiss cheeses. Repeat the layers.

3 Cover and bake at 350° for 40 minutes. Uncover; bake 10 minutes longer or a meat thermometer reads 160°. Let stand for 15 minutes before serving. Sprinkle with remaining parsley.

YIELD: 12 SERVINGS.

saucy southwestern pork chops

PREP: 15 MIN. COOK: 25 MIN.

This recipe with a Southwestern kick was an instant hit with my husband.

Jeannette Mitchell, Frederic, Wisconsin

4 bone-in pork loin chops (3/4 inch thick and 7 ounces each)

1/4 teaspoon pepper

2 teaspoons olive oil, divided

1 large onion, halved and sliced

1 can (14-1/2 ounces) stewed tomatoes, cut up

1 can (4 ounces) chopped green chilies

1/3 cup water

2 tablespoons enchilada sauce mix

4 tablespoons sliced ripe olives, divided

1 small green pepper, sliced into eight rings

1/2 cup reduced-fat sour cream

2 cups hot cooked rice

1 Sprinkle pork chops with pepper. In a nonstick skillet coated with cooking spray, brown chops in 1 teaspoon oil over medium heat for 2-3 minutes on each side. Remove and keep warm.

2 In same skillet, saute onion in remaining oil until tender. Stir in tomatoes, chilies, water, sauce mix and 2 tablespoons olives. Bring to a boil. Reduce heat; simmer, uncovered, for 3 minutes. Return chops to pan; top with pepper rings. Cover and simmer for 9-12 minutes or until meat is tender.

3 Remove chops and pepper rings; keep warm. Stir sour cream into sauce until blended. Serve with pork and rice. Garnish with remaining olives.

YIELD: 4 SERVINGS.

In this meal, tomato bisque, milk and cheese make a creamy sauce for macaroni, Italian sausage and broccoli. This is a dish your family is sure to love.

Margie Haen, Menomonee Falls, Wisconsin

sausage macaroni supper

PREP/TOTAL TIME: 25 MIN.

2 cups uncooked elbow macaroni

1 pound bulk Italian sausage

1 cup chopped onion

2 teaspoons canola oil

1 can (11 ounces) condensed cream of tomato bisque soup, undiluted

1/2 cup 2% milk

1/2 cup shredded Parmesan cheese

2 teaspoons Italian seasoning

4 cups frozen broccoli florets, thawed

1 Cook macaroni according to package directions. Meanwhile, in a Dutch oven, cook sausage and onion over medium heat in oil until meat is no longer pink; drain.

2 Stir in the soup, milk, cheese and Italian seasoning. Bring to a boil; reduce heat. Drain macaroni; add to sausage mixture. Stir in broccoli; heat through.

YIELD: 6 SERVINGS.

This dish is convenient because it uses packaged au gratin potatoes. You can alter the flavor by substituting a different mix, such as scalloped potatoes with sour cream and chives.

Sue Ross, Casa Grande, Arizona

smoky potato skillet

PREP: 10 MIN. COOK: 25 MIN.

1 package (16 ounces) smoked sausage links, cut into 1-inch pieces
2 celery ribs, chopped
1 medium onion, chopped
1 tablespoon butter
2 cups hot water
2/3 cup 2% milk
1 package (4.9 ounces) au gratin potatoes

1 In a large skillet, saute the sausage, celery and onion in butter until vegetables are tender. Stir in the water, milk and contents of sauce mix from potatoes. Bring to a boil. Stir in potatoes. Reduce heat; cover and simmer for 20-25 minutes or until potatoes are tender, stirring once.

YIELD: 4-6 SERVINGS.

spiral stromboli

PREP: 15 MIN. BAKE: 20 MIN.

My mother gave me this recipe to try and everyone loves it. It is so easy and quick to make.

Beth Bruhn, Willmar, Minnesota

1 tube (11 ounces) crusty French loaf
3/4 cup shredded part-skim mozzarella cheese
3/4 cup shredded cheddar cheese
1/4 pound thinly sliced hard salami
1/4 pound thinly sliced deli ham
1 jar (2 ounces) diced pimientos, drained
1 tablespoon butter, melted
3 tablespoons shredded Parmesan cheese

1 Unroll dough on a lightly floured surface. Pat into a 14-in. x 12-in. rectangle; sprinkle mozzarella and cheddar cheeses to within 1/2 in. of edges. Layer with salami, ham and pimientos.

2 Roll up tightly jelly-roll style, starting from a short side; pinch seam to seal. Place seam side down on an ungreased baking sheet. Brush with butter; sprinkle with Parmesan cheese.

3 Bake at 375° for 20-25 minutes or until golden brown. Cool on a wire rack for 5 minutes. Cut with a serrated knife. Serve warm. Refrigerate leftovers.

YIELD: 6 SERVINGS.

TIP

You can personalize Spiral Stromboli to suit your family's taste. Switch out the deli meats for sliced deli turkey, roast pork or beef, and change the shredded mozzarella for cheddar, Swiss or Colby/Jack.

broccoli ham pockets

PREP/TOTAL TIME: 30 MIN.

These hearty sandwiches not only taste great, they're attractive, too. The creamy filling has wonderful flavor.

Nancy Robaidek, Krakow, Wisconsin

- 1/3 cup diced fully cooked ham
- 3 tablespoons finely chopped fresh broccoli
- 2 tablespoons shredded cheddar cheese
- 1 tablespoon diced sweet red pepper
- 2 tablespoons mayonnaise
- 1/4 teaspoon Dijon mustard, optional
- 1 tube (4 ounces) refrigerated crescent rolls
- 1 egg white, lightly beaten
- 1-1/2 teaspoons sliced almonds

1 In a small bowl, combine the ham, broccoli, cheese, pepper, mayonnaise and mustard if desired. Unroll, crescent dough into two rectangles; seal seams and perforations. Spread filling down center of each rectangle. Fold dough over filling and pinch to seal; tuck ends under.

2 Place seam side down on an ungreased baking sheet. Brush tops with egg white; sprinkle with almonds. Bake at 375° for 11-13 minutes or until golden brown.

YIELD: 2 SERVINGS.

You can easily feed a crowd with this simple recipe that's ready in about 40 minutes. Its comforting sauce will become a fast favorite at your next potluck or weeknight dinner.

Charlane Gathy, Lexington, Kentucky

creamy pepperoni ziti

PREP: 15 MIN. BAKE: 25 MIN.

- 1 package (16 ounces) ziti or small tube pasta
- 1 can (10-3/4 ounces) condensed cream of mushroom soup, undiluted
- 3/4 cup shredded part-skim mozzarella cheese
- 3/4 cup chopped pepperoni
- 1/2 cup each chopped onion, mushrooms, green pepper and tomato
- 1/2 cup half-and-half cream
- 1/4 cup chicken broth
- 1/4 teaspoon salt
- 1/4 teaspoon garlic powder
- 1/4 teaspoon pepper
- 1/2 cup grated Parmesan cheese

1 Cook pasta according to package directions; drain. In a bowl, combine pasta, soup, mozzarella cheese, pepperoni, onion, mushrooms, green pepper, tomato, cream, broth and seasonings.

2 Transfer to a greased 13-in. x 9-in. baking dish. Sprinkle with Parmesan cheese. Cover and bake at 350° for 20 minutes. Uncover; bake 5-10 minutes longer or until bubbly.

YIELD: 9 SERVINGS.

1 In a 3-qt. slow cooker, combine the ham, broccoli, soup, cheese sauce, water chestnuts, rice, milk, celery, onion and pepper. Cover and cook on high for 2-3 hours or until the rice is tender. Let stand for 10 minutes before serving. Sprinkle with the paprika.

YIELD: 6-8 SERVINGS.

pork fajita pasta

PREP/TOTAL TIME: 30 MIN.

One night, my husband and I started making fajitas before we realized we didn't have any tortillas. We improvised and served the pork mixture over noodles instead. It soon become a family favorite.

Janice Thompson, Lansing, Michigan

1 package (7 ounces) angel hair pasta
4 boneless pork loin chops (1/2 inch thick and 4 ounces each), cut into thin strips
1 medium green pepper, julienned
1 medium onion, sliced and separated into rings
1 envelope (1.4 ounces) fajita seasoning
1/3 cup water
1 cup (4 ounces) shredded cheddar cheese
1 medium tomato, seeded and chopped

1 Cook pasta according to package directions. Meanwhile, in a large skillet, cook pork over medium heat until juices run clear. Add green pepper and onion; cook and stir for 1-2 minutes or until vegetables are crisp-tender.

2 Stir in fajita seasoning and water; cook 1 minute longer. Drain pasta. In a large bowl, layer the pasta, pork mixture, cheese and tomato.

YIELD: 4 SERVINGS.

This sensational dish is so wonderful to come home to, especially on a cool fall or winter day. It's a delicious way to use up leftover holiday ham, too.

Jill Pennington, Jacksonville, Florida

slow-cooked ham & broccoli

PREP: 10 MIN. COOK: 2 HOURS + STANDING

3 cups cubed fully cooked ham
3 cups frozen chopped broccoli, thawed
1 can (10-3/4 ounces) condensed cream of mushroom soup, undiluted
1 jar (8 ounces) process cheese sauce
1 can (8 ounces) sliced water chestnuts, drained
1-1/4 cups uncooked instant rice
1 cup 2% milk
1 celery rib, chopped
1 medium onion, chopped
1/8 to 1/4 teaspoon pepper
1/2 teaspoon paprika

pesto sausage pizza

PREP: 20 MIN. BAKE: 25 MIN.

1/2 pound bulk Italian sausage

1 cup chopped onion

1 loaf (1 pound) frozen bread dough, thawed

1 package (8 ounces) cream cheese, softened

1/4 cup prepared pesto

1 cup roasted garlic Parmesan spaghetti sauce

2 cups sliced fresh mushrooms

1 can (2-1/4 ounces) sliced ripe olives, drained

1-1/2 cups (6 ounces) shredded Monterey Jack cheese

1 In a large skillet, cook sausage and onion over medium heat until meat is no longer pink; drain.

2 On a lightly floured surface, roll dough into a 16-in. x 11-in. rectangle. Transfer to a greased 15-in. x 10-in. x 1-in. baking pan. Build up the edges slightly.

3 In a small bowl, beat cream cheese and pesto until blended. Spread over dough. Layer with spaghetti sauce, sausage mixture, mushrooms, olives and Monterey Jack cheese.

4 Bake at 400° for 25-30 minutes or until crust is golden brown and cheese is melted.

YIELD: **12 SLICES.**

pork tenderloin fajitas

PREP: 15 MIN. + MARINATING GRILL: 25 MIN.

- 1 can (8 ounces) sliced pineapple
- 1 envelope fajita seasoning mix
- 1 pork tenderloin (1 pound)
- 1 medium sweet red pepper, sliced
- 1 medium onion, sliced
- 4 flour tortillas (8 inches), warmed
- 1 cup (4 ounces) shredded Monterey Jack cheese
- 1 medium ripe avocado, peeled and sliced

1 Drain pineapple, reserving juice; set pineapple aside. In a large resealable plastic bag, combine seasoning mix and reserved juice; add the pork. Seal bag and turn to coat; refrigerate for 15 minutes.

2 Meanwhile, place the red pepper, onion and pineapple on a double thickness of heavy-duty foil (about 12 in. square). Fold foil around mixture and seal tightly.

3 Prepare grill for indirect heat. Drain and discard marinade from pork. Grill pork and foil packet, covered, over indirect medium heat for 25-40 minutes or until a meat thermometer inserted in the pork reads 160° and vegetables are tender. Remove from the grill. Cover pork and let stand for 5 minutes.

4 Cut tenderloin into strips; place on tortillas. Top with vegetable mixture, cheese and avocado; fold in sides.

YIELD: 4 SERVINGS.

almost homemade

upside-down pizza bake

PREP: 20 MIN. BAKE: 25 MIN.

This super-easy, but exceptionally delicious, recipe is one I've been preparing and serving to my children, and now to my grandchildren, for many years.

Sandy Bastian, Tinley Park, Illinois

- 1/2 pound Italian sausage links, cut into 1/4-inch slices
- 1 cup spaghetti sauce
- 1/2 cup sliced fresh mushrooms
- 1/2 cup julienned green pepper
- 1 cup (4 ounces) shredded part-skim mozzarella cheese, divided
- 1 cup biscuit/baking mix
- 1 egg
- 1/2 cup 2% milk

1 In a large skillet, cook sausage over medium heat until meat is no longer pink; drain.

2 Pour spaghetti sauce into a greased 8-in. square baking dish. Layer with mushrooms, green pepper, sausage and 1/2 cup cheese.

3 In a small bowl, combine the biscuit mix, egg and milk until blended. Pour over top. Sprinkle with remaining cheese.

4 Bake, uncovered, at 400° for 25-30 minutes or until golden brown.

YIELD: 4 SERVINGS.

Sized right for two, this rustic and comforting entree is treated to a combination of apples, raisins and nuts. The fruited sauce adds great flavor. I serve this often, and when I double it for guests, it's greeted with appreciation.

Tiffany Anderson-Taylor, Gulfport, Florida

- 1/4 cup chopped pecans
- 1/4 teaspoon ground cinnamon

1 Rub salt and pepper over pork. Place in a large resealable plastic bag; add apple juice. Seal bag and turn to coat. Refrigerate for 30 minutes.

2 Drain and discard apple juice. Place pork on a rack in a roasting pan. Combine the pie filling, raisins, pecans and cinnamon; spoon over pork.

3 Bake, uncovered, at 400° for 40-45 minutes or until a meat thermometer reads 160°. Let stand for 5 minutes before slicing.

YIELD: 2 SERVINGS.

autumn pork tenderloin

PREP: 5 MIN. + MARINATING BAKE: 40 MIN.

- 1/2 teaspoon salt
- 1/4 teaspoon pepper
- 1 pork tenderloin (3/4 pound)
- 1/2 cup unsweetened apple juice
- 1 cup apple pie filling
- 1/4 cup raisins

This must-try casserole tastes so good when it's hot and bubbly from the oven. The cheddar french-fried onions lend a cheesy, crunchy touch.

Margaret Wilson
Sun City, California

penne and smoked sausage

PREP: 15 MIN. BAKE: 30 MIN.

2 cups uncooked penne pasta

1 pound smoked sausage, cut into 1/4-inch slices

1-1/2 cups 2% milk

1 can (10-3/4 ounces) condensed cream of celery soup, undiluted

1-1/2 cups cheddar french-fried onions, divided

1 cup (4 ounces) shredded part-skim mozzarella cheese, divided

1 cup frozen peas

1 Cook pasta according to package directions. Meanwhile, in a large skillet, brown sausage over medium heat for 5 minutes; drain. In a large bowl, combine milk and soup. Stir in 1/2 cup onions, 1/2 cup cheese, peas and sausage. Drain pasta; stir into sausage mixture.

2 Transfer to a greased 13-in. x 9-in. baking dish. Cover and bake at 375° for 25-30 minutes or until bubbly. Sprinkle with remaining onions and cheese. Bake, uncovered, 3-5 minutes longer or until cheese is melted.

YIELD: 6 SERVINGS.

TIP

If your family eats dinner at different times, make up Penne and Smoked Sausage and divide the mixture between two greased 8-in. square or 9-in. round baking dishes. Heat one for an early dinner and refrigerate the second dish for serving later that night (remove from refrigerator 30 minutes before heating). Check after baking 20 minutes.

snap peas & ham alfredo

PREP/TOTAL TIME: 20 MIN.

This fast-to-fix entree comes together in a jiffy with help from a frozen pasta and veggie medley. Adding ham and fresh sugar snap peas really jazzes it up. Add some red pepper flakes to the creamy mixture for an extra kick.

Taste of Home Test Kitchen

1 package (24 ounces) frozen pasta, broccoli and Alfredo sauce
2 cups fresh sugar snap peas
1/4 cup water
2 cups cubed fully cooked ham
1/2 teaspoon dried oregano
1/8 teaspoon pepper

1 Prepare pasta and sauce according to package directions. Meanwhile, place peas and water in a microwave-safe dish. Cover and microwave on high for 2-3 minutes or until crisp-tender; drain.

2 Stir the peas, ham, oregano and pepper into pasta mixture; cook and stir for 3-4 minutes or until heated through.

YIELD: 4 SERVINGS.

EDITOR'S NOTE: This recipe was tested in a 1,100-watt microwave.

I got this recipe from my mother and love it because it's easy and I've usually have the ingredients on hand. Also, it freezes well and I can have it ready to bake when extra guests show up. Everyone always likes it; there are never leftovers.

Jan Schoshke, Brookville, Kansas

ham & cheese casseroles

PREP: 20 MIN. BAKE: 25 MIN.

1-1/2 pounds uncooked egg noodles
3 pounds cubed fully cooked ham
4 cans (10-3/4 ounces each) condensed cream of chicken soup, undiluted
4 cups frozen cut green beans, thawed
1 cup 2% milk
1/4 cup butter, melted
2 cups (8 ounces) shredded Colby-Monterey Jack cheese

1 Cook pasta according to package directions. Meanwhile, in a large bowl, combine the ham, soup, beans and milk. Drain pasta; pour over ham mixture and toss to coat. Transfer to two greased 13-in. x 9-in. baking dishes. Drizzle each with butter; sprinkle with cheese.

2 Cover and freeze one casserole for up to 3 months. Bake the remaining casserole, uncovered, at 350° for 25-30 minutes or until heated through.

3 **To use frozen casserole:** Thaw in the refrigerator overnight. Remove from the refrigerator 30 minutes before baking. Bake, uncovered, at 350° for 40-45 minutes or until heated through.

YIELD: 2 CASSEROLES (8 SERVINGS EACH).

rice-stuffed pork chops

PREP: 20 MIN. BAKE: 35 MIN.

Seasoned coating and rice mixes speed up these mouthwatering chops. They really impressed my husband when we were first dating.

Becky Aderman, Niagara, Wisconsin

- 2-1/4 cups water
- 1 tablespoon butter
- 1 package (5.3 ounces) instant chicken and Parmesan risotto rice
- 4 bone-in pork loin chops (1 inch thick each)
- 1 envelope seasoned coating mix

1 In a saucepan, combine water, butter and rice with contents of sauce mix. Bring to a boil; stir. Reduce heat; cover and simmer for 4 minutes or until the rice is almost tender. Let stand for 5 minutes.

2 Meanwhile, moisten pork chops with water; dip in coating mix. Cut a pocket in each chop; fill with rice mixture. Place in an ungreased 13-in. x 9-in. baking dish. Spoon remaining rice around chops. Bake, uncovered, at 425° for 35-40 minutes or until meat juices run clear.

YIELD: 4 SERVINGS.

EDITOR'S NOTE: This recipe was tested with Lipton risotto mix and Shake 'n' Bake seasoned coating mix.

Purchased pork roast in gravy gives this satisfying skillet supper a handy head start, making it terrific for busy weeknights.

Taste of Home Test Kitchen

pork noodle skillet

PREP/TOTAL TIME: 15 MIN.

- 1/2 pound sliced fresh mushrooms
- 1 cup shredded carrots
- 3 tablespoons butter
- 1 package (17 ounces) ready-to-serve pork roast in gravy
- 2 cups cooked egg noodles
- 2 tablespoons minced fresh parsley
- 1/4 teaspoon pepper

1 In a large skillet, saute mushrooms and carrots in butter for 5 minutes or until mushrooms are tender. Cut pork roast into small pieces; add pork and gravy to the skillet. Stir in the noodles, parsley and pepper. Cook for 5 minutes or until heated through.

YIELD: 4 SERVINGS.

TIP

Dress up the rice stuffing for the pork chops above. In a little butter, saute about 2 tablespoons each minced onion and celery and 2 thinly sliced mushrooms. Stir into the rice before you stuff the pork chops.

This hearty stromboli isn't difficult to make and is great for a large group. With a popuar combination of cheese and deli meats, it is sure to be a hit.

Lee Gregory
Ashland, Ohio

ham & sausage stromboli

PREP: 25 MIN. BAKE: 35 MIN + COOLING

- 1 package (16 ounces) hot roll mix
- 1-1/4 cups warm water (120° to 130°)
- 3 tablespoons olive oil, divided
- 1/3 pound sliced deli ham
- 1/3 pound sliced salami
- 4 slices process American cheese, cut into thin strips
- 1 cup (4 ounces) shredded part-skim mozzarella or provolone cheese
- 1/4 pound bulk Italian sausage, cooked and crumbled
- 2 tablespoons grated Parmesan cheese
- 1 teaspoon dried oregano
- 1/2 teaspoon garlic powder
- 1/4 teaspoon coarsely ground pepper

1 In a large bowl, combine the contents of the roll mix and yeast packets. Stir in warm water and 2 tablespoons oil until dough pulls away from sides of bowl.

2 Turn onto a floured surface; knead until smooth and elastic, about 5 minutes. Cover and let rest for 5 minutes. Press into a lightly greased 15-in. x 10-in. x 1-in. baking pan.

3 Layer ham, salami, American cheese, mozzarella cheese and Italian sausage over dough. Roll up jelly-roll style, starting with a long side; pinch seam to seal. Place diagonally in pan. Brush dough with remaining oil; sprinkle with Parmesan cheese, oregano, garlic powder and pepper.

4 Bake at 375° for 35-40 minutes or until golden brown. Let stand for 10 minutes before slicing.

YIELD: 18 SERVINGS.

1/4 teaspoon curry powder

2 tablespoons grated Parmesan cheese

1 Prepare rice according to package directions, omitting the butter. In a 13-in. x 9-in. baking dish coated with cooking spray, layer the rice, broccoli, chicken, ham, cheddar cheese and mushrooms.

2 In a small bowl, combine the soup, yogurt, mayonnaise, mustard and curry powder. Spread evenly over top of casserole; sprinkle with the Parmesan cheese.

3 Bake, uncovered, at 350° for 40-45 minutes or until heated through.

YIELD: 6 SERVINGS.

sausage manicotti

PREP: 15 MIN. BAKE: 65 MIN.

When you want an Italian entree without much fuss, turn to this classic dish. It's so tasty and easy to fix. My gang always enjoys it.

Carolyn Henderson, Maple Plain, Minnesota

1 pound bulk pork sausage

2 cups (16 ounces) 4% cottage cheese

1 package (8 ounces) manicotti shells

1 jar (26 ounces) Italian baking sauce

1 cup (4 ounces) shredded part-skim mozzarella cheese

1 In a large bowl, combine sausage and cottage cheese. Stuff into the manicotti shells. Place shells in a greased 13-in. x 9-in. baking dish. Top with the baking sauce.

2 Cover and bake at 350° for 55-60 minutes or until a meat thermometer inserted into the center of a shell reads 160°.

3 Uncover; sprinkle with mozzarella cheese. Bake 8-10 minutes longer or until cheese is melted. Let stand for 5 minutes before serving.

YIELD: 7 SERVINGS.

This wonderful casserole is a fun way to chase away chilly evenings. It's full of ham, chicken, broccoli and rice.

Ruth Andrewson, Leavenworth, Washington

company casserole

PREP: 35 MIN. BAKE: 40 MIN.

1 package (6 ounces) long grain and wild rice mix

4 cups frozen broccoli florets, thawed and drained

1-1/2 cups cubed cooked chicken breast

1 cup cubed fully cooked lean ham

1/2 cup shredded reduced-fat cheddar cheese

1 cup sliced fresh mushrooms

1 can (10-3/4 ounces) reduced-fat reduced-sodium condensed cream of mushroom soup, undiluted

2/3 cup reduced-fat plain yogurt

1/3 cup reduced-fat mayonnaise

1 teaspoon prepared mustard

ham salad croissants

PREP/TOTAL TIME: 30 MIN.

Men and women alike savor this crunchy, full-flavored ham salad. It's a favorite sandwich at church dinners and family gatherings, and a great use for leftover ham.

Jo Riley, Hart, Texas

3 cups ground fully cooked ham
2 cups (8 ounces) shredded cheddar cheese
2 celery ribs, finely chopped
8 green onions, chopped
1/3 cup unsalted sunflower kernels
1/3 cup finely chopped green pepper
1/3 cup chopped dill pickle
1/3 cup mayonnaise
1/3 cup sour cream
1 jar (4 ounces) diced pimientos, drained
1 teaspoon ranch salad dressing mix
1 teaspoon coarsely ground pepper
1 teaspoon minced fresh parsley
8 lettuce leaves
8 croissants, split

1 In a large bowl, combine the ham, cheese, celery, onions, sunflower kernels, green pepper and dill pickle. In a small bowl, combine the mayonnaise, sour cream, pimientos, salad dressing mix, pepper and parsley. Pour over ham mixture; toss to coat. Serve on lettuce-lined croissants.

YIELD: 8 SERVINGS.

Who needs hot dog buns when you serve these saucy chili dogs over french fries from the freezer section? Folks of all ages will truly like this hearty combo.

Taste of Home Test Kitchen

chili dog fries

PREP/TOTAL TIME: 30 MIN.

4 cups frozen french-fried potatoes
1 can (15 ounces) vegetarian chili with beans
5 hot dogs, halved lengthwise and sliced
1/2 cup chopped onion
1 cup (4 ounces) shredded cheddar cheese

1 Prepare fries according to package directions. Meanwhile, in a microwave-safe dish, combine the chili, hot dogs and onion. Cover and microwave on high for 5-6 minutes or until heated through, stirring once. Serve over fries; sprinkle with cheese.

YIELD: 4 SERVINGS.

EDITOR'S NOTE: This recipe was tested in a 1,100-watt microwave.

1. Cook tortellini according to package directions. Meanwhile, in a large skillet, cook sausage in oil over medium heat until no longer pink; drain. Cut into 1/4-in. slices.

2. Place the red peppers in a blender; cover and process until smooth. Drain tortellini. Add the tortellini, pureed peppers and pizza sauce to the skillet; stir to combine. Cook for 5 minutes or until heated through. Sprinkle with cheeses; cover and heat until cheese is melted.

YIELD: 6 SERVINGS.

italian sausage calzone

PREP: 20 MIN. BAKE: 30 MIN. + STANDING

My teenage daughter and I have been experimenting in the kitchen to re-create some old-time family dishes. This calzone with spinach and sausage is definitely a favorite. Using a refrigerated pizza crust, it's a cinch to prepare. For a crowd, just make several of them.

Terri Gallagher, King George, Virginia

- 1 tube (13.8 ounces) refrigerated pizza crust
- 1 can (8 ounces) pizza sauce
- 1 package (10 ounces) frozen chopped spinach, thawed and squeezed dry
- 1 pound bulk Italian sausage, cooked and drained
- 1 jar (4-1/2 ounces) sliced mushrooms, drained
- 2 cups (8 ounces) shredded part-skim mozzarella cheese

1. Unroll pizza dough onto an ungreased baking sheet; pat into a 14-in. x 11-in. rectangle. Spread pizza sauce over one long side of dough to within 1/2 in. of edges.

2. Layer the spinach, sausage, mushrooms and cheese over sauce. Fold dough over filling; pinch seams to seal.

3. Bake at 400° for 30-35 minutes or until golden brown. Let stand for 10-15 minutes before slicing.

YIELD: 6 SERVINGS.

Refrigerated tortellini cooks quickly, but you can also use dried cheese tortellini in this entree.

Taste of Home Test Kitchen

roasted pepper tortellini

PREP/TOTAL TIME: 25 MIN.

- 1 package (20 ounces) refrigerated cheese tortellini
- 5 Italian sausage links
- 2 tablespoons olive oil
- 2 jars (7 ounces each) roasted sweet red peppers, drained
- 1 can (15 ounces) pizza sauce
- 1 cup (4 ounces) shredded part-skim mozzarella cheese
- 2 tablespoons shredded Parmesan cheese

green bean ham quiche

PREP: 20 MIN. BAKE: 35 MIN.

Ham tastes just as good the next day in this robust quiche that's great at any meal. I added the green beans for a unique touch, and they pair perfectly with ham, mushrooms and Swiss cheese.

Sandy Flick, Toledo, Ohio

1/2 pound fresh green beans, trimmed and cut into 1-inch pieces

1 cup cubed fully cooked ham

1 jar (6 ounces) sliced mushrooms, drained

1 cup (4 ounces) shredded Swiss cheese

1/2 cup finely chopped onion

1/8 teaspoon garlic powder

3 eggs, lightly beaten

1-1/2 cups 2% milk

3/4 cup biscuit/baking mix

1/2 teaspoon salt

1/4 teaspoon pepper

1 Place beans in a large saucepan and cover with water. Bring to a boil; cook, uncovered, for 5 minutes or until crisp-tender.

2 Meanwhile, in a large bowl, combine the ham, mushrooms, cheese, onion and garlic powder. Drain the beans; stir into the ham mixture. Transfer to a 9-in. deep-dish pie plate coated with cooking spray.

3 In a small bowl, combine the eggs, milk, biscuit mix, salt and pepper just until blended; pour over ham mixture.

4 Bake 400° for 35-40 minutes or until a knife inserted near the center comes out clean. Let stand for 5 minutes before cutting.

YIELD: 8 SERVINGS.

Hearty and comforting, this meat-and-potatoes supper is rich with homemade goodness...and it takes only a few minutes to get it ready for the oven. Sometimes I use chicken thighs instead of the pork chops called for in the recipe.

Joyce Valentine, Sanford, Colorado

creamy pork chop dinner

PREP: 15 MIN. BAKE: 1 HOUR

2 medium potatoes, peeled and cut into 1/4-inch slices

2 medium carrots, sliced

2 boneless pork loin chops (3/4 inch thick and 4 ounces each)

1 tablespoon onion soup mix

1-1/2 teaspoons cornstarch

1 can (10-3/4 ounces) ready-to-serve creamy chicken soup

1 Place the potatoes and carrots in a 1-qt. baking dish coated with cooking spray. In a skillet coated with cooking spray, brown pork chops on both sides. Place over vegetables.

2 In a small bowl, combine remaining ingredients. Pour over pork chops. Cover and bake at 350° for 1 hour or until meat and potatoes are tender.

YIELD: 2 SERVINGS.

sausage rice casserole

PREP: 30 MIN. BAKE: 40 MIN.

I fiddled around with this dish, trying to adjust it to my family's tastes. When my pickiest child cleaned her plate, I knew I'd found the right flavor combination.

Jennifer Trost, West Linn, Oregon

- 2 packages (7.2 ounces each) rice pilaf
- 2 pounds bulk pork sausage
- 6 celery ribs, chopped
- 4 medium carrots, sliced
- 1 can (10-3/4 ounces) condensed cream of chicken soup, undiluted
- 1 can (10-3/4 ounces) condensed cream of mushroom soup, undiluted
- 2 teaspoons onion powder
- 1/2 teaspoon garlic powder
- 1/4 teaspoon pepper

1 Prepare rice mixes according to package directions. Meanwhile, in a large skillet, cook the sausage, celery and carrots over medium heat until meat is no longer pink; drain.

2 In a large bowl, combine the sausage mixture, rice, soups, onion powder, garlic powder and pepper. Transfer to two greased 11-in. x 7-in. baking dishes.

3 Cover and freeze one casserole for up to 3 months. Cover and bake the remaining casserole at 350° for 40-45 minutes or until the vegetables are tender.

4 **To use frozen casserole:** Thaw in the refrigerator overnight. Remove from the refrigerator 30 minutes before baking. Bake as directed in step 3.

YIELD: 2 CASSEROLES (6-8 SERVINGS EACH).

This golden loaf relies on the convenience of refrigerated dough that's stuffed with ham and cheese. I created the recipe by experimenting with a few simple ingredients my family loves. It makes a delicious hot sandwich in no time.

Gloria Lindell, Welcome, Minnesota

ham and cheese loaf

PREP: 15 MIN. BAKE: 30 MIN.

- 1 tube (13.8 ounces) refrigerated pizza crust
- 10 slices deli ham
- 1/4 cup sliced green onions
- 1 cup (4 ounces) shredded part-skim mozzarella cheese
- 1 cup (4 ounces) shredded cheddar cheese
- 4 slices provolone cheese
- 1 tablespoon butter, melted

1 Unroll dough onto a greased baking sheet; top with the ham, onions and cheeses. Roll up tightly jelly-roll style, starting with a long side; pinch seam to seal and tuck ends under. Brush with butter.

2 Bake at 350° for 30-35 minutes or until loaf is golden brown. Let stand for 5 minutes; cut the loaf into 1-in. slices.

YIELD: 6 SERVINGS.

almost homemade

Porcini mushrooms surround these luscious pork chops with earthy undertones and a delectable essence. Hints of rosemary and Parmesan cheese make polenta a sophisticated accompaniment to this restaurant-quality meal.

Casandra Rittenhouse
North Hollywood
California

porcini-crusted pork with polenta

PREP: 20 MIN. BAKE: 20 MIN.

1 package (1 ounce) dried porcini mushrooms
1/4 teaspoon salt
1/4 teaspoon pepper
4 bone-in pork loin chops (7 ounces each)
2 teaspoons olive oil
1 tube (1 pound) polenta
1/2 cup grated Parmesan cheese
1/4 teaspoon dried rosemary, crushed

1 Process mushrooms in a food processor until coarsely chopped. Transfer to a shallow bowl; stir in salt and pepper. Press one side of each pork chop into mushroom mixture.

2 In a large ovenproof skillet coated with cooking spray, heat oil over medium-high heat. Place chops, mushroom side down, in skillet; cook for 2 minutes. Turn over; cook 2 minutes longer. Bake, uncovered, at 375° for 20-25 minutes or until a meat thermometer reads 160°.

3 Prepare polenta according to package directions for soft polenta. Stir in cheese and rosemary. Serve with pork chops.

YIELD: 4 SERVINGS.

sweet & saucy sausage sandwiches

PREP: 20 MIN. COOK: 30 MIN.

- 2 Italian sausage links (4 ounces each), sliced
- 1/4 cup coarsely chopped onion
- 1/4 cup coarsely chopped green pepper
- 1/3 cup ginger ale
- 1/3 cup chili sauce
- 1/4 cup apricot preserves
- 1 tablespoon onion soup mix
- 1 French roll, split
- 1/4 cup shredded cheddar cheese

1 In a large saucepan, saute the sausage, onion and green pepper over medium heat until meat is no longer pink; drain. Stir in the ginger ale, chili sauce, preserves and soup mix. Bring to a boil. Reduce heat; simmer, uncovered, for 30 minutes or until slightly thickened, stirring occasionally.

2 Place roll halves cut side up on an ungreased baking sheet; top with sausage mixture and cheese. Broil 4 in. from the heat for 1-2 minutes or until cheese is melted.

YIELD: 2 SERVINGS.

TIP

Sometimes, it can be messy to eat an open-faced sausage or meatball sandwich. If you remove some of the bread to hollow out each roll half, the filling will nestle into the sandwich and will be a little easier to enjoy.

roast pork with cherry-almond glaze

PREP: 10 MIN. BAKE: 65 MIN. + STANDING

Your pork roast will never dry out during cooking with this sweet cherry glaze. You can also spoon the sauce over slices of baked ham.

Joan Laurenzo, Johnstown, Ohio

- 1 boneless whole pork loin roast (3-1/2 pounds)
- 1 teaspoon salt
- 1 jar (12 ounces) cherry preserves
- 1/4 cup cider vinegar
- 2 tablespoons light corn syrup
- 1/4 teaspoon each ground cinnamon, nutmeg and cloves
- 1/4 cup slivered almonds

1 Sprinkle the roast with salt; place on a rack in a shallow roasting pan. Bake, uncovered, at 350° for 30 minutes.

2 In a small saucepan, bring the preserves, vinegar, corn syrup and spices to a boil. Reduce heat; simmer, uncovered, for 2 minutes. Set aside 3/4 cup cherry mixture for serving. Stir the almonds into the remaining mixture.

3 Brush roast with some of the glaze. Bake 35-50 minutes longer or until a meat thermometer reads 160°, brushing frequently with remaining glaze. Let stand for 10 minutes before slicing. Serve with reserved cherry mixture.

YIELD: 10 SERVINGS.

Fresh rosemary flavors these moist, golden-crusted pork chops, which are special enough to serve company, but fast enough for weekdays.

Terri McKitrick, Delafield, Wisconsin

parmesan pork chops

PREP/TOTAL TIME: 30 MIN.

- 1/4 cup biscuit/baking mix
- 1 egg, lightly beaten
- 1 cup shredded Parmesan cheese
- 1/4 cup dry bread crumbs
- 2 teaspoons minced fresh rosemary
- 4 boneless pork loin chops (1/2 inch thick and 6 ounces each)
- 2 tablespoons canola oil

1 Place biscuit mix and egg in separate shallow bowls. In another shallow bowl, combine the cheese, bread crumbs and rosemary. Coat pork chops with biscuit mix, dip in egg, then coat with cheese mixture.

2 In a large skillet, brown pork chops on both sides in oil. Cook, uncovered, over medium heat for 10-15 minutes or until juices run clear, turning once.

YIELD: 4 SERVINGS.

ramen pork & peppers

PREP/TOTAL TIME: 30 MIN.

- 1 package (3 ounces) ramen noodles
- 1 teaspoon cornstarch
- 1/4 cup orange juice
- 4-1/2 teaspoons reduced-sodium soy sauce
- 1 tablespoon balsamic vinegar
- 1-1/2 teaspoons honey
- 1/8 teaspoon pepper
- 1/2 cup each chopped green, sweet red and yellow pepper
- 1-1/2 teaspoons canola oil
- 1/2 pound cooked pork, cubed

1 Cook noodles according to package directions (discard seasoning packet or save for another use); drain and set aside.

2 In a small bowl, combine the cornstarch, orange juice, soy sauce, vinegar, honey and pepper until smooth; set aside.

3 In a large skillet, saute the peppers in oil until crisp-tender. Stir the cornstarch mixture and add to the skillet. Add the pork. Bring to a boil; cook and stir for 2 minutes or until sauce is thickened. Stir in noodles; heat through.

YIELD: 2 SERVINGS.

poultry

spicy chicken bundles

PREP: 25 MIN. BAKE: 15 MIN.

- 1 package (3 ounces) cream cheese, softened
- 2 tablespoons 2% milk
- 1 tablespoon pickled jalapeno slices, chopped
- 1/4 teaspoon pepper
- 2 cups cubed cooked chicken
- 1/2 cup chopped onion
- 2 tubes (8 ounces each) refrigerated crescent rolls
- 1 tablespoon butter, melted
- 4 teaspoons seasoned bread crumbs

MUSHROOM SAUCE:

- 1 can (10-3/4 ounces) condensed cream of mushroom soup, undiluted
- 1/2 cup 2% milk

1 In a large bowl, beat the cream cheese, milk, jalapenos and pepper until blended. Stir in chicken and onion.

2 Separate crescent dough into eight rectangles; seal perforations. Spoon 1/4 cup chicken mixture onto the center of each rectangle; bring corners up to the center and pinch edges to seal.

3 Place on an ungreased baking sheet. Brush with butter; sprinkle with bread crumbs. Bake at 375° for 15-20 minutes or until golden brown.

4 In a small saucepan, combine soup and milk. Cook and stir over medium heat until heated through. Serve with bundles.

YIELD: 8 SERVINGS.

EDITOR'S NOTE: When cutting hot peppers, disposable gloves are recommended. Avoid touching your face.

sloppy joe mac and cheese

PREP: 1 HOUR BAKE: 30 MIN.

- 1 package (16 ounces) elbow macaroni
- 3/4 pound lean ground turkey
- 1/2 cup finely chopped celery
- 1/2 cup shredded carrot
- 1 can (14-1/2 ounces) diced tomatoes, undrained
- 1 can (6 ounces) tomato paste
- 1/2 cup water
- 1 envelope sloppy joe mix
- 1 small onion, finely chopped
- 1 tablespoon butter
- 1/3 cup all-purpose flour
- 1 teaspoon ground mustard
- 3/4 teaspoon salt
- 1/4 teaspoon pepper
- 4 cups 2% milk
- 1 tablespoon Worcestershire sauce
- 8 ounces reduced-fat process cheese (Velveeta), cubed
- 2 cups (8 ounces) shredded cheddar cheese, divided

1 Cook macaroni according to package directions. Meanwhile, in a large nonstick skillet, cook the turkey, celery and carrot over medium heat until meat is no longer pink and vegetables are tender; drain. Add the tomatoes, tomato paste, water and sloppy joe mix. Bring to a boil. Reduce heat; cover and simmer for 10 minutes, stirring occasionally.

2 Drain macaroni; set aside. In a large saucepan, saute onion in butter until tender. Stir in the flour, mustard, salt and pepper until smooth. Gradually add milk and Worcestershire sauce. Bring to a boil; cook and stir for 1-2 minutes or until thickened. Remove from the heat. Stir in the process cheese until melted. Add macaroni and 1 cup cheddar cheese; mix well.

Lean ground turkey is a good alternative to beef for those concerned about calories and fat, but it still makes a hearty meal. This family-pleasing dish is a comforting dinner on a chilly night.

Taste of Home Test Kitchen

3 Spread two-thirds of the macaroni mixture in a 13-in. x 9-in. baking dish coated with cooking spray. Spread turkey mixture to within 2 in. of edges. Spoon remaining macaroni mixture around edges of pan.

4 Cover and bake at 375° for 30-35 minutes or until bubbly. Uncover; sprinkle with remaining cheddar cheese. Cover and let stand until cheese is melted.

YIELD: 10 SERVINGS.

1 In a large bowl, combine the rice, contents of seasoning packet, cream soups and water. Spread into a greased 13-in. x 9-in. baking dish. Top with chicken; sprinkle with onion soup mix.

2 Cover and bake at 350° for 2 hours or until a meat thermometer reads 180° and rice is tender.

YIELD: 4 SERVINGS.

au gratin turkey skillet

PREP/TOTAL TIME: 30 MIN.

Leftover turkey is in store for a tasty treatment. The creamy comfort food comes together in a snap with a package of au gratin potatoes, some seasonings and a handful of kitchen staples.

Ann Wood, Pleasant Hill, Oregon

    2-1/2 cups water
    1 package (4.9 ounces) au gratin potatoes
    1/2 cup chopped onion
    1/2 cup 2% milk
    2 tablespoons butter
    1/2 teaspoon poultry seasoning
    1/4 teaspoon dried rosemary, crushed
    2 cups cubed cooked turkey
    2 cups frozen peas, thawed

1 In a large skillet, combine the water, potatoes with contents of sauce mix, onion, milk, butter, poultry seasoning and rosemary. Bring to a boil. Reduce heat; cover and simmer for 15 minutes or until potatoes are tender. Gently stir in turkey and peas; heat through.

YIELD: 4 SERVINGS.

Chicken and rice has never been so easy, or so delicious! This very tender chicken is served over creamy wild rice. Finish the meal with steamed carrots or another favorite veggie.

Sharon Juart, Rochester Mills, Pennsylvania

golden chicken with rice

PREP: 10 MIN. BAKE: 2 HOURS

    1 package (6 ounces) long grain and wild rice mix
    1 can (10-3/4 ounces) condensed cream of mushroom soup, undiluted
    1 can (10-3/4 ounces) condensed cream of celery soup, undiluted
    1-1/2 cups water
    4 chicken leg quarters
    1 envelope onion soup mix

corn bread chicken tenders

PREP/TOTAL TIME: 15 MIN.

These golden tenders are cooked in just a tiny bit of oil, and they crisp up in about six minutes.

Angela Bottger, New Canaan, Connecticut

1/4 cup corn bread/muffin mix
3 tablespoons prepared ranch salad dressing
6 chicken tenderloins
2 teaspoons canola oil

1 Place corn bread mix and salad dressing in separate shallow bowls. Dip chicken in dressing, then roll in corn bread mix.

2 In a large skillet, cook chicken in oil over medium heat for 3-4 minutes on each side or until meat is no longer pink.

YIELD: 2 SERVINGS.

Seasoned chicken, guacamole and salsa add finger-lickin' Southwest flavor and flair to these zesty wraps.

Taste of Home Test Kitchen

turkey biscuit bake

PREP/TOTAL TIME: 30 MIN.

As a college student, I appreciate stick-to-your-ribs foods like this that are also easy on the budget. I often double the recipe to ensure leftovers.

Andy Zinkle, Mt. Pleasant, Iowa

1 can (10-3/4 ounces) condensed cream of chicken soup, undiluted
1 cup diced cooked turkey or chicken
1 can (4 ounces) mushroom stems and pieces, drained
1/2 cup frozen peas
1/4 cup milk
Dash each ground cumin, dried basil and thyme
1 tube (12 ounces) refrigerated biscuits

1 In a large bowl, combine the soup, turkey, mushrooms, peas, milk, cumin, basil and thyme. Pour into a greased 8-in. square baking dish. Arrange biscuits over the top. Bake, uncovered, at 350° for 20-25 minutes or until biscuits are golden brown.

YIELD: 5 SERVINGS.

guacamole chicken wraps

PREP/TOTAL TIME: 10 MIN.

1/2 cup guacamole
4 spinach tortillas (8 inches)
1/2 cup salsa
1 cup (4 ounces) shredded Mexican cheese blend
2 packages (6 ounces each) ready-to-use Southwestern chicken strips
4 lettuce leaves

1 Spread guacamole over half of each tortilla. Layer with salsa, cheese, chicken and lettuce to within 2 in. of edges. Roll up tightly.

YIELD: 4 SERVINGS.

EDITOR'S NOTE: This recipe was prepared with Louis Rich cooked chicken breast.

soup. Fluff stuffing with a fork; spoon over soup. Sprinkle with cheese.

3 Bake, uncovered, at 350° for 30-35 minutes or until heated through.

YIELD: 6 SERVINGS.

pesto turkey pasta

PREP/TOTAL TIME: 25 MIN.

Give this family-friendly entree a try tonight. With a few ingredients and short start-to-finish time, we're sure it'll become a supper staple.

Taste of Home Test Kitchen

3 cups uncooked tricolor spiral pasta
1 package (17.6 ounces) turkey breast cutlets, cut into thin strips
3 tablespoons prepared Italian salad dressing
1 jar (12 ounces) roasted sweet red peppers, drained and cut into thin strips
1/2 cup prepared pesto
1/2 teaspoon salt
1/4 teaspoon pepper
3 tablespoons pine nuts, toasted
Shredded Parmesan cheese, optional

1 Cook pasta according to package directions. Meanwhile, in a large skillet, saute turkey in salad dressing until no longer pink.

2 Drain pasta; add to the skillet. Stir in the red peppers, pesto, salt and pepper; heat through. Sprinkle with pine nuts and Parmesan cheese if desired.

YIELD: 6 SERVINGS.

All ages really seem to go for this comforting, scrumptious meal-in-one. It takes just a handful of ingredients and minutes to put together. I've found that adding dried cranberries to the stuffing mix also adds flavor and color.

Jenn Schlachter, Big Rock, Illinois

broccoli chicken casserole

PREP: 15 MIN. BAKE: 30 MIN.

1-1/2 cups water
1 package (6 ounces) chicken stuffing mix
2 cups cubed cooked chicken
1 cup frozen broccoli florets, thawed
1 can (10-3/4 ounces) condensed broccoli cheese soup, undiluted
1 cup (4 ounces) shredded cheddar cheese

1 In a small saucepan, bring water to a boil. Stir in stuffing mix. Remove from the heat; cover and let stand for 5 minutes.

2 Meanwhile, layer chicken and broccoli in a greased 11-in. x 7-in. baking dish. Top with

open-faced turkey tacos

PREP/TOTAL TIME: 20 MIN.

1 pound lean ground turkey
1 medium onion, chopped
1 can (16 ounces) fat-free refried beans
1 jar (16 ounces) salsa
10 flour tortillas (6 inches), warmed
2 cups shredded lettuce
2 medium tomatoes, chopped
2 medium green peppers, chopped
2 medium sweet red peppers, chopped
10 tablespoons fat-free sour cream

1 In a large skillet, cook turkey and onion over medium heat until meat is no longer pink; drain. Add beans and salsa; cook and stir until heated through. Spread 1/2 cup turkey mixture over each tortilla. Top with lettuce, tomatoes, peppers and sour cream.

YIELD: **10 SERVINGS.**

until crisp-tender. Drain pineapple, reserving the juice in a 2-cup measuring cup; set the pineapple aside. Add enough water to the juice to measure 1-1/3 cups; stir in the vinegar, soy sauce and ketchup.

2 In a large bowl, combine brown sugar and cornstarch. Stir in pineapple juice mixture until smooth. Gradually add to the skillet. Bring to a boil; cook and stir for 2 minutes or until thickened. Add pineapple. Reduce heat; simmer, uncovered, for 4-5 minutes or until heated through.

3 Meanwhile, microwave chicken according to package directions. Stir into pineapple mixture. Serve immediately.

YIELD: 4 SERVINGS.

turkey potpie

PREP: 15 MIN. BAKE: 30 MIN.

People are always asking me for this recipe. If you don't have any turkey on hand, you can use chicken or ham.

Vanita Davis, Camden, Arkansas

- 1 cup frozen mixed vegetables
- 1 cup cubed cooked turkey breast
- 2/3 cup condensed cream of chicken soup, undiluted
- 1/4 cup chicken broth
- 1/2 cup biscuit/baking mix
- 1/4 cup 2% milk
- 2 teaspoons butter, melted

1 Place the vegetables in a steamer basket; place in a small saucepan over 1 in. of water. Bring to a boil; cover and steam for 2-3 minutes. In another small saucepan, combine the turkey, soup, broth and vegetables; cook until bubbly. Transfer to a 1-qt. baking dish coated with cooking spray.

2 In a small bowl, combine biscuit mix and milk just until blended. Spread over turkey mixture; drizzle with butter. Bake, uncovered, at 350° for 30-40 minutes or until filling is bubbly and crust is golden brown.

YIELD: 3 SERVINGS.

Precooked, frozen popcorn chicken simmered in a thick, homemade sweet-and-sour sauce is the secret to this fast and fabulous entree. And what a great way to dress up frozen chicken nuggets. This is one menu item you'll find yourself returning to time and again.

Amy Corlew-Sherlock, Lapeer, Michigan

sweet-and-sour popcorn chicken

PREP/TOTAL TIME: 25 MIN.

- 1 medium green pepper, cut into 1-inch pieces
- 1 small onion, thinly sliced
- 1 tablespoon canola oil
- 1 can (20 ounces) unsweetened pineapple chunks
- 3 tablespoons white vinegar
- 2 tablespoons soy sauce
- 2 tablespoons ketchup
- 1/3 cup packed brown sugar
- 2 tablespoons cornstarch
- 1 package (12 ounces) frozen popcorn chicken

1 In a large skillet or wok, stir-fry green pepper and onion in oil for 3-4 minutes or

wild rice chicken dinner

PREP/TOTAL TIME: 30 MIN.

With chicken, green beans and the nice crunch of water chestnuts and almonds, this casserole has everything you need. Using ready-to-serve wild rice makes putting it together a breeze.

Lorraine Hanson, Independence, Iowa

2 packages (8.8 ounces each) ready-to-serve long grain and wild rice

2 packages (16 ounces each) frozen French-style green beans, thawed

2 cans (10-3/4 ounces each) condensed cream of celery soup, undiluted

2 cans (8 ounces each) sliced water chestnuts, drained

2/3 cup chopped onion

2 jars (4 ounces each) sliced pimientos, drained

1 cup mayonnaise

1/2 cup 2% milk

1 teaspoon pepper

6 cups cubed cooked chicken

1 cup slivered almonds, divided

1 Heat rice according to package directions. Meanwhile, in a Dutch oven, combine the green beans, soup, water chestnuts, onion, pimientos, mayonnaise, milk and pepper. Bring to a boil. Reduce heat; cover and simmer for 5 minutes. Stir in chicken and rice; cook 3-4 minutes longer or until chicken is heated through.

2 Transfer half of the mixture to a serving dish; sprinkle with 1/2 cup almonds. Serve immediately. Pour the remaining mixture into a greased 13-in. x 9-in. baking dish; cool. Sprinkle with remaining almonds. Cover and freeze for up to 3 months.

3 **To use frozen casserole:** Thaw in the refrigerator overnight. Cover and bake at 350° for 40-45 minutes or until heated through.

YIELD: 2 CASSEROLES (6-8 SERVINGS EACH).

With only a handful of everyday items, you can turn a ho-hum entree into a tasty dish that's bursting with flavor. Serve with a side of rice to round out the meal.

Frances Roberts, Silver Spring, Maryland

catalina chicken

PREP: 10 MIN. BAKE: 25 MIN.

2 boneless skinless chicken breast halves (5 ounces each)

2 teaspoons canola oil

1/4 cup Catalina salad dressing

4-1/2 teaspoons onion soup mix

1 tablespoon grape jelly

1 In a large nonstick skillet, brown chicken in oil. Transfer to a shallow baking dish coated with cooking spray. Combine the salad dressing, soup mix and jelly; pour over chicken.

2 Bake, uncovered, at 350° for 25-30 minutes or until a meat thermometer reads 170°.

YIELD: 2 SERVINGS.

Here's Southern comfort food at its best! This casserole is delicious made with chicken or turkey. It's often on the menu when I cook for my husband, our children and our grandkids.

Ann Hillmeyer
Sandia Park, New Mexico

chicken & corn bread bake

PREP: 25 MIN. BAKE: 25 MIN.

2-1/2 cups reduced-sodium chicken broth
1 small onion, chopped
1 celery rib, chopped
1/8 teaspoon pepper
4-1/2 cups corn bread stuffing mix, divided
4 cups cubed cooked chicken
1-1/2 cups (12 ounces) sour cream
1 can (10-3/4 ounces) condensed cream
  of chicken soup, undiluted
3 green onions, thinly sliced
1/4 cup butter, cubed

1 In a large saucepan, combine the broth, onion, celery and pepper. Bring to a boil. Reduce heat; cover and simmer for 5-6 minutes or until vegetables are tender. Stir in 4 cups stuffing mix.

2 Transfer to a greased 13-in. x 9-in. baking dish. Top with chicken. In a small bowl, combine the sour cream, soup and green onions. Spread over chicken. Sprinkle with remaining stuffing mix; dot with butter.

3 Bake, uncovered, for 325° for 25-30 minutes or until heated through.

YIELD: 8 SERVINGS.

chicken and rice dish

PREP/TOTAL TIME: 20 MIN.

Serve this colorful dish anytime you need to put something fast and flavorful on the table in a hurry.

Dorothy Morley, Sault Saint Marie, Michigan

- 1 package (5.7 ounces) broccoli cheddar rice and sauce mix
- 2 cups frozen mixed vegetables
- 2 cups cubed cooked chicken

1 Prepare the rice mix according to package directions. Stir in vegetables and chicken; heat through.

YIELD: 3 SERVINGS.

EDITOR'S NOTE: This recipe was tested with Lipton rice mix.

ranch turkey pasta dinner

PREP/TOTAL TIME: 20 MIN.

Leftover turkey has never tasted so good. I also use chicken if I have that on hand instead. Sprinkle grated cheese over the top of each helping if you like.

Peggy Key, Grant, Alabama

- 2-1/2 cups uncooked penne pasta
- 6 to 8 tablespoons butter, cubed
- 1 envelope ranch salad dressing mix
- 1 cup frozen peas and carrots, thawed
- 3 cups cubed cooked turkey

1 Cook pasta according to package directions. Meanwhile, in a large skillet, melt butter. Stir in salad dressing mix until smooth. Add peas and carrots; cook and stir for 2-3 minutes. Drain pasta and add to skillet. Stir in turkey; cook for 3-4 minutes or until heated through.

YIELD: 4 SERVINGS.

This is a fantastic five-ingredient recipe that takes almost no time to prep for the oven.

Taste of Home Test Kitchen

oregano roasting chicken

PREP: 10 MIN. BAKE: 2-1/4 HOURS

- 1/4 cup butter, melted
- 1 envelope Italian salad dressing mix
- 2 tablespoons lemon juice
- 1 roasting chicken (6 to 7 pounds)
- 2 teaspoons dried oregano

1 In a bowl, combine first three ingredients. Place chicken on a rack in an ungreased roasting pan. Spoon butter mixture over chicken. Cover and bake at 350° for 45 minutes. Uncover; sprinkle with oregano. Bake, uncovered, for 1-1/2 to 1-3/4 hours or until a meat thermometer reads 180°.

YIELD: 6 SERVINGS.

These warm open-faced sandwiches make a quick and filling entree before evening activities. Starting with garlic bread from the frozen food section hurries along the preparation.

Taste of Home Test Kitchen

provolone turkey sandwiches

PREP/TOTAL TIME: 20 MIN.

- 1 loaf (10 ounces) frozen garlic bread, thawed
- 1 pound thinly sliced deli turkey
- 1 cup fresh baby spinach
- 1/2 cup roasted sweet red peppers, drained and patted dry
- 4 slices provolone cheese

1 Bake the garlic bread according to package directions. Layer with the turkey, spinach, red peppers and cheese.

2 Bake 3-4 minutes longer or until the cheese is melted. Cut into serving-size pieces.

YIELD: 4 SERVINGS.

chicken pesto pasta

PREP/TOTAL TIME: 25 MIN.

This is one of my favorite recipes because it's so easy, but it looks and tastes like I spent all day cooking it. And it has all of my favorite things in it.

Barbara Christensen, Arvada, Colorado

- 1 package (16 ounces) bow tie pasta
- 1 cup cut fresh asparagus (1-inch pieces)
- 1-1/4 cups sliced fresh mushrooms
- 1 medium sweet red pepper, sliced
- 2 tablespoons olive oil
- 1-1/2 teaspoons minced garlic
- 2 cups cubed cooked chicken
- 1 can (14 ounces) water-packed artichoke hearts, rinsed, drained and quartered
- 2 jars (3-1/2 ounces each) prepared pesto
- 1 jar (7 ounces) oil-packed sun-dried tomatoes, drained and chopped
- 1 teaspoon salt
- 1/8 teaspoon crushed red pepper flakes
- 1 cup (4 ounces) shredded Parmesan cheese
- 2/3 cup pine nuts, toasted

1 Cook pasta according to package directions, adding asparagus during the last 3 minutes of cooking.

2 Meanwhile, in a large skillet, saute mushrooms and red pepper in oil until tender. Add garlic; cook 1 minute longer. Reduce heat; stir in the chicken, artichokes, pesto, tomatoes, salt and pepper flakes. Cook 2-3 minutes longer or until heated through.

3 Drain pasta; toss with chicken mixture. Sprinkle with cheese and pine nuts.

YIELD: 8 SERVINGS.

Condensed soups and frozen vegetables make this creamy main dish a weeknight delight. I like this simple casserole so much that I've requested it for my birthday dinner. I serve it with biscuits for a meal my family loves.

Michelle Summers
Chattanooga, Tennessee

veggie turkey casserole

PREP: 10 MIN. BAKE: 30 MIN.

3 cups cubed cooked turkey

2 cups frozen mixed vegetables

2 cups frozen broccoli florets

1 can (10-3/4 ounces) condensed cream of chicken soup, undiluted

1 can (10-3/4 ounces) condensed cream of mushroom soup, undiluted

1/2 cup chopped onion

1/4 teaspoon garlic powder

1/4 teaspoon celery seed

1 In a large bowl, combine all the ingredients. Transfer to a greased 11-in. x 7-in. baking dish. Bake, uncovered, at 350° for 30-35 minutes or until heated through. Stir before serving.

YIELD: 4 SERVINGS.

TIP

Feel free to substitute frozen green beans or frozen cauliflower florets for the broccoli in saucy Veggie Turkey Casserole.

poultry seasoning and pepper. Bring to a boil. Reduce heat; simmer, uncovered. Add the chicken.

2 For dumplings, combine biscuit mix and milk. Drop by tablespoonfuls onto simmering broth. Cover and simmer for 10-15 minutes or until a toothpick inserted into a dumpling comes out clean (do not lift cover while simmering).

YIELD: 6 SERVINGS.

turkey potato tetrazzini

PREP: 20 MIN. BAKE: 1 HOUR 5 MIN.

This casserole is a great contribution to a potluck. The dish features layers of sliced potatoes, cooked turkey, broccoli and Swiss cheese with creamy Alfredo sauce spooned over it all.

Karen Bundy, Cabot, Pennsylvania

- 1 jar (16 ounces) Alfredo sauce
- 1 cup 2% milk
- 7 medium potatoes, peeled and thinly sliced
- 4 tablespoons grated Parmesan cheese, divided
- 1-1/2 cups diced cooked turkey or chicken
- 2 cups (8 ounces) shredded Swiss cheese, divided
- 3 cups frozen chopped broccoli, thawed

1 In a large bowl, combine Alfredo sauce and milk; spread 1/4 cup into a greased 13-in. x 9-in. baking dish. Top with a third of the potatoes; sprinkle with 1 tablespoon Parmesan cheese.

2 In another bowl, combine the turkey, 1-1/2 cups Swiss cheese and broccoli; spoon about 2 cups over potatoes. Top with about 2/3 cup sauce mixture. Repeat layers twice.

3 Cover and bake at 400° for 45 minutes. Top with remaining cheeses (dish will be full). Bake, uncovered, 20-25 minutes longer or until potatoes are tender. Let stand for 5 minutes before serving.

YIELD: 12-15 SERVINGS.

Perfect for autumn nights, this main course is speedy, low in fat and a delicious one-dish meal.

Nancy Tuck, Elk Falls, Kansas

easy chicken and dumplings

PREP/TOTAL TIME: 30 MIN.

- 3 celery ribs, chopped
- 1 cup sliced fresh carrots
- 3 cans (14-1/2 ounces each) reduced-sodium chicken broth
- 1/2 teaspoon poultry seasoning
- 1/8 teaspoon pepper
- 3 cups cubed cooked chicken breast
- 1-2/3 cups reduced-fat biscuit/baking mix
- 2/3 cup fat-free milk

1 In a Dutch oven coated with cooking spray, saute celery and carrots for 5 minutes. Stir in the broth,

colorful chicken pizza

PREP/TOTAL TIME: 25 MIN.

I threw this delightful pizza together on a hot summer night when I needed something quick for supper.

Kelli Stone, Boise, Idaho

1 prebaked 12-inch pizza crust

2 tablespoons olive oil

1 package (6 ounces) ready-to-use grilled chicken breast strips

1/2 cup barbecue sauce

1/3 cup chopped onion

1-1/2 teaspoons minced garlic

1-1/2 cups (6 ounces) shredded pizza cheese blend

1/4 cup chopped sweet red pepper

1/4 cup chopped green pepper

2 ounces smoked Gouda cheese, shredded

2 tablespoons minced fresh basil

1 Place the crust on an ungreased 12-in. pizza pan. Brush with oil. Combine the chicken, barbecue sauce, onion and garlic; spoon half over crust. Sprinkle with pizza cheese. Top with remaining chicken mixture. Sprinkle with peppers, Gouda cheese and basil. Bake at 450° for 10-12 minutes or until cheese is melted.

YIELD: 6 SLICES.

linguine pesto with italian chicken strips

PREP/TOTAL TIME: 20 MIN.

8 ounces uncooked linguine

1 package (6 ounces) ready-to-use grilled Italian chicken strips

1 cup (4 ounces) shredded sharp cheddar cheese

3/4 cup frozen corn, thawed

1 jar (3-1/2 ounces) prepared pesto

1/4 cup seasoned bread crumbs

1/4 teaspoon crushed red pepper flakes

1/4 teaspoon pepper

This dish happened by chance one night when I was scrambling to make dinner. It's one of the best pasta entrees I've created and is incredibly fast and tasty!

Beckie Perez, Port Washington, Wisconsin

1 Cook linguine according to package directions; drain. Add the chicken, cheese, corn, pesto, bread crumbs, red pepper flakes and pepper. Toss to coat.

YIELD: 4 SERVINGS.

TIP

Pesto sauce is available in more than the classic basil-pine nut flavor. To add a new twist to Linguine Pesto with Italian Chicken Strips, try one of these varieties: sun-dried tomato, olive or pepper.

1 Cook pasta according to package directions. Meanwhile, in a large bowl, combine the chicken, dip, milk and salt.

2 Drain pasta; return to pan. Stir in chicken mixture and toss to coat. Top with black beans, tomato, onions and cheese; heat through.

YIELD: 6 SERVINGS.

blackened chicken and beans

PREP/TOTAL TIME: 15 MIN.

My husband loves any spicy food. And this is one quick-to-fix and low-fat recipe we both enjoy.

Christine Zongker, Spring Hill, Kansas

2 teaspoons chili powder

1/4 teaspoon salt

1/4 teaspoon pepper

4 boneless skinless chicken breast halves (4 ounces each)

1 tablespoon canola oil

1 can (15 ounces) black beans, rinsed and drained

1 cup frozen corn, thawed

1 cup chunky salsa

1 Combine the chili powder, salt and pepper; rub over both sides of chicken. In a large nonstick skillet, cook chicken in oil over medium heat for 4-5 minutes on each side or until a meat thermometer reads 170°. Remove and keep warm.

2 Add the beans, corn and salsa to skillet; bring to a boil. Reduce heat; cover and simmer for 2-3 minutes or until heated through. Transfer to a serving dish; serve with chicken.

YIELD: 4 SERVINGS.

This flavorful, hearty pasta meal is packed with chicken, veggies and cheese. It's also creamy, colorful and quick.

Marti Gutwein, Rensselaer, Indiana

mexican chicken penne

PREP/TOTAL TIME: 25 MIN.

1 package (16 ounces) penne pasta

2 cups cubed cooked chicken

1-1/4 cups salsa con queso dip

1/2 cup 2% milk

1/4 teaspoon salt

1 can (15 ounces) black beans, rinsed and drained

1 large tomato, chopped

3 green onions, sliced

1/4 cup shredded cheddar cheese

turkey tostadas

PREP/TOTAL TIME: 25 MIN.

Have a delicious fiesta in moments with this dish. Here it is made with tostadas, but it is just as tasty with tortillas. This simple Mexican classic will be requested by your family again and again!

Liz Raisig, New York, New York

1 package (20 ounces) lean ground turkey
1/2 cup chopped onion
1/2 cup chopped green pepper
1 teaspoon canola oil
3/4 cup water
1 envelope taco seasoning
1 can (15-1/2 ounces) hominy, rinsed
  and drained
12 tostada shells
3 cups shredded lettuce
1 cup (4 ounces) shredded Mexican cheese blend
1 cup chopped tomato
1 cup cubed avocado

1 In a large skillet, cook the turkey, onion and green pepper in oil over medium heat for 5 minutes or until meat is no longer pink; drain. Stir in the water, taco seasoning and hominy. Bring to a boil. Reduce heat; simmer, uncovered, for 5 minutes or until heated through.

2 On each tostada shell, layer the lettuce, about 1/3 cup turkey mixture, cheese, tomato and avocado.

YIELD: 6 SERVINGS.

parmesan chicken pasta

PREP/TOTAL TIME: 25 MIN.

2 packages (4.3 ounces each) Parmesan
  cheese pasta sauce mix
1 pound boneless skinless chicken breasts,
  cut into strips
1 cup sliced fresh mushrooms

Pasta mixes simplify assembly of this skillet supper that's loaded with tender chicken. Be sure you have water, milk and butter to prepare the mixes as directed on the package.

Taste of Home Test Kitchen

1 cup fresh green beans, cut into 1-inch pieces
2 tablespoons canola oil
1 medium tomato, chopped

1 Prepare pasta mix according to package directions. Meanwhile, in a large skillet, cook the chicken, mushrooms and green beans in oil over medium heat for 10-15 minutes or until meat is no longer pink and vegetables are tender; drain. Add to pasta and sauce. Stir in tomato.

YIELD: 4 SERVINGS.

EDITOR'S NOTE: This recipe was tested with Lipton Pasta Sides Fettuccine and Spinach Pasta in a Parmesan Cheese Sauce mix.

2 Drain gnocchi; add to skillet. Cover and cook for 10-15 minutes or until heated through. Serve with cheese if desired.

YIELD: 4 SERVINGS.

turkey cabbage bake

PREP: 30 MIN. BAKE: 15 MIN.

I revised this old recipe by using ground turkey instead of ground beef to make it healthier, and by adding thyme to round out the flavor. Crescent rolls help it come together quickly, and my family requests it often.

Irene Gutz, Fort Dodge, Iowa

- 2 tubes (8 ounces each) refrigerated crescent rolls
- 1-1/2 pounds ground turkey
- 1/2 cup chopped onion
- 1/2 cup finely chopped carrot
- 1 teaspoon minced garlic
- 2 cups finely chopped cabbage
- 1 can (10-3/4 ounces) condensed cream of mushroom soup, undiluted
- 1/2 teaspoon dried thyme
- 1 cup (4 ounces) shredded part-skim mozzarella cheese

1 Unroll one tube of crescent dough into one long rectangle; seal seams and perforations. Press onto the bottom of a greased 13-in. x 9-in. baking dish. Bake at 425° for 6-8 minutes or until golden brown.

2 Meanwhile, in a large skillet, cook the turkey, onion and carrot over medium heat until meat is no longer pink. Add garlic; cook 1 minute longer. Drain. Add the cabbage, soup and thyme. Pour over crust; sprinkle with cheese.

3 On a lightly floured surface, press second tube of crescent dough into a 13-in. x 9-in. rectangle, sealing the seams and perforations. Place over the casserole.

4 Bake, uncovered, at 375° for 14-16 minutes or until crust is golden brown.

YIELD: 6 SERVINGS.

Potato gnocchi are little dumplings made from a dough of potatoes, flour and sometimes eggs. They are irregularly shaped balls or oval disks. They are usually boiled or baked. Look for gnocchi in the pasta, ethnic or frozen section of your grocery store.

Taste of Home Test Kitchen

gnocchi chicken skillet

PREP/TOTAL TIME: 25 MIN.

- 1 package (10 ounces) potato gnocchi
- 1 pound ground chicken
- 1/2 cup chopped onion
- 2 tablespoons olive oil
- 1 jar (26 ounces) spaghetti sauce
- 1/4 to 1/2 teaspoon dried oregano
- 1/4 teaspoon salt
- Shredded Parmesan cheese, optional

1 Prepare gnocchi according to package directions. Meanwhile, in a large skillet, cook chicken and onion in oil over medium heat until chicken is no longer pink. Stir in the spaghetti sauce, oregano and salt.

oven-fried chicken

PREP: 25 MIN. BAKE: 35 MIN.

1 cup all-purpose flour

2 envelopes (.6 ounce each) individual serving cream of chicken soup mix

2 envelopes Italian salad dressing mix

1-1/2 teaspoons paprika

1 teaspoon seasoned salt

1 teaspoon dried thyme

1 teaspoon rubbed sage

1/2 teaspoon onion powder

1/2 teaspoon curry powder, optional

1 cup 2% milk

2 broiler/fryer chickens (4 pounds each), cut up

1/4 cup butter, melted

1 Line two 15-in. x 10-in. x 1-in. baking pans with foil and grease the foil; set aside.

2 In a large resealable plastic bag, combine the flour, soup mix, dressing mix and seasonings. Place milk in a shallow dish. Dip chicken into milk, then add to flour mixture, a few pieces at a time, and shake to coat. Place in prepared pans. Drizzle with butter.

3 Bake at 350° for 35-50 minutes or until juices run clear.

YIELD: 8 SERVINGS.

chicken over curly noodles

PREP/TOTAL TIME: 30 MIN.

- 1/4 cup packed brown sugar
- 1/4 cup creamy peanut butter
- 1/4 cup soy sauce
- 1 teaspoon minced garlic
- 1/2 cup dry bread crumbs
- 3 packages (3 ounces each) chicken ramen noodles
- 4 boneless skinless chicken breast halves (5 ounces each)
- 1 tablespoon olive oil
- 1 can (14 ounces) bean sprouts, rinsed and drained

1 In a small bowl, combine the brown sugar, peanut butter, soy sauce and garlic; set aside. In a large resealable plastic bag, combine bread crumbs and contents of two noodle seasoning packets (discard the remaining packet or save for another use). Add chicken, one piece at a time, and shake to coat.

2 In a large skillet, cook chicken in oil over medium heat for 5-6 minutes on each side or until juices run clear. Meanwhile, cook noodles according to package directions.

3 Remove chicken and keep warm. Add peanut butter mixture to skillet; cook and stir until heated through. Drain noodles. Add noodles and bean sprouts to skillet; toss to coat. Serve with chicken.

YIELD: 4 SERVINGS.

stuffed cornish hens

PREP: 15 MIN. BAKE: 1-1/2 HOURS

Cornish hens, basted with a delicious glaze of apricot preserves and cloves, make dinner for two something special. I use convenient packaged herb stuffing to complement the flavorful meat.

Gusty Crum, Dover, Ohio

2 cups seasoned stuffing croutons
5 tablespoons water
2 tablespoons butter, melted
2 Cornish game hens (20 ounces each)
GLAZE:
1 envelope brown gravy mix
1/2 cup water
1/2 cup apricot preserves
Dash ground cloves

1 In a large bowl, combine the croutons, water and butter. Loosely stuff into hens. Place hens breast side up on a rack in a shallow roasting pan; tie the drumsticks together.

2 In a small saucepan, combine the glaze ingredients. Bring to a boil. Spoon half over hens. Bake, uncovered, at 350° for 1-1/2 hours or until a meat thermometer reads 180° for hens and 165° for stuffing, basting occasionally with remaining glaze.

YIELD: 2 SERVINGS.

A crispy coating flecked with minced fresh parsley tops this tasty chicken, which is finished with a drizzle of a simple fruit sauce.

Briana Roell, Indianapolis, Indiana

apricot chicken

PREP/TOTAL TIME: 30 MIN.

4 boneless skinless chicken breast halves (6 ounces each)
6 tablespoons butter, melted, divided
1 cup biscuit/baking mix
1 tablespoon minced fresh parsley
1 tablespoon canola oil
1/4 cup apricot preserves
2 tablespoons orange juice

1 Flatten chicken to 1/4-in. thickness; set aside. Pour 5 tablespoons butter into a shallow bowl. In another shallow bowl, combine biscuit mix and parsley. Dip chicken in butter, then coat with biscuit mixture.

2 In a large skillet, cook chicken in oil and remaining butter over medium heat for 9-10 minutes on each side or until no longer pink.

3 Meanwhile, in a small microwave-safe bowl, combine preserves and orange juice. Cover and microwave on high for 30-40 seconds or until the preserves are melted; stir until combined. Drizzle over the chicken; cook 1-2 minutes longer or until heated through.

YIELD: 4 SERVINGS.

1. Cook mostaccioli according to package directions. Meanwhile, in a large skillet, saute onion and red pepper in oil until tender. Add garlic; cook 1 minute longer. Stir in the soup, chicken and water. Bring to a boil. Reduce heat; cover and simmer for 8 minutes.

2. Stir in beans; heat through. Drain mostaccioli; transfer to a serving bowl; top with chicken mixture. Sprinkle with cheese if desired.

YIELD: 6 SERVINGS.

cheddar-apple turkey salad

PREP: 20 MIN. + CHILLING

I like to serve this unique salad when my group gets together for lunch. I have to watch out for my son though... he loves it and always takes a hearty serving for himself. The apples add interest and a little crunch.

Luci Knepper, Salem, Ohio

1 package (3 ounces) ramen noodles
1-1/2 cups cubed red apples
1-1/4 cups cubed cooked turkey breast
1/2 cup reduced-fat cheddar cheese
1/2 cup frozen peas, thawed
1/4 cup sliced green onions
1/4 cup chopped sweet red pepper
1/2 cup fat-free poppy seed salad dressing
2 tablespoons reduced-fat sour cream
1/4 teaspoon salt

1. Prepare noodles according to package directions (discard seasoning packet or save for another use). Drain and rinse in cold water.

2. In a large bowl, combine the noodles, apples, turkey, cheese, peas, green onions and red pepper. In a small bowl, combine the dressing, sour cream and salt. Stir into noodle mixture. Cover and refrigerate for at least 1 hour.

YIELD: 4 SERVINGS.

This saucy Southwestern dish is ready in minutes due to help from packaged grocery items.

Mike Kirschbaum, Cary, North Carolina

pepper jack chicken pasta

PREP/TOTAL TIME: 25 MIN.

3 cups uncooked mostaccioli
1/4 cup chopped onion
1/4 cup chopped sweet red pepper
1 tablespoon canola oil
1/2 teaspoon minced garlic
1 can (10-3/4 ounces) condensed nacho cheese soup, undiluted
1 package (9 ounces) ready-to-use Southwestern chicken strips
3/4 cup water
1 can (15 ounces) black beans, rinsed and drained
1/4 cup shredded Monterey Jack cheese, optional

hearty turkey casserole

PREP: 20 MIN. BAKE: 35 MIN.

This casserole is a creamy, cheesy delight for guests of all ages. It makes frequent appearances on my dinner table.

Eunice Holmberg, Willmar, Minnesota

2 cups uncooked elbow macaroni

2 cups cubed cooked turkey breast

2 cups 2% milk

1 can (10-3/4 ounces) condensed cream of mushroom soup, undiluted

1 can (10-3/4 ounces) condensed cream of celery soup, undiluted

1 can (8 ounces) sliced water chestnuts, drained

1/2 pound process cheese (Velveeta), cubed

3 hard-cooked eggs, chopped

1 jar (2 ounces) diced pimientos, drained

1 teaspoon grated onion

1 Cook macaroni according to package directions; drain and place in a large bowl. Add the remaining ingredients. Transfer to a greased 13-in. x 9-in. baking dish. Bake, uncovered, at 350° for 35-40 minutes or until bubbly.

YIELD: 9 SERVINGS.

Take advantage of convenience foods to serve a special entree even when time is tight. A colorful mixture of fresh vegetables and purchased cooked turkey and gravy is spooned into puff pastry shells from the freezer section.

Taste of Home Test Kitchen

turkey and gravy baskets

PREP/TOTAL TIME: 20 MIN.

1 package (10 ounces) frozen puff pastry shells

2 cups fresh broccoli florets

1/2 cup chopped onion

1/2 cup chopped sweet red pepper

4 teaspoons canola oil

1 package (18 ounces) refrigerated turkey breast slices in gravy

1/2 cup turkey gravy

1 Bake four pastry shells according to package directions; save remaining shells for another use. Meanwhile, in a large skillet, saute the broccoli, onion and red pepper in oil for 5 minutes or until crisp-tender.

2 Cut turkey slices into bite-size pieces; add to skillet with gravy from package and additional gravy. Heat through. Serve in pastry shells.

YIELD: 4 SERVINGS.

TIP

Frozen puff pastry shells make fun baskets for all sorts of food, such as stews or saucy casseroles. You can even use them for desserts. Simply fill with some prepared instant pudding, then top with fresh fruit and a dollop of whipped topping.

2 Stir in the soup, peas, milk, garlic powder, salt and pepper. Bring to a boil. Reduce heat; simmer, uncovered, for 1-2 minutes or until heated through. Stir in cheese. Drain pasta; add to chicken mixture and toss to coat.

3 Serve half of the mixture immediately. Cool remaining mixture; transfer to a freezer container. Cover and freeze for up to 3 months.

4 **To use frozen casserole:** Thaw in refrigerator overnight. Transfer to an ungreased shallow 3-qt. microwave-safe dish. Cover and microwave on high for 8-10 minutes or until heated through, stirring once.

YIELD: 2 CASSEROLES (6 SERVINGS EACH).

EDITOR'S NOTE: This recipe was tested in a 1,100-watt microwave.

I first made this recipe when I was a professional nanny. It comes together quickly at dinnertime when the kids are hungry.

Danette Forbes, Overland Park, Kansas

dijon chicken with grapes

PREP/TOTAL TIME: 20 MIN.

This deliciously different entree features sweet grapes in a creamy Dijon sauce served atop golden chicken breast halves.

Margaret Wilson, Sun City, California

4 boneless skinless chicken breast halves (4 ounces each)
1 teaspoon olive oil
1/2 cup refrigerated nondairy creamer
2 tablespoons Dijon mustard
3/4 cup seedless red grapes, halved
3/4 cup seedless green grapes, halved

1 In a large nonstick skillet coated with cooking spray, cook chicken in oil over medium heat for 4-5 minutes on each side or until a meat thermometer reads 170°. Remove and keep warm.

2 Add creamer to the skillet; cook over medium-low heat, stirring to loosen browned bits from pan. Whisk in mustard until blended. Add grapes; cook and stir until heated through. Serve with chicken.

YIELD: 4 SERVINGS.

chicken and bows

PREP/TOTAL TIME: 25 MIN.

1 package (16 ounces) bow tie pasta
2 pounds boneless skinless chicken breasts, cut into strips
1 cup chopped sweet red pepper
1/4 cup butter, cubed
2 cans (10-3/4 ounces each) condensed cream of chicken soup, undiluted
2 cups frozen peas
1-1/2 cups 2% milk
1 teaspoon garlic powder
1/4 to 1/2 teaspoon salt
1/4 teaspoon pepper
2/3 cup grated Parmesan cheese

1 Cook pasta according to package directions. Meanwhile, in a Dutch oven, cook chicken and red pepper in butter over medium heat for 5-6 minutes or until chicken is no longer pink.

almost homemade

penne chicken with sun-dried tomatoes

PREP: 20 MIN. BAKE: 50 MIN.

3-3/4 cups uncooked penne pasta

1 jar (6 ounces) sliced mushrooms, drained

1 tablespoon butter

2 jars (15 ounces each) sun-dried tomato Alfredo sauce

2 packages (9 ounces each) ready-to-use Southwestern chicken strips

2 cups oil-packed sun-dried tomatoes, drained and chopped

4 green onions, sliced

1/8 teaspoon pepper

1-1/2 cups shredded Parmesan cheese

1 Cook pasta according to package directions. Meanwhile, in a small skillet, saute mushrooms in butter; set aside.

2 In a large bowl, combine the Alfredo sauce, chicken, tomatoes, green onions, pepper and reserved mushrooms. Drain pasta; stir into chicken mixture. Spoon into a greased 13-in. x 9-in. baking dish.

3 Cover and bake at 350° for 45-50 minutes or until heated through. Uncover; sprinkle with cheese. Bake 5-8 minutes longer or until cheese is melted.

YIELD: 8 SERVINGS.

Start the night right with this mouthwatering dish. Lemon pie filling is the secret ingredient to the moist chicken's full-bodied sauce.

Taste of Home Test Kitchen

lemon chicken with rice

PREP: 25 MIN. BAKE: 40 MIN.

1/3 cup biscuit/baking mix
1 teaspoon seasoned salt
1/2 teaspoon pepper
4 bone-in chicken breast halves (12 ounces each), skin removed
1/4 cup olive oil
1-1/3 cups lemon pie filling
1/2 cup water
1/3 cup cider vinegar
1/4 cup soy sauce
TOMATO PARSLEY RICE:
2 cups water

1 teaspoon chicken bouillon granules
1/8 teaspoon pepper
2 cups uncooked instant rice
1 medium tomato, seeded and chopped
3 tablespoons minced fresh parsley

1 In a large resealable plastic bag, combine the biscuit mix, seasoned salt and pepper. Add chicken, one piece at a time, and shake to coat.

2 In a large skillet, brown chicken in oil on both sides; drain. Transfer to a 13-in. x 9-in. baking dish. In a small bowl, combine the pie filling, water, vinegar and soy sauce; pour over chicken. Bake, uncovered, at 375° for 40-45 minutes or until a meat thermometer reads 170°.

3 In a large saucepan, bring the water, bouillon and pepper to a boil. Stir in the rice, tomato and parsley. Cover and remove from the heat; let stand for 5 minutes. Fluff with a fork. Serve with chicken.

YIELD: 4 SERVINGS.

turkey stir-fry

PREP/TOTAL TIME: 20 MIN.

Need a nourishing meal in minutes? Toss together these seven ingredients for a colorful and scrumptious main dish the whole family will love.

Mildred Sherrer, Fort Worth, Texas

1 pound turkey breast tenderloins, cubed
1 tablespoon canola oil
1 package (16 ounces) frozen stir-fry vegetable blend
1 medium onion, cut into wedges
1/2 cup stir-fry sauce
1/3 cup shredded carrot
Hot cooked rice

1 In a large skillet or wok, stir-fry turkey in oil for 3-4 minutes or until no longer pink. Remove with a slotted spoon. Stir-fry the mixed vegetables, onion, stir-fry sauce and carrot for 4-6 minutes or until vegetables are tender. Add turkey; heat through. Serve with rice.

YIELD: 4 SERVINGS.

crescent-topped turkey amandine

PREP: 20 MIN. BAKE: 30 MIN.

Quick to prepare, this tasty entree is loaded with turkey flavor and a nice crunch from celery and water chestnuts. Topped with a golden crescent roll crust and a sprinkling of almonds and cheese, it's bound to become a favorite.

Becky Larson, Mallard, Iowa

3 cups cubed cooked turkey
1 can (10-3/4 ounces) condensed cream of
  mushroom soup, undiluted
1 can (8 ounces) sliced water chestnuts, drained
2/3 cup mayonnaise
1/2 cup chopped celery
1/2 cup chopped onion
1 tube (4 ounces) refrigerated crescent rolls
2/3 cup shredded Swiss cheese
1/2 cup sliced almonds
1/4 cup butter, melted

1 In a large saucepan, combine the turkey, soup, water chestnuts, mayonnaise, celery and onion; heat through. Transfer to a greased 2-qt. baking dish. Unroll the crescent dough and place over the turkey mixture.

2 In a small bowl, combine the cheese, almonds and butter. Spoon over dough. Bake, uncovered, at 375° for 30-35 minutes or until crust is golden brown and filling is bubbly.

YIELD: 4 SERVINGS.

My husband calls me an aerobic cook because I can make this Italian dish in just 30 minutes. No one will accuse you of cutting corners. It tastes like it's been simmering deliciously for hours.

Regina Cowles, Boulder, Colorado

roasted pepper chicken penne

PREP/TOTAL TIME: 30 MIN.

1-1/2 pounds boneless skinless chicken breasts,
  cut into 1-inch strips
1/4 cup balsamic vinegar
1 package (16 ounces) penne pasta
1 medium onion, sliced
3 garlic cloves, sliced
1/4 cup olive oil
1 can (28 ounces) crushed tomatoes
1 cup julienned roasted sweet red peppers
1 cup chicken broth
3 teaspoons Italian seasoning
1/4 teaspoon salt
1 cup shredded Parmesan cheese

1 Place chicken in a large resealable plastic bag; add vinegar. Seal bag and turn to coat; refrigerate for 15 minutes.

2 Cook pasta according to package directions. Meanwhile, in a large skillet, saute onion and garlic in oil for 1 minute. Drain and discard vinegar. Add chicken to skillet; cook for 4-5 minutes or until meat is no longer pink.

3 Stir in the tomatoes, red peppers, broth, Italian seasoning and salt. Bring to a boil over medium heat; cook and stir for 4-5 minutes or until heated through. Drain pasta; toss with chicken mixture. Sprinkle with cheese.

YIELD: 8 SERVINGS.

Frozen spinach and a jar of spaghetti sauce speed up the prep time for these tender, nutritious turkey meatballs. Freeze leftovers for another busy night.

Taste of Home Test Kitchen

marinara
turkey meatballs

PREP: 20 MIN. COOK: 25 MIN.

- 1 package (10 ounces) frozen chopped spinach, thawed and squeezed dry
- 1/2 cup seasoned bread crumbs
- 1 small onion, finely chopped
- 3 tablespoons minced fresh parsley
- 2 garlic cloves, minced
- 1/4 teaspoon ground nutmeg
- 1/4 teaspoon ground allspice
- 1/4 teaspoon pepper
- 1-1/4 pounds lean ground turkey
- 1 jar (26 ounces) meatless spaghetti sauce
- 9 ounces uncooked spaghetti

1 In a large bowl, combine spinach, bread crumbs, onion, parsley, garlic, nutmeg, allspice and pepper. Crumble turkey over mixture and mix well.

2 Shape into 24 meatballs. Place on a broiler pan coated with cooking spray. Broil 4-6 in. from the heat for 8 minutes. Turn; broil 3-5 minutes longer or until meat is no longer pink.

3 Transfer meatballs to a Dutch oven; add spaghetti sauce. Bring to a boil. Reduce heat; cover and simmer for 10 minutes. Meanwhile, cook spaghetti according to package directions; drain. Serve with meatballs and sauce.

YIELD: 6 SERVINGS.

seafood

If you've ever tasted potato-crusted sea bass in a restaurant and wished you could have it at home, this version is for you. Store-bought potato flakes and a salad dressing mix combine for a great coating that's a breeze to whip up.

Judi Markert
Mentor-on-the-Lake, Ohio

golden sea bass

PREP/TOTAL TIME: 25 MIN.

1 cup mashed potato flakes
1 envelope Italian salad dressing mix
1/4 teaspoon pepper
1 egg
2 pounds sea bass fillets or halibut steaks
2 tablespoons butter, melted
Paprika

1 In a shallow bowl, combine the potato flakes, dressing mix and pepper. In another bowl, beat the egg. Dip fillets into egg, then coat with potato flake mixture.

2 Place in a single layer in a 15-in. x 10-in. x 1-in. baking pan coated with cooking spray. Drizzle with butter; sprinkle with paprika. Bake, uncovered, at 450° for 10-14 minutes or until fish flakes easily with a fork.

YIELD: 8 SERVINGS.

TIP

When buying fresh fish fillets or steaks, choose ones that have firm, elastic and moist-looking flesh. If there is skin, it should be shiny and bright. Fresh fish should have a mild aroma. Avoid fish with a strong fishy odor, bruised skin and flesh with drying edges.

wild rice shrimp bake

PREP: 20 MIN. BAKE: 20 MIN.

Fresh shrimp lends a special touch to this effortless entree that starts with a boxed wild rice mix. The creamy hot dish is topped off with a handful of crunchy croutons.

Lee Stearns, Mobile, Alabama

- 1 package (6 ounces) long grain and wild rice mix
- 1 pound uncooked medium shrimp, peeled and deveined
- 1 medium green pepper, chopped
- 1 medium onion, chopped
- 1 can (4 ounces) mushroom stems and pieces, drained
- 1/4 cup butter
- 1 can (10-3/4 ounces) condensed cream of chicken soup, undiluted
- 1/2 cup seasoned stuffing croutons

1 Prepare rice according to package directions. Meanwhile, in a large skillet, saute the shrimp, green pepper, onion and mushrooms in butter until shrimp turn pink. Add the soup to the rice; stir into the shrimp mixture.

2 Transfer to a greased 2-qt. baking dish. Sprinkle with croutons. Bake, uncovered, at 350° for 20-25 minutes or until heated through.

YIELD: 6 SERVINGS.

Enjoy the comforting flavor of tuna noodle casserole in minutes with this rich stovetop version. It's easy to make with prepared Alfredo sauce, frozen peas and canned tuna.

Ruth Simon, Buffalo, New York

tuna noodle skillet

PREP/TOTAL TIME: 30 MIN.

- 2 jars (16 ounces each) Alfredo sauce
- 1 can (14-1/2 ounces) chicken broth
- 1 package (16 ounces) wide egg noodles
- 1 package (10 ounces) frozen peas
- 1/4 teaspoon pepper
- 1 can (12 ounces) solid white water-packed tuna, drained and flaked

1 In a large skillet over medium heat, bring Alfredo sauce and broth to a boil. Add noodles; cover and cook for 7-8 minutes. Reduce heat; stir in peas and pepper. Cover and cook 4 minutes longer or until noodles are tender. Stir in tuna; heat through.

YIELD: 6 SERVINGS.

1. Cook pasta shells according to package directions. Meanwhile, in a small skillet over medium heat, cook scallops in butter for 1-2 minutes or until opaque. Transfer to a large bowl.

2. Place one egg and half of the cottage cheese, ricotta, nutmeg and pepper in a blender; cover and process until smooth. Add to the scallops. Repeat with the remaining egg, cottage cheese, ricotta, nutmeg and pepper. Add to the scallops. Stir in the crab and shrimp.

3. Drain shells and rinse in cold water. Stuff with seafood mixture. Place in a greased 13-in. x 9-in. baking dish. Top with Alfredo sauce. Cover and bake at 350° for 30-35 minutes or until bubbly.

YIELD: 10 SERVINGS.

curried shrimp

PREP/TOTAL TIME: 15 MIN.

If you like curry, you'll enjoy the rich flavor of this creamy shrimp mixture that is delicious served over rice. I garnish it with bacon bits and chopped hard-cooked eggs.

Sue Friend, Lynden, Washington

- 1 small onion, chopped
- 1 tablespoon canola oil
- 1 can (10-3/4 ounces) condensed cream of shrimp soup, undiluted
- 1 teaspoon curry powder
- 1 package (1 pound) frozen uncooked small shrimp, thawed, peeled and deveined
- 1 cup (8 ounces) sour cream
- Hot cooked rice

1. In a large saucepan, saute onion in oil until tender. Stir in soup and curry powder; bring to a boil. Add the shrimp; cook and stir until shrimp turn pink. Reduce heat. Stir in sour cream; heat through. Serve with rice.

YIELD: 4 SERVINGS.

These stuffed shells are really good, and we have them often. Even if you don't care for fish, you'll love this dish.

Mrs. Ezra Weaver, Wolcott, New York

seafood-stuffed shells

PREP: 35 MIN. BAKE: 30 MIN.

- 30 uncooked jumbo pasta shells
- 1/2 pound bay scallops
- 2 teaspoons butter
- 2 eggs
- 2 cups (16 ounces) cream-style cottage cheese
- 1 carton (15 ounces) ricotta cheese
- 1/2 teaspoon ground nutmeg
- 1/4 teaspoon pepper
- 1 can (6 ounces) lump crabmeat, drained
- 3/4 pound frozen cooked small shrimp, thawed
- 1 jar (15 ounces) Alfredo sauce

almost homemade

tuna patties

PREP/TOTAL TIME: 30 MIN.

My family likes anything involving stuffing mix, so these tuna burgers are a popular request. It takes only minutes to form the moist patties, brown them in a skillet and mix up the easy sauce to serve on the side.

Sonya Sherrill, Sioux City, Iowa

 2 eggs, lightly beaten
 1 can (10-3/4 ounces) condensed cream of
    mushroom soup, undiluted, divided
 3/4 cup milk, divided
 2 cups stuffing mix
 1 can (12 ounces) tuna, drained and flaked
 2 tablespoons butter

1 In a large bowl, combine the eggs, a third of the soup and 1/4 cup milk. Stir in stuffing mix and tuna. Shape into eight patties.

2 In a large skillet, brown patties in butter for 3-4 minutes on each side or until heated through. Meanwhile, in a small saucepan, heat remaining soup and milk. Serve with patties.

YIELD: 4 SERVINGS.

I needed a quick meal one night when my husband was coming home late with the kids. So I threw together this tasty gumbo with ingredients I had on hand, and my family really relished it.

Lori Costo, Spring, Texas

speedy seafood gumbo

PREP/TOTAL TIME: 15 MIN.

 3 cups water, divided
 1 tablespoon butter
 1/4 teaspoon salt
 1 cup uncooked instant rice
 4 cans (10-3/4 ounces each) condensed
    chicken gumbo soup, undiluted
 1 pound frozen cooked shrimp, peeled
    and deveined
 1 package (10 ounces) frozen cut okra
 1 package (8 ounces) imitation crabmeat, flaked
 1 tablespoon dried minced onion
 1 teaspoon Cajun seasoning
 1/2 teaspoon garlic powder

1 In a small saucepan, bring 1 cup of water, butter and salt to a boil. Stir in rice; cover and remove from the heat. Let stand for 5 minutes.

2 Meanwhile, in a Dutch oven, combine the soup, shrimp, okra, crab, onion, Cajun seasoning, garlic powder and remaining water. Bring to a boil. Reduce heat; cover and cook over medium heat until heated through. Stir in cooked rice.

YIELD: 12 SERVINGS (3 QUARTS).

Mixed veggies perk up this classic tuna salad sandwich. Serve alongside fruit cups and your favorite chips.

Taste of Home Test Kitchen

creamy shrimp & spaghetti

PREP/TOTAL TIME: 25 MIN.

As a single parent, cooking quick and easy meals is something I've done for a long time. This recipe has remained a tradition—it's fast to fix and everyone loves it.

David Burgess, Olympia, Washington

- 1 package (7 ounces) spaghetti
- 1 cup sliced fresh mushrooms
- 1/2 cup julienned green pepper
- 2 tablespoons butter, divided
- 1 envelope (1.6 ounces) garlic-herb pasta sauce mix
- 2 tablespoons all-purpose flour
- 2-1/2 cups 2% milk
- 1/4 cup water
- 3/4 pound frozen cooked small shrimp, thawed
- 1/4 teaspoon white pepper
- 1/2 cup grated Parmesan cheese

1 Cook spaghetti according to package directions. Meanwhile, in a large skillet, saute mushrooms and green pepper in 1 tablespoon butter for 3-4 minutes or until crisp-tender.

2 In a small bowl, whisk pasta sauce mix, flour, milk and water until blended. Stir into skillet. Bring to a boil; cook and stir for 2 minutes or until thickened. Add the shrimp, white pepper and remaining butter; cook 2-3 minutes longer or until the shrimp are heated through.

3 Drain spaghetti; toss with shrimp mixture. Sprinkle with cheese.

YIELD: 3 SERVINGS.

hot tuna sandwiches

PREP/TOTAL TIME: 25 MIN.

- 1 can (12 ounces) white water-packed tuna, drained and flaked
- 1/2 cup frozen mixed vegetables, thawed and chopped
- 1/3 cup mayonnaise
- 2 tablespoons finely chopped onion
- 1 tablespoon ranch salad dressing mix
- 4 hamburger buns, split

1 In a large bowl, combine the tuna, vegetables, mayonnaise, onion and salad dressing mix. Spoon tuna mixture onto bun bottoms; replace tops.

2 Place each sandwich on a piece of heavy-duty foil (about 12 in. square). Fold foil around each sandwich and seal tightly; place packets on a baking sheet. Bake at 400° for 10-15 minutes or until heated through.

YIELD: 4 SERVINGS.

TIP

If you like the flavor of ranch salad dressing, feel free to increase the amount you use in the Hot Tuna Sandwiches. For every tablespoon you increase the dressing, reduce the mayonnaise by the same amount.

This zippy stew is very simple to prepare. The hardest part is peeling and dicing the potatoes, and even that can be done the night before.

Bonnie Marlow
Ottoville, Ohio

spicy seafood stew

PREP: 30 MIN. COOK: 4-3/4 HOURS

2 pounds potatoes, peeled and diced

1 pound carrots, sliced

1 jar (26 ounces) spaghetti sauce

2 jars (6 ounces each) sliced mushrooms, drained

1-1/2 teaspoons ground turmeric

1-1/2 teaspoons minced garlic

1 teaspoon cayenne pepper

3/4 teaspoon salt

1-1/2 cups water

1 pound sea scallops

1 pound uncooked medium shrimp, peeled and deveined

1 In a 5-qt. slow cooker, combine the potatoes, carrots, spaghetti sauce, mushrooms and seasonings. Cover and cook on low for 4-1/2 to 5 hours or until potatoes are tender.

2 Stir in the water, scallops and shrimp. Cover and cook for 15-20 minutes or until scallops are opaque and shrimp turn pink.

YIELD: **9 SERVINGS.**

Your family will love this hearty and smoky dish that comes together in a snap. A basic red beans and rice mix gets a quick makeover for a wonderful meal.

Taste of Home Test Kitchen

jiffy jambalaya

PREP/TOTAL TIME: 30 MIN.

- 1 package (8 ounces) red beans and rice mix
- 1/2 pound smoked sausage, sliced
- 1/2 cup chopped onion
- 1 tablespoon olive oil
- 1/2 pound cooked medium shrimp, peeled and deveined
- 1 can (14-1/2 ounces) diced tomatoes, drained
- 1 teaspoon brown sugar
- 1/4 teaspoon Louisiana-style hot sauce, optional

1 Cook the red beans and rice mix according to package directions.

2 Meanwhile, in a large skillet, saute sausage and onion in oil until onion is tender. Add the shrimp, tomatoes, brown sugar and hot sauce if desired. Cook for 3-4 minutes or until heated through. Stir in rice mixture.

YIELD: 4 SERVINGS.

TIP

To give your jambalaya a little more spice, substitute andouille sausage for the smoked sausage. Look for andouille sausage in the refrigerated section of your supermarket where smoked and Polish sausages are sold.

almost
homemade

spicy shrimp wraps

PREP/TOTAL TIME: 20 MIN.

This easy recipe is deliciously big on flavor. The tasty shrimp are tucked inside a tortilla wrap, along with coleslaw and dressed-up bottled salsa.

Frankie Allen Mann, Warrior, Alabama

This is one of my favorite ways to prepare perch. Taco seasoning and cornmeal make the coating zesty and unique.

Jim Lord, Mancheseter, New Hampshire

1 cup salsa

1 medium ripe mango, peeled, pitted and diced

1 tablespoon ketchup

1 envelope reduced-sodium taco seasoning

1 tablespoon olive oil

1 pound uncooked medium shrimp, peeled and deveined

6 flour tortillas (10 inches), warmed

1-1/2 cups coleslaw mix

6 tablespoons reduced-fat sour cream

1 In a small bowl, combine the salsa, mango and ketchup; set aside. In a large resealable plastic bag, combine taco seasoning and oil; add shrimp. Seal bag and shake to coat.

2 In a nonstick skillet or wok, cook shrimp over medium-high heat for 2-3 minutes or until shrimp turn until pink. Top tortillas with coleslaw mix, salsa mixture and shrimp. Fold bottom third of tortilla up over filling; fold sides over. Serve with sour cream.

YIELD: 6 SERVINGS.

southwestern fried perch

PREP/TOTAL TIME: 30 MIN.

1 envelope taco seasoning

1 pound lake perch fillets

1 egg, lightly beaten

1/2 cup yellow cornmeal

1/4 cup all-purpose flour

3 tablespoons canola oil

1 Place taco seasoning in a large resealable bag; add perch fillets, one at a time, and shake to coat.

2 Place the egg in a shallow bowl. In another shallow bowl, combine cornmeal and flour. Dip fillets in egg, then coat with cornmeal mixture. Place in a single layer on a plate; refrigerate for 15 minutes.

3 In a large skillet, heat oil over medium-high heat. Fry fillets for 2-3 minutes on each side or until fish flakes easily with a fork.

YIELD: 4 SERVINGS.

1. In a small bowl, combine spinach and 3/4 cup cream cheese. Spoon onto each fillet; roll up. Place seam side down in a greased 8-in. square baking dish. Bake, uncovered, at 375° for 25-30 minutes or until fish flakes easily with a fork.

2. In a small microwave-safe bowl, combine the milk, lemon juice, salt, pepper and remaining cream cheese. Microwave on high for 30-60 seconds; stir until smooth. Spoon over fish.

YIELD: 4 SERVINGS.

broccoli tuna roll-ups

PREP: 15 MIN. BAKE: 40 MIN.

For a family-pleasing main dish that's on the lighter side, consider these cheesy tortilla wraps. They're a fun and tasty alternative to the usual tuna casserole.

Mary Wilhelm, Sparta, Wisconsin

- 1 can (10-3/4 ounces) reduced-fat reduced-sodium condensed cream of mushroom soup, undiluted
- 1 cup fat-free milk
- 2 cans (5 ounces each) light water-packed tuna, drained and flaked
- 3 cups frozen chopped broccoli, thawed and drained
- 2/3 cup shredded reduced-fat cheddar cheese, divided
- 1/3 cup sliced almonds, divided
- 6 flour tortillas (7 inches)
- 1 large tomato, seeded and chopped

1. In a small bowl, combine the soup and milk; set aside. Combine the tuna, broccoli, 1/3 cup cheese and 3 tablespoons almonds. Stir in half of the soup mixture.

2. Spoon filling down the center of each tortilla; roll up. Place seam side down in an 11-in. x 7-in. baking dish coated with cooking spray. Pour remaining soup mixture over top; sprinkle with tomato.

3. Cover and bake at 350° for 35 minutes. Uncover; sprinkle with remaining cheese and almonds. Bake 5 minutes longer or until cheese is melted.

YIELD: 6 SERVINGS.

A mixture of vegetable cream cheese and healthful chopped spinach lends rich flavor to these tender fish fillets. You'll have an elegant meal on the table in just over 30 minutes.

Bobby Taylor, Michigan City, Indiana

flounder florentine

PREP: 10 MIN. BAKE: 25 MIN.

- 1 package (10 ounces) frozen chopped spinach, thawed and squeezed dry
- 1 carton (8 ounces) spreadable garden vegetable cream cheese, divided
- 4 flounder or sole fillets (3 ounces each)
- 2 tablespoons 2% milk
- 1/2 teaspoon lemon juice
- 1/8 teaspoon salt
- 1/8 teaspoon pepper

flavorful fish fillets

PREP/TOTAL TIME: 20 MIN.

I like to make this entree whenever there's a special occasion in my large family. The fish has an impressive taste without the time-consuming preparation of other dishes, and people always ask for the recipe.

Nella Parker, Hersey, Michigan

1 package (18.7 ounces) frozen breaded
   fish fillets
3 tablespoons olive oil
1 jar (26 ounces) spaghetti sauce
3 tablespoons prepared horseradish
1 cup (4 ounces) shredded part-skim
   mozzarella cheese

1 In a large skillet, cook fish in oil for 4 minutes on each side or until crisp and golden brown. Meanwhile, in a large saucepan, combine the spaghetti sauce and horseradish; cook until heated through.

2 Spoon over fish; sprinkle with cheese. Cover and remove from the heat. Let stand for 5 minutes or until cheese is melted.

YIELD: 4-5 SERVINGS.

Purchased Alfredo sauce adds creaminess to this crab casserole while red pepper flakes kick up the heat. Summer squash and zucchini bring garden-fresh goodness to the comforting main dish.

Bernadette Bennett, Waco, Texas

crab & penne casserole

PREP: 20 MIN. BAKE: 40 MIN.

1-1/2 cups uncooked penne pasta
1 jar (15 ounces) Alfredo sauce
1-1/2 cups imitation crabmeat, chopped
1 medium yellow summer squash, sliced
1 medium zucchini, sliced
1 tablespoon dried parsley flakes
1/8 to 1/4 teaspoon crushed red pepper flakes
1-1/2 cups (6 ounces) shredded part-skim
   mozzarella cheese
2 tablespoons dry bread crumbs
2 teaspoons butter, melted

1 Cook pasta according to package directions. Meanwhile, in a large bowl, combine the Alfredo sauce, crab, yellow squash, zucchini, parsley and pepper flakes. Drain pasta; add to sauce mixture and toss to coat.

2 Transfer to a greased 13-in. x 9-in. baking dish. Sprinkle with cheese. Cover and bake at 325° for 35 minutes.

3 Toss bread crumbs and butter; sprinkle over casserole. Bake, uncovered, 5-6 minutes longer or until browned.

YIELD: 6 SERVINGS.

Roasted red peppers give this hearty sandwich fantastic taste. The fish is surprisingly mild, so kids won't be bothered by the spices.

Taste of Home Test Kitchen

fish sandwich loaf

PREP/TOTAL TIME: 30 MIN.

1 loaf (1 pound) Italian bread
2 packages (7.6 ounces each) frozen Cajun blackened grilled fish fillets
3 tablespoons butter, melted
1 teaspoon minced garlic
1/2 cup roasted sweet red peppers, patted dry
1 cup (4 ounces) shredded part-skim mozzarella cheese

1 Cut the top half off the loaf of bread; carefully hollow out top and bottom, leaving a 1/2-in. shell (save removed bread for another use).

2 Microwave fish fillets according to package directions. Meanwhile, combine butter and garlic; spread over cut sides of bread. In bread bottom, layer fish, red peppers and cheese. Replace bread top.

3 Wrap loaf in foil. Bake at 350° for 15-20 minutes or until cheese is melted. Slice and serve immediately.

YIELD: 6 SERVINGS.

seafood alfredo baskets

PREP: 10 MIN. BAKE: 25 MIN.

They'll think you slaved over this sophisticated entree of shellfish on flaky puff pastry shells. But with only five convenient ingredients—it goes together in a heartbeat.

Diana Smarrito, Blackwood, New Jersey

4 frozen puff pastry shells
6 cups water
1/2 pound bay scallops
1/4 pound uncooked medium shrimp, peeled and deveined
1 cup Alfredo sauce, warmed
1/2 to 1 teaspoon garlic powder

1 Bake puff pastry shells according to package directions. Meanwhile, in a large saucepan, bring water to a boil. Add scallops and shrimp. Cook, uncovered, for 2-5 minutes or until scallops are firm and opaque and shrimp turn pink; drain.

2 Combine Alfredo sauce and garlic powder; drizzle over puff pastry shells. Top with seafood.

YIELD: 2 SERVINGS.

tuna & pea casserole

PREP: 20 MIN. BAKE: 40 MIN.

8 ounces uncooked egg noodles

2 cans (10-3/4 ounces each) condensed cream of mushroom soup, undiluted

1/2 cup mayonnaise

1/2 cup 2% milk

2 to 3 teaspoons prepared horseradish

1/2 teaspoon dill weed

1/8 teaspoon pepper

1 cup frozen peas, thawed

1 can (4 ounces) mushroom stems and pieces, drained

1 small onion, chopped

1 jar (2 ounces) diced pimientos, drained

2 cans (6 ounces each) tuna, drained and flaked

1/4 cup dry bread crumbs

1 tablespoon butter, melted

1 Cook noodles according to package directions. In a large bowl, combine the soup, mayonnaise, milk, horseradish, dill and pepper. Stir in the peas, mushrooms, onion, pimientos and tuna.

2 Drain noodles; stir into soup mixture. Transfer to a greased 2-qt. baking dish. Toss bread crumbs and butter; sprinkle over the top. Bake, uncovered, at 375° for 40-45 minutes or until bubbly.

YIELD: 6 SERVINGS.

Orange roughy is a great fish for this mild, yet tasty meal. Flounder, sole or red snapper will also work in this recipe.

Taste of Home Test Kitchen

orange roughy with rice

PREP/TOTAL TIME: 25 MIN.

1 package (5.7 ounces) instant creamy chicken-flavored rice and sauce mix

2 cups water

1 tablespoon butter, optional

1 cup fresh broccoli florets

1/4 teaspoon onion salt

1/4 teaspoon pepper

1/8 teaspoon dill weed

1/8 teaspoon paprika

4 orange roughy fillets (6 ounces each)

1 tablespoon olive oil

1 In a large saucepan, combine the rice mix, water and butter if desired. Bring to a boil; stir in broccoli. Reduce heat; cover and simmer for 7 minutes or until rice is tender.

2 Meanwhile, combine the onion salt, pepper, dill and paprika; sprinkle over fillets. In a large skillet, cook fillets in oil over medium heat for 4-6 minutes on each side or until fish flakes easily with a fork.

3 Remove rice from the heat; let stand for 2 minutes. Serve with fish.

YIELD: 4 SERVINGS.

meatless

These cute bundles are stuffed with a savory asparagus-cream cheese mixture. They're wonderful for a brunch or even as a fun side dish.

Cynthia Linthicum
Towson, Maryland

asparagus brunch pockets

PREP: 20 MIN. BAKE: 15 MIN.

1 pound fresh asparagus, trimmed and cut into 1-inch pieces

4 ounces cream cheese, softened

1 tablespoon 2% milk

1 tablespoon mayonnaise

1 tablespoon diced pimientos

1 tablespoon finely chopped onion

1/8 teaspoon salt

Dash pepper

1 tube (8 ounces) refrigerated crescent rolls

2 teaspoons butter, melted

1 tablespoon seasoned bread crumbs

1 In a large saucepan, bring 1/2 in. of water to a boil. Add asparagus; cover and boil for 3 minutes. Drain and set aside.

2 In a small bowl, beat the cream cheese, milk and mayonnaise until smooth. Stir in the pimientos, onion, salt and pepper.

3 Unroll crescent dough and separate into triangles; place on an ungreased baking sheet. Spoon 1 teaspoon of cream cheese mixture into the center of each triangle; top with asparagus. Top each with another teaspoonful of cream cheese mixture. Bring three corners of dough together and twist; pinch edges to seal.

4 Brush with butter; sprinkle with bread crumbs. Bake at 375° for 15-18 minutes or until golden brown.

YIELD: 8 SERVINGS.

spinach feta turnovers

PREP/TOTAL TIME: 30 MIN.

These quick and easy turnovers are a favorite with my wife, who says they are delicious and melt in your mouth.

David Baruch, Weston, Florida

2 eggs or 1/2 cup egg substitute
1 package (10 ounces) frozen leaf spinach, thawed, squeezed dry and chopped
3/4 cup crumbled feta cheese
2 garlic cloves, minced
1/4 teaspoon pepper
1 tube (13.8 ounces) refrigerated pizza crust

1 In a bowl, whisk eggs; reserve 1 tablespoon egg and set aside. In a large bowl, combine the spinach, feta cheese, garlic, pepper and remaining eggs.

2 Unroll pizza dough; roll into a 12-in. square. Cut into four 3-in. squares. Top each square with about 1/3 cup spinach mixture. Fold into a triangle and pinch edges to seal. Cut slits in top; brush with reserved egg.

3 Place on a greased baking sheet. Bake at 425° for 8-10 minutes or until golden brown.

YIELD: 4 SERVINGS.

black bean veggie burger salad

PREP/TOTAL TIME: 15 MIN.

2 frozen spicy black bean veggie burgers
3 cups spring mix salad greens
3/4 cup grape tomatoes, halved
1/3 cup frozen corn, thawed
1/4 cup finely chopped red onion
1/2 cup coarsely crushed nacho tortilla chips
1/2 cup shredded Mexican cheese blend
1/3 cup ranch salad dressing
1/3 cup salsa
1 teaspoon taco seasoning

This low-fat version of a traditional taco salad doesn't lose any of the flavor. The creamy, tasty dressing complements the unique use of a veggie burger as well.

Mary Bilyeu, Ann Arbor, Michigan

1 Cook the veggie burgers according to package directions. Divide the salad greens, tomatoes, corn and onion between two serving plates. Crumble burgers; sprinkle each salad with burgers, chips and cheese. In a bowl, combine salad dressing, salsa and taco seasoning; serve with salad.

YIELD: 2 SERVINGS.

2 Bring to a boil; cover and simmer for 10 minutes. Discard bay leaf. Drain spaghetti; top with sauce and cheese.

YIELD: 6 SERVINGS.

enchiladas florentine

PREP: 25 MIN. BAKE: 35 MIN.

After tasting wonderful enchiladas at a Mexican restaurant, I created this lighter version at home. Topped with a zesty lime and cilantro sauce, the main course is perfect alongside reduced-fat refried beans.

Debbie Purdue, Westland, Michigan

- 1 carton (15 ounces) reduced-fat ricotta cheese
- 1 package (10 ounces) frozen chopped spinach, thawed and squeezed dry
- 1-1/2 cups (6 ounces) shredded reduced-fat Mexican cheese blend, divided
- 2 egg whites, lightly beaten
- 10 flour tortillas (8 inches)
- 1 tablespoon cornstarch
- 1 cup vegetable broth
- 1 bottle (7 ounces) mild green taco sauce
- 1/4 cup minced fresh cilantro
- 1 tablespoon lime juice
- 1/2 pound sliced fresh mushrooms
- 2 teaspoons canola oil

1 In a large bowl, combine the ricotta, spinach, 1 cup cheese and egg whites. Spoon down the center of each tortilla. Roll up and place seam side down in a 13-in. x 9-in. baking dish coated with cooking spray.

2 In a small saucepan, combine the cornstarch and broth until smooth. Stir in taco sauce. Bring to a boil; cook and stir for 2 minutes or until thickened. Stir in cilantro and lime juice. Pour over enchiladas. In a nonstick skillet, saute mushrooms in oil until tender; arrange evenly over enchiladas.

3 Cover and bake at 350° for 30-35 minutes or until heated through. Uncover; sprinkle with remaining cheese. Bake 5 minutes longer or until the cheese is melted.

YIELD: 10 SERVINGS.

Who says spaghetti needs meat to be good? I streamlined the original recipe for this deliciously different dish to reduce its 2-hour simmer time to just 10 minutes.

Margaret Wilson, Sun City, California

vegetarian spaghetti

PREP/TOTAL TIME: 25 MIN.

- 1 package (16 ounces) spaghetti
- 1 cup chopped onion
- 1/2 cup chopped celery
- 1 teaspoon garlic powder
- 3 tablespoons canola oil
- 1 jar (26 ounces) meatless spaghetti sauce
- 1 can (15 ounces) garbanzo beans or chickpeas, rinsed and drained
- 1 can (14-1/2 ounces) diced tomatoes with garlic and onion, undrained
- 1 teaspoon sugar
- 1/2 teaspoon salt
- 1/2 teaspoon dried oregano
- 1 bay leaf
- 1/4 cup grated Parmesan cheese

1 Cook spaghetti according to package directions. Meanwhile, in a large skillet, saute the onion, celery and garlic powder in oil until tender. Add the next seven ingredients.

artichoke blue cheese fettuccine

PREP/TOTAL TIME: 20 MIN.

Store-bought Alfredo sauce speeds along this flavorful meatless entree. I start with dry pasta, but you can use refrigerated fettuccine to make this recipe even faster.

Jolanthe Erb, Harrisonburg, Virginia

1 package (12 ounces) fettuccine
1 can (14 ounces) water-packed artichoke hearts, rinsed, drained and chopped
1 cup sliced fresh mushrooms
1-1/2 cups Alfredo sauce
1/4 cup crumbled blue cheese

1 Cook fettuccine according to package directions. Meanwhile, in a large nonstick skillet coated with cooking spray, saute artichokes and mushrooms until tender. Stir in Alfredo sauce. Bring to a boil. Reduce heat; simmer, uncovered, for 4-5 minutes or until heated through, stirring occasionally.

2 Drain fettuccine; add to artichoke mixture; toss to coat. Sprinkle with blue cheese.

YIELD: 4 SERVINGS.

This grilled sandwich uses fresh eggplant and savory marinara to make a hearty dinner sandwich for four. If you can't find smoked mozzarella, regular works just fine.

Taste of Home Test Kitchen

eggplant-portobello sandwich loaf

PREP: 25 MIN. GRILL: 20 MIN.

1 loaf (1 pound) Italian bread
1/2 cup olive oil
2 teaspoons minced garlic
1 teaspoon Italian seasoning
1/2 teaspoon salt
1/4 teaspoon pepper
1 large eggplant (1 pound), cut into 1/2-inch slices
1 package (6 ounces) sliced portobello mushrooms
1 cup marinara sauce
2 tablespoons minced fresh basil
4 ounces smoked fresh mozzarella cheese, cut into 1/4-inch slices

1 Cut bread lengthwise in half. Carefully hollow out top and bottom, leaving a 1/2-in. shell; set aside. In a small bowl, combine the oil, garlic, Italian seasoning, salt and pepper. Brush over eggplant and mushrooms.

2 Grill, covered, over medium heat for 3-5 minutes on each side or until vegetables are tender. Spread half of the marinara sauce over bottom of bread. Top with eggplant and mushrooms. Spread with remaining sauce; top with the basil and cheese. Replace bread top.

3 Wrap loaf in a large piece of heavy-duty foil (about 28 in. x 18 in.); seal tightly. Grill, covered, over medium heat for 4-5 minutes on each side.

YIELD: 4 SERVINGS.

gnocchi with pesto sauce

PREP/TOTAL TIME: 20 MIN.

Prepared pesto makes a flavorful sauce for gnocchi and vegetables. If you don't have pine nuts, substitute any nut you like, such as walnuts, pecans or almonds.

Taste of Home Test Kitchen

1 package (16 ounces) potato gnocchi
1 cup diced zucchini
1/2 cup chopped sweet yellow pepper
2 teaspoons olive oil
1/4 cup prepared pesto
1 cup chopped tomatoes
Toasted pine nuts, optional

1 Cook gnocchi according to package directions. Meanwhile, in a large skillet, saute zucchini and yellow pepper in oil until crisp-tender. Drain gnocchi; add to skillet with the pesto. Gently stir until coated. Stir in tomatoes. Sprinkle with pine nuts if desired.

YIELD: 4 SERVINGS.

This tasty pizza is so easy to prepare. My family, including my young daughter, loves it. What an easy way to make a delicious veggie meal.

Dawn Bartholomew, Raleigh, North Carolina

spinach pizza

PREP/TOTAL TIME: 25 MIN.

1 package (6-1/2 ounces) pizza crust mix
1/2 cup Alfredo sauce
4 cups chopped fresh spinach
2 medium tomatoes, chopped
2 cups (8 ounces) shredded Italian cheese blend

1 Prepare pizza dough according to package directions. With floured hands, press dough onto a greased 12-in. pizza pan.

2 Spread Alfredo sauce over dough to within 1 in. of edges. Top with spinach, tomatoes and cheese. Bake at 450° for 10-15 minutes or until cheese is melted and crust is golden brown.

YIELD: 4-6 SERVINGS.

These Italian-inspired roll-ups are fast and fun to make. They may look elegant, but they are also very kid-friendly.

Cindy Romberg
Mississauga, Ontario

spinach lasagna roll-ups

PREP: 25 MIN. + CHILLING BAKE: 35 MIN.

- 1 package (10 ounces) frozen chopped spinach, thawed and squeezed dry
- 1 cup (4 ounces) shredded part-skim mozzarella cheese
- 1 cup (8 ounces) 2% cottage cheese
- 3/4 cup grated Parmesan cheese, divided
- 1 egg, lightly beaten
- 6 lasagna noodles, cooked and drained
- 2 cans (15 ounces each) seasoned tomato sauce for lasagna

1 In a small bowl, combine the spinach, mozzarella, cottage cheese, 1/2 cup Parmesan cheese and egg. Spread a heaping 1/3 cupful over each noodle. Roll up and secure with toothpicks. Place seam side down in an 11-in. x 7-in. baking dish coated with cooking spray. Cover and refrigerate overnight.

2 Remove from the refrigerator 30 minutes before baking. Pour tomato sauce over roll-ups. Cover and bake at 350° for 33-38 minutes or until bubbly. Sprinkle with remaining Parmesan cheese. Discard the toothpicks.

YIELD: 6 SERVINGS.

EDITOR'S NOTE: This recipe was tested with Hunt's seasoned tomato sauce for lasagna.

veggie calzones

PREP: 25 MIN. + RISING BAKE: 35 MIN.

- 1/2 pound fresh mushrooms, chopped
- 1 medium onion, chopped
- 1 medium green pepper, chopped
- 2 tablespoons canola oil
- 3 plum tomatoes, seeded and chopped
- 1 can (6 ounces) tomato paste
- 1 cup (4 ounces) shredded Monterey Jack cheese
- 1 cup (4 ounces) shredded part-skim mozzarella cheese
- 1/2 cup grated Parmesan cheese
- 2 loaves (1 pound each) frozen bread dough, thawed
- 1 egg
- 1 tablespoon water

1 In a large skillet, saute the mushrooms, onion and green pepper in oil until tender. Add tomatoes; cook and stir for 3 minutes. Stir in tomato paste; set aside. Combine cheeses and set aside.

2 On a lightly floured surface, divide dough into eight pieces. Roll each piece into a 7-in. circle. Spoon a scant 1/2 cup vegetable mixture and 1/4 cup cheese mixture over one side of each circle. Brush edges of dough with water; fold dough over filling and press edges with a fork to seal. Place calzones 3 in. apart on greased baking sheets. Cover and let rise in a warm place for 20 minutes.

3 Whisk egg and water; brush over calzones. Bake at 375° for 15 minutes. Cool desired number of calzones; place in freezer bags. Seal and freeze for up to 3 months. Bake the remaining calzones 18-22 minutes longer or until golden brown. Serve immediately.

4 **To use frozen calzones:** Place 2 in. apart on a greased baking sheet. Bake at 350° for 30-35 minutes or until golden brown.

YIELD: 8 SERVINGS.

almost homemade

four-cheese baked ziti

PREP: 20 MIN. BAKE: 30 MIN.

This pasta dish, made with Alfredo sauce, is deliciously different from typical tomato-based recipes. It's extra cheesy and goes together quickly.

Lisa Varner, Charleston, South Carolina

- 1 package (16 ounces) ziti or small tube pasta
- 2 cartons (10 ounces each) refrigerated Alfredo sauce
- 1 cup (8 ounces) sour cream
- 2 eggs, lightly beaten
- 1 carton (15 ounces) ricotta cheese
- 1/2 cup grated Parmesan cheese, divided
- 1/4 cup grated Romano cheese
- 1/4 cup minced fresh parsley
- 1-3/4 cups shredded part-skim mozzarella cheese

1 Cook pasta according to package directions; drain and return to the pan. Stir in Alfredo sauce and sour cream. Spoon half into a lightly greased 3-qt. baking dish.

2 Combine the eggs, ricotta cheese, 1/4 cup Parmesan cheese, Romano cheese and parsley; spread over pasta. Top with the remaining pasta mixture; sprinkle with mozzarella and remaining Parmesan.

3 Cover and bake at 350° for 25 minutes or until a thermometer reads 160°. Uncover; bake 5-10 minutes longer or until bubbly.

YIELD: 12 SERVINGS.

Pasta, black beans and nacho cheese soup combine in this speedy six-ingredient supper. Servings of this zippy casserole will be friendly to your grocery budget.

Melodie Gay, Salt Lake City, Utah

black bean nacho bake

PREP: 15 MIN. BAKE: 30 MIN.

- 1 package (7 ounces) small pasta shells, cooked and drained
- 1 can (15 ounces) black beans, rinsed and drained
- 1 can (11 ounces) condensed nacho cheese soup, undiluted
- 1/3 cup 2% milk
- 1/2 cup crushed tortilla chips
- 1/2 cup shredded cheddar cheese

1 In a large bowl, combine macaroni and beans. In a small bowl, combine soup and milk; stir into macaroni mixture.

2 Transfer to a greased 8-in. square baking dish. Cover and bake at 350° for 25 minutes. Uncover; sprinkle with tortilla chips and cheese. Bake 5-10 minutes longer or until pasta is tender and cheese is melted.

YIELD: 4 SERVINGS.

vegetable pizza

PREP: 15 MIN. BAKE: 15 MIN. + STANDING

1 tube (13.8 ounces) refrigerated pizza crust
1/2 cup sliced fresh mushrooms
1/2 cup chopped onion
1/2 cup chopped fresh broccoli
1/2 cup chopped green pepper
1/2 cup chopped fresh baby spinach
1 cup meatless spaghetti sauce
2 plum tomatoes, thinly sliced
2 cups (8 ounces) shredded part-skim
  mozzarella cheese

1 Unroll pizza crust into a 15-in. x 10-in. x 1-in. baking pan coated with cooking spray; flatten dough and build up edges slightly. Bake at 400° for 8 minutes.

2 Meanwhile, in a nonstick skillet coated with cooking spray, saute mushrooms, onion, broccoli, green pepper and spinach until crisp-tender.

3 Spread spaghetti sauce over crust. Top with sauteed vegetables, tomatoes and cheese. Bake for 15-20 minutes or until crust is golden brown and cheese is melted. Let pizza stand for 10 minutes before serving.

YIELD: 8 SLICES.

TIP

When buying fresh vegetables, look for firm, plump, crisp ones. Avoid those with soft spots, bruises and discolorations. Also reject any vegetables that look shriveled.

sides

creamy blueberry gelatin salad

PREP: 30 MIN. + CHILLING

- 2 packages (3 ounces each) grape gelatin
- 2 cups boiling water
- 1 can (21 ounces) blueberry pie filling
- 1 can (20 ounces) unsweetened crushed pineapple, undrained

TOPPING:
- 1 package (8 ounces) cream cheese, softened
- 1 cup (8 ounces) sour cream
- 1/2 cup sugar
- 1 teaspoon vanilla extract
- 1/2 cup chopped walnuts

1 In a large bowl, dissolve gelatin in boiling water. Cool for 10 minutes. Stir in the pie filling and pineapple until blended. Transfer to a 13-in. x 9-in. dish. Cover and refrigerate until partially set, about 1 hour.

2 For topping, in a small bowl, combine the cream cheese, sour cream, sugar and vanilla. Carefully spread over gelatin; sprinkle with walnuts. Cover and refrigerate until firm.

YIELD: 12-15 SERVINGS.

almost homemade

golden corn casserole

PREP: 10 MIN. BAKE: 35 MIN.

This terribly moist dish is super easy to prepare. It went over so well at Thanksgiving one year that it's now served at all our gatherings.

Marcia Braun, Scott City, Kansas

> 3 eggs
> 1 carton (8 ounces) French onion dip
> 1/4 cup butter, softened
> 1 package (8-1/2 ounces) corn bread/muffin mix
> 1/2 teaspoon salt
> 1/2 teaspoon pepper
> 1 can (15-1/4 ounces) whole kernel corn, drained
> 1 can (14-3/4 ounces) cream-style corn

1 In a large bowl, beat the eggs, dip, butter, corn bread mix, salt and pepper until combined. Stir in the corn.

2 Pour into a greased 11-in. x 7-in. baking dish. Bake, uncovered, at 350° for 35-40 minutes or until a thermometer reads 160°.

YIELD: 8-10 SERVINGS.

I created this side while trying to make broccoli Alfredo. I kept adding fresh vegetables, and the result was this creamy pasta dish!

Tammy Perrault, Lancaster, Ohio

garden primavera fettuccine

PREP/TOTAL TIME: 30 MIN.

> 1 package (12 ounces) fettuccine
> 1 cup fresh cauliflowerets
> 1 cup fresh broccoli florets
> 1/2 cup julienned carrot
> 1 small sweet red pepper, julienned
> 1/2 small yellow summer squash, sliced
> 1/2 small zucchini, sliced
> 1 cup Alfredo sauce
> 1 teaspoon dried basil
> Shredded Parmesan cheese, optional

1 In a large saucepan, cook fettuccine according to package directions, adding vegetables during the last 4 minutes. Drain and return to the pan.

2 Add Alfredo sauce and basil; toss to coat. Cook over low heat for 1-2 minutes or until heated through. Sprinkle with cheese if desired.

YIELD: 10 SERVINGS.

2 Cover and refrigerate overnight. Just before serving, add tomatoes and olives; toss to coat.

YIELD: 12 SERVINGS.

holiday green bean bake

PREP: 15 MIN. BAKE: 50 MIN.

Ham and a blend of seasonings make a plain green bean bake spectacular! The recipe has been in my family for more than a generation.

Frances Whitson, Tiptonville, Tennessee

6 cups frozen cut green beans, thawed
1 cup cubed fully cooked ham
3 tablespoons butter, divided
1 tablespoon all-purpose flour
1/2 cup 2% milk
1 can (10-3/4 ounces) condensed cream of mushroom soup, undiluted
4 ounces process cheese (Velveeta), cubed
1 jar (4 ounces) diced pimientos, drained
1 teaspoon Worcestershire sauce
1/2 teaspoon salt
1/4 teaspoon pepper
1/2 cup dry bread crumbs

1 In a large bowl, combine the beans and ham; set aside. In a large saucepan, melt 1 tablespoon butter. Stir in flour until smooth; gradually add milk. Bring to a boil; cook and stir for 1 minute or until thickened. Reduce heat; add the soup, cheese, pimientos, Worcestershire sauce, salt and pepper. Cook and stir until cheese is melted. Pour over bean mixture; toss to coat.

2 Transfer to a greased 2-qt. baking dish. Bake, uncovered at 350° for 40 minutes, stirring twice. Melt the remaining butter; toss with bread crumbs. Sprinkle over top. Bake 10-15 minutes longer or until golden brown.

YIELD: 8-10 SERVINGS.

This is a perfect salad for potlucks and other occasions year-round. In winter, the ingredients are available when many other vegetables aren't in season...and in summer, it's a delicious picnic food.

Muggs Nash, Bloomington, Minnesota

marinated italian salad

PREP: 30 MIN. + MARINATING

4 cups fresh broccoli florets
3 cups fresh cauliflowerets
1/2 pound sliced fresh mushrooms
2 celery ribs, chopped
4 green onions, thinly sliced
1 can (8 ounces) sliced water chestnuts, drained
1 bottle (16 ounces) Italian salad dressing
1 envelope Italian salad dressing mix
1 pint cherry tomatoes, halved
1 can (2-1/4 ounces) sliced ripe olives, drained

1 In a large serving bowl, combine the broccoli, cauliflower, mushrooms, celery, onions and water chestnuts. In a small bowl, whisk the salad dressing and dressing mix; drizzle over vegetables and toss to coat.

biscuit corn bread dressing

PREP: 45 MIN. + STANDING BAKE: 1 HOUR

This mouthwatering and slightly sweet recipe was my mother's. It's just not Christmas at our house without this favorite dressing...and it goes great with goose, too.

Karen Andrews, Arlington, Texas

- 1 package (8-1/2 ounces) corn bread/muffin mix
- 1 tube (7-1/2 ounces) refrigerated buttermilk biscuits
- 2 medium onions, chopped
- 4 celery ribs with leaves, chopped
- 1/4 cup butter
- 1/2 teaspoon salt
- 1/4 teaspoon pepper
- 1/4 teaspoon curry powder
- 1/4 teaspoon dried basil
- 1/4 teaspoon dried thyme
- 1 can (14-1/2 ounces) chicken broth
- 1/2 cup water
- 3/4 cup egg substitute

1 Prepare corn bread according to package directions; cool on a wire rack. Crumble into a large bowl. Prepare biscuits according to package directions; cool on a wire rack. Crumble biscuits over corn bread; stir gently to combine.

2 In a large skillet, saute onions and celery in butter. Stir in the salt, pepper, curry powder, basil and thyme. Add to corn bread mixture. Stir in broth and water (mixture should be the consistency of corn bread batter). Let stand for 1 hour.

3 Stir in egg substitute. Pour into a greased shallow 2-qt. baking dish. Bake, uncovered, at 350° for 1 hour or until golden brown and a knife inserted near the center comes out clean.

YIELD: 8-10 SERVINGS.

Here's a creamy side dish that pairs well with many entrees. It's easy to make and can be prepared ahead.

Maretta Ballinger, Visalia, California

broccoli supreme

PREP/TOTAL TIME: 30 MIN.

- 1 package (16 ounces) frozen chopped broccoli, thawed and drained
- 1 can (10-3/4 ounces) condensed cream of mushroom soup, undiluted
- 1/2 cup sour cream
- 1/2 cup chopped celery
- 1 jar (2 ounces) diced pimientos, drained
- 1/2 teaspoon salt
- 1/2 teaspoon pepper
- 1/2 cup shredded cheddar cheese

1 In a bowl, combine the broccoli, soup, sour cream, celery, pimientos, salt and pepper; stir to coat.

2 Transfer to a greased 1-1/2-qt. baking dish. Sprinkle with cheese. Bake, uncovered, at 350° for 20 minutes or until heated through.

YIELD: 4-6 SERVINGS.

This creamy, sweet salad, with crisp apple crunch, is a real people-pleaser. It makes a lot, which is good because it will go fast!

Cyndi Fynaardt, Oskaloosa, Iowa

candy bar apple salad

PREP/TOTAL TIME: 15 MIN.

- 1-1/2 cups cold 2% milk
- 1 package (3.4 ounces) instant vanilla pudding mix
- 1 carton (8 ounces) frozen whipped topping, thawed
- 4 large apples, chopped (about 6 cups)
- 4 Snickers candy bars (2.07 ounces each), cut into 1/2-inch pieces

1 In a large bowl, whisk milk and pudding mix for 2 minutes. Let stand for 2 minutes or until soft-set. Fold in whipped topping. Fold in apples and candy bars. Refrigerate until serving.

YIELD: 12 SERVINGS (3/4 CUP EACH).

marvelous shells & cheese

PREP: 25 MIN. BAKE: 30 MIN.

This macaroni dish is so good! I adapted the recipe from one my mother makes, but she agrees that my version is rich and delicious.

Lauren Versweyveld, Delavan, Wisconsin

- 1 package (16 ounces) medium pasta shells
- 1 package (8 ounces) process cheese (Velveeta), cubed
- 1/3 cup 2% milk
- 2 cups (16 ounces) 2% cottage cheese
- 1 can (10-3/4 ounces) condensed cream of onion soup, undiluted
- 3 cups (12 ounces) shredded Mexican cheese blend
- 2/3 cup dry bread crumbs
- 1/4 cup butter, melted

1 Cook pasta according to package directions. Meanwhile, in a large saucepan, combine process cheese and milk; cook and stir over low heat until melted. Remove from the heat. Stir in cottage cheese and soup.

2 Drain pasta and add to cheese sauce; stir until coated. Transfer to a greased 13-in. x 9-in. baking dish. Sprinkle with Mexican cheese blend. Toss bread crumbs with butter; sprinkle over the top.

3 Bake, uncovered, at 350° for 30-35 minutes or until heated through.

YIELD: 8 SERVINGS.

green bean & corn bake

PREP: 15 MIN. BAKE: 30 MIN.

1 can (14-1/2 ounces) French-style green beans, drained

1 can (11 ounces) shoepeg corn, drained

1 can (10-3/4 ounces) condensed cream of celery soup, undiluted

1/2 cup sliced celery

1/2 cup chopped onion

1/2 cup sour cream

1/2 cup shredded cheddar cheese

1 jar (2 ounces) diced pimientos, drained

1/2 teaspoon salt

1/2 teaspoon pepper

1/2 cup crushed butter-flavored crackers (about 13 crackers)

2 tablespoons butter, melted

1 In a large bowl, combine the beans, corn, soup, celery, onion, sour cream, cheese, pimientos, salt and pepper. Transfer mixture to a greased 1-1/2-qt. baking dish.

2 Combine the cracker crumbs and butter; sprinkle over vegetable mixture. Bake, uncovered, at 350° for 30-35 minutes or until topping is golden brown.

YIELD: 6 SERVINGS.

brown and wild rice medley

PREP: 20 MIN. COOK: 30 MIN.

- 1 package (6.7 ounces) mushroom-flavored brown and wild rice mix
- 1 large onion, chopped
- 1 cup cut fresh green beans (1/2-inch pieces)
- 1 tablespoon olive oil
- 1 cup sliced fresh mushrooms
- 2 medium carrots, shredded
- 1/4 cup chopped sweet red pepper
- 1/4 cup slivered almonds, toasted

1 In a large saucepan, cook rice mix according to package directions, omitting butter.

2 Meanwhile, in a large nonstick skillet, saute onion and green beans in oil for 2 minutes. Add the mushrooms, carrots and pepper; saute 3-5 minutes longer or until vegetables are tender. Add vegetables and almonds to the cooked rice; stir until blended.

YIELD: 8 SERVINGS.

TIP

If you don't like chopping fresh onions or would like to streamline your cooking prep time, try using frozen chopped onions, which are available in the frozen vegetable section of supermarkets. A small onion yields about 1/3 cup chopped; a medium onion about 1/2 cup chopped; and a large onion 1 to 1-1/4 cups chopped.

summer squash stuffing bake

PREP: 25 MIN. BAKE: 25 MIN.

A convenient stuffing mix adds comforting taste to this creamy yellow squash bake. The simple side is great with chicken or pork.

Ruth Peterson, Jenison, Michigan

- 3/4 cup water
- 1/4 teaspoon salt
- 4 medium yellow summer squash, cut into 1/4-inch slices
- 1/4 cup chopped onion
- 1 package (8 ounces) stuffing mix
- 2 tablespoons butter, melted
- 1 can (10-3/4 ounces) reduced-fat reduced-sodium condensed cream of celery soup, undiluted
- 1 cup (8 ounces) fat-free sour cream
- 2 medium carrots, finely shredded

1 In a large saucepan, bring water and salt to a boil. Add squash and onion. Reduce heat; cover and simmer for 3-5 minutes or until squash is crisp-tender. In a small bowl, combine stuffing mix and butter; set aside.

2 In a large bowl, combine the soup, sour cream and carrots. Drain squash mixture; gently stir into soup mixture. Place half of the stuffing mixture in a 3-qt. baking dish coated with cooking spray. Layer with squash mixture and remaining stuffing mixture.

3 Bake, uncovered, at 350° for 25-30 minutes or until heated through and golden brown (cover loosely with foil if top browns too quickly).

YIELD: 8 SERVINGS.

This thick, smooth mixture has the flavor of ranch dressing and is a breeze to blend together. Use it to top mixed greens or as a dip for fresh vegetables.

Vickie Floden, Story City, Iowa

buttermilk salad dressing

PREP: 10 MIN. + CHILLING

- 3/4 cup buttermilk
- 2 cups (16 ounces) 2% cottage cheese
- 1 envelope ranch salad dressing mix
- Salad greens and vegetables of your choice

1 In a blender, combine the buttermilk, cottage cheese and salad dressing mix; cover and process for 20 seconds or until smooth. Pour into a small pitcher or bowl. Cover and refrigerate for 1 hour. Stir before serving with salad.

YIELD: 2-3/4 CUPS.

glazed baby carrots

PREP/TOTAL TIME: 20 MIN.

With only two ingredients, this side is ideal for nights when you need something quick. People always want to know the secret to our wonderful carrots...here it is!

Linda Hoffman, Logansport, Indiana

- 2 packages (16 ounces each) baby carrots
- 1 jar (12 ounces) orange marmalade

1 Place 1 in. of water in a large saucepan; add carrots. Bring to a boil. Reduce heat; cover and simmer for 12-15 minutes or until crisp-tender.

2 Drain carrots and place in a large serving bowl; stir in marmalade. Serve with a slotted spoon.

YIELD: 8 SERVINGS.

corn fritter patties

PREP/TOTAL TIME: 30 MIN.

Pancake mix gives you a head start when you prepare this Southern staple. Corn fritters make a homey side and are delicious with many entrees.

Megan Hamilton, Pineville, Missouri

- 1 cup pancake mix
- 1 egg, lightly beaten
- 1/4 cup plus 2 tablespoons 2% milk
- 1 can (7 ounces) whole kernel corn, drained
- 2 cups canola oil

1 In a small bowl, combine the pancake mix, egg and milk just until moistened. Stir in the corn.

2 In an electric skillet or deep-fat fryer, heat 1/4 in. of oil to 375°. Drop batter by 1/4 cupfuls into oil; press lightly to flatten. Cook for 2 minutes on each side or until golden brown.

YIELD: 7 PATTIES.

This recipe is easy and tasty. What a clever way to use up all that zucchini from the garden.

Grace Bryant, Merritt Island, Florida

zucchini pancakes

PREP/TOTAL TIME: 20 MIN.

- 1 cup shredded zucchini
- 3 tablespoons biscuit/baking mix
- 1 egg
- 2 tablespoons shredded cheddar cheese
- 1/4 teaspoon dried basil, optional
- 1/8 teaspoon salt
- 1/8 teaspoon pepper

1 Place zucchini in a colander to drain; squeeze to remove excess liquid. Pat dry. In a small bowl, combine the zucchini, biscuit mix, egg, cheese, basil if desired, salt and pepper.

2 Spoon by 1/3 cupful onto a large skillet coated with cooking spray. Cook over medium heat for 3-4 minutes on each side or until golden brown.

YIELD: 2 SERVINGS.

creamy vegetable medley

PREP: 10 MIN. BAKE: 35 MIN.

With its rich, cheesy sauce and golden onion topping, this casserole has broad appeal. Because of that, I frequently rely on it for many functions.

Pay Waymire, Yellow Springs, Ohio

1 package (16 ounces) frozen broccoli, carrot and cauliflower blend
1 can (10-3/4 ounces) condensed cream of mushroom soup, undiluted
1 cup (4 ounces) shredded Swiss cheese, divided
1/3 cup sour cream
1 jar (2 ounces) diced pimientos, drained
1/4 teaspoon salt
1/4 teaspoon pepper
1 can (2.8 ounces) french-fried onions, divided

1 In a large bowl, combine the vegetables, soup, 1/2 cup cheese, sour cream, pimientos, salt, pepper and half of the onions. Pour into a greased 1-1/2-qt. baking dish.

2 Cover and bake at 350° for 30-40 minutes or until the edges are browned. Uncover; sprinkle with remaining cheese and onions. Bake 5 minutes longer or until cheese is melted.

YIELD: 8 SERVINGS.

cherry ribbon salad

PREP: 10 MIN. + CHILLING

1 package (3 ounces) cherry gelatin
2-1/4 cups boiling water, divided
1 can (21 ounces) cherry pie filling
1 package (3 ounces) orange gelatin
1 can (8 ounces) crushed pineapple, undrained
1 cup whipped topping
1/3 cup mayonnaise
1/4 cup chopped pecans, optional

Filled with pineapple, pecans and cherry pie filling, this colorful salad mold adds fun, fruity flavor to any potluck menu.

Virginia Luke, Red Level, Alabama

1 In a large bowl, dissolve cherry gelatin in 1-1/4 cups boiling water. Stir in pie filling. Pour into a 7-cup ring mold coated with cooking spray; refrigerate for about 1 hour or until thickened but not set.

2 In a large bowl, dissolve orange gelatin in remaining boiling water. Stir in pineapple. Chill for about 1 hour or until thickened but not set.

3 Combine the whipped topping, mayonnaise and pecans if desired; fold into orange mixture. Spoon over cherry layer. Refrigerate for at least 1 hour or until firm. Unmold onto a serving plate.

YIELD: 12 SERVINGS.

3 Transfer to a greased 1-qt. baking dish. Sprinkle with the cheese. Broil 4 in. from the heat for 3-4 minutes or until cheese is melted.

YIELD: 6 SERVINGS.

EDITOR'S NOTE: This recipe was tested in a 1,100-watt microwave.

buttery-onion corn on the cob

PREP/TOTAL TIME: 20 MIN.

My mom has been making this recipe for years. Every time I make it for company, they rave and can't believe how easy it is!

Lisa Denson, Decatur, Alabama

1/2 cup butter, melted
1 envelope onion soup mix
4 medium ears sweet corn, husks removed

1 In a small bowl, combine butter and soup mix; rub over corn. Place each ear of corn on a 12-in. x 10-in. piece of heavy-duty foil. Fold foil over corn and seal tightly. Bake at 450° for 15-20 minutes or until corn is tender, turning once.

YIELD: 4 SERVINGS.

Turn garlic-seasoned instant mashed potatoes into a comforting casserole that people will think is from scratch. Just stir in cream cheese before topping the dish with shredded cheddar cheese and broiling it until melted.

Debbie Pataky, Lookout Mountain, Georgia

creamy mashed potatoes

PREP/TOTAL TIME: 15 MIN.

3 cups water
1 cup 2% milk
1 package (7.6 ounces) roasted garlic instant mashed potatoes
4 ounces cream cheese, cubed
1 cup (4 ounces) shredded Mexican cheese blend

1 In a large saucepan, bring water and milk to a rolling boil. Remove from the heat. Add the contents of both envelopes from the potato package. Let stand for 1 minute; whip the potato mixture with a fork.

2 Place cream cheese in a microwave-safe bowl; cover and heat at 70% power for 30 seconds or until softened. Stir into potato mixture.

My mother-in-law gave me the directions for this hearty dish more than 35 years ago. It was the only way I could get my husband to eat broccoli—by hiding it in the stuffing!

Sheron Hutcheson
Newark, Delaware

cheesy broccoli casserole

PREP: 10 MIN. BAKE: 50 MIN.

3 cups frozen chopped broccoli, thawed, drained and patted dry

2 cups (8 ounces) shredded reduced-fat cheddar cheese

1 package (6 ounces) reduced-sodium stuffing mix

1 small onion, finely chopped

1 egg, lightly beaten

1/8 teaspoon ground nutmeg

Dash pepper

1 cup fat-free milk

1 cup reduced-sodium chicken broth

2 bacon strips, cooked and crumbled

1 In a large bowl, combine the broccoli, cheese, stuffing mix, onion, egg, nutmeg and pepper. Gradually stir in milk and broth.

2 Transfer to a 2-qt. baking dish coated with cooking spray. Bake, uncovered, at 325° for 50-55 minutes or until a thermometer reads 160°. Sprinkle with the bacon.

YIELD: 7 SERVINGS.

1. Cook pasta according to package directions. Meanwhile, in a large skillet, saute the mushrooms, salt and pepper in butter until tender. Add cheese spread and broth; cook and stir until blended. Drain pasta; add to skillet and toss to coat.

YIELD: 9 SERVINGS.

early-bird asparagus supreme

PREP/TOTAL TIME: 25 MIN.

This is the best spring vegetable side dish! The fresh asparagus is so delicious in the springtime.

Joyce Speckman, Holt, California

3 pounds fresh asparagus, cut into 1-inch pieces
3 tablespoons butter, melted
1 envelope onion soup mix
1 cup (4 ounces) shredded part-skim mozzarella or Monterey Jack cheese

1. In a large saucepan, bring 1/2 in. of water to a boil. Add asparagus; cover and boil for 3 minutes. Drain and immediately place asparagus in ice water. Drain and pat dry.

2. Place in a 13-in. x 9-in. baking dish coated with cooking spray. Combine butter and soup mix; drizzle over asparagus. Sprinkle with cheese. Bake, uncovered, at 425° for 10-12 minutes or until asparagus is tender and cheese is melted.

YIELD: 6-8 SERVINGS.

This pasta dish has become one of our favorites. It is so simple! But it tastes like it took much longer in the kitchen than it does. Some of our friends don't eat red meat, so I sometimes serve this as a meatless main dish. It's wonderful with a salad and a loaf of French bread.

Dodi Mahan Walker, Peachtree City, Georgia

creamy mushroom bow ties

PREP/TOTAL TIME: 20 MIN.

6 cups uncooked bow tie pasta
1 pound sliced fresh mushrooms
1/2 teaspoon salt
1/4 teaspoon pepper
2 tablespoons butter
1 package (4.4 ounces) garlic-herb cheese spread
1/4 cup chicken broth

TIP

When you shred most cheese either by hand or with the shredding disk in a food processor, it will be less crumbly if it is well-chilled before shredding. Hard cheeses, like Romano or Parmesan, shred more easily if they are at room temperature.

spinach-pine nut pasta

PREP/TOTAL TIME: 20 MIN.

I assure you this is a fantastic recipe. It's easy to prepare and delivers a taste that rivals dishes served in fancy Italian restaurants.

Katie Graczyk, Darien, Illinois

8 ounces uncooked gemelli or spiral pasta

1/2 cup sun-dried tomatoes (not packed in oil), chopped

8 ounces coarsely chopped fresh spinach

1-1/2 cups fat-free milk

1 package (1.6 ounces) Alfredo sauce mix

1/2 cup pine nuts, divided

1/4 teaspoon salt

1 Cook pasta according to package directions, stirring in the tomatoes and spinach during the last 4 minutes of cooking time.

2 Meanwhile, in a small saucepan, combine milk and Alfredo sauce mix. Bring to a boil; cook and stir for 1 minute or until thickened. Stir in 1/4 cup pine nuts and salt.

3 Drain pasta and vegetables; toss with Alfredo sauce. Sprinkle with remaining pine nuts.

YIELD: 5 SERVINGS.

Add your favorite cheese to prepared mashed potatoes, which can be found in the refrigerated meat section of your local grocery store.

Taste of Home Test Kitchen

blue cheese mashed potatoes

PREP/TOTAL TIME: 10 MIN.

1 package (2 pounds) refrigerated mashed potatoes

1/3 cup crumbled blue cheese

1 Heat potatoes according to package directions; stir in blue cheese. Serve immediately.

YIELD: 6 SERVINGS.

EDITOR'S NOTE: This recipe was tested in a 1,100-watt microwave.

Few foods capture the flavor of the season like cranberries. This lightened up version is one of my family's holiday favorite. You'll love the taste of cranberry, apple and pineapple covered in a sweet and creamy dressing.

Alexandra Lypecky
Dearborn, Michigan

creamy cranberry salad

PREP: 15 MIN. + CHILLING

3 cups fresh or frozen cranberries, thawed and coarsely chopped

1 can (20 ounces) unsweetened crushed pineapple, drained

2 cups miniature marshmallows

1 medium apple, chopped

Sugar substitute equivalent to 1/2 cup sugar

1/8 teaspoon salt

1 carton (8 ounces) frozen reduced-fat whipped topping, thawed

1/4 cup chopped walnuts

1 In a large bowl, combine the cranberries, pineapple, marshmallows, apple, sugar substitute and salt. Cover and refrigerate overnight.

2 Just before serving, fold in the whipped topping and walnuts.

YIELD: 12 SERVINGS.

EDITOR'S NOTE: This recipe was tested with Splenda no-calorie sweetener.

fresh floret salad

PREP: 25 MIN. + CHILLING

The dressing for this crisp vegetable salad blends refreshing lemon with hearty Italian seasonings.

Mary Tallman, Arbor Vitae, Wisconsin

- 1 cup fresh broccoli florets
- 1 cup fresh cauliflowerets
- 3 tablespoons sliced celery
- 2 tablespoons finely chopped onion
- 1 hard-cooked egg, chopped
- 1/3 cup prepared Italian salad dressing
- 2 tablespoons plain yogurt
- 2-1/2 teaspoons Italian salad dressing mix
- 2 teaspoons lemon juice

1 In a small bowl, combine the vegetables and egg. In another bowl, whisk the salad dressing, yogurt, dressing mix and lemon juice. Pour over broccoli mixture and toss to coat. Cover and refrigerate for 4 hours or overnight.

YIELD: 2 SERVINGS.

broccoli rice casserole

PREP: 15 MIN. BAKE: 30 MIN.

- 1-1/2 cups water
- 1/2 cup butter, cubed
- 1 tablespoon dried minced onion
- 2 cups uncooked instant rice
- 1 package (16 ounces) frozen chopped broccoli, thawed
- 1 can (10-3/4 ounces) condensed cream of mushroom soup, undiluted
- 1 jar (8 ounces) process cheese sauce

1 In a large saucepan, bring the water, butter and onion to a boil. Stir in rice. Remove from the heat; cover and let stand for 5 minutes or until the water is absorbed.

When I was little, serving this dish was the only way my mother could get me to eat broccoli. It's an excellent recipe to serve anytime and is especially good with poultry.

Jennifer Fuller, Ballston Spa, New York

2 Stir in the broccoli, soup and cheese sauce. Transfer to a greased 2-qt. baking dish. Bake, uncovered, at 350° for 30-35 minutes or until the casserole is bubbly.

YIELD: 8 SERVINGS.

festive peas and onions

PREP: 35 MIN. BAKE: 40 MIN.

The first time I tried this side, my friend finished half of it while my back was turned! That was many years ago, but the dish is just as popular today.

Caramella Robichaud, Richibucto, New Brunswick

- 1 package (16 ounces) frozen pearl onions
- 2 cups water
- 1 package (10 ounces) frozen peas, thawed
- 1 can (10-3/4 ounces) condensed cream of celery soup, undiluted
- 1 jar (2 ounces) diced pimientos, divided
- 1/3 cup shredded sharp cheddar cheese

1 Prepare onions according to package directions. Drain, reserving 1/4 cup liquid. In a large bowl, combine the onions, peas, soup, 2 tablespoons pimientos and reserved cooking liquid; stir to coat. Transfer to a greased 1-1/2-qt. baking dish.

2 Bake, uncovered, at 350° for 35 minutes. Sprinkle with cheese and remaining pimientos. Bake 5 minutes longer or until the cheese is melted.

YIELD: 4-6 SERVINGS.

I came up with this recipe when I tried re-creating a pasta salad I had at a wedding rehearsal. It's easy to make and I'm always asked to bring it to potlucks and parties.

Danielle Weets, Grandview, Washington

pesto tortellini salad

PREP/TOTAL TIME: 20 MIN.

- 1 package (19 ounces) frozen cheese tortellini
- 3/4 cup shredded Parmesan cheese
- 1 can (2-1/4 ounces) sliced ripe olives, drained
- 5 bacon strips, cooked and crumbled
- 1/4 cup prepared pesto

1 Cook tortellini according to package directions; drain and rinse in cold water. Place in a small bowl. Add remaining ingredients; toss to coat.

YIELD: 5 SERVINGS.

balsamic salad dressing

PREP/TOTAL TIME: 5 MIN.

My tomato juice-based dressing offers a nice combination of tangy and tart with only a trace of fat. We like our salad dressing that way, but you may want to add a little more sugar if that suits you family's tastes better.

Alice Coate, Bryan, Texas

- 3/4 cup tomato juice
- 1/4 cup balsamic vinegar
- 1 envelope Italian salad dressing mix
- 2 teaspoons sugar

1 In a jar with a tight-fitting lid, combine all the ingredients; shake well. Store in the refrigerator.

YIELD: 1 CUP.

This colorful and tasty salad is always well received at picnics and gatherings. Corn bread salads have long been popular in the South but may be new to people in other regions. No matter where you live, I think you'll like this one.

Jennifer Horst
Goose Creek
South Carolina

corn bread confetti salad

PREP: 15 MIN. BAKE: 15 MIN. + COOLING

- 1 package (8-1/2 ounces) corn bread/muffin mix
- 2 cans (15-1/2 ounces each) whole kernel corn, drained
- 2 cans (15 ounces each) pinto beans, rinsed and drained
- 1 can (15 ounces) black beans, rinsed and drained
- 3 small tomatoes, chopped
- 1 medium green pepper, chopped
- 1 medium sweet red pepper, chopped
- 1/2 cup chopped green onions
- 10 bacon strips, cooked and crumbled
- 2 cups (8 ounces) shredded cheddar cheese

DRESSING:
- 1 cup (8 ounces) sour cream
- 1 cup mayonnaise
- 1 envelope ranch salad dressing mix

1 Prepare corn bread according to the package directions. Cool completely; crumble.

2 In a large bowl, combine the corn, beans, tomatoes, peppers, onions, bacon, cheese and crumbled corn bread.

3 In a small bowl, combine the dressing ingredients until well blended. Just before serving, pour dressing over salad and toss.

YIELD: 20-22 SERVINGS.

colorful braised vegetables

PREP/TOTAL TIME: 20 MIN.

1/3 cup chopped onion
1 tablespoon butter
2 cups coleslaw mix
1 medium carrot, shredded
2 tablespoons minced fresh parsley
1/4 teaspoon salt
1/8 teaspoon pepper
1/3 cup water

1 In a saucepan, saute onion in butter until tender. Stir in the coleslaw mix, carrot, parsley, salt and pepper. Add water. Bring to a boil. Reduce heat; cover and simmer for 3 minutes. Uncover; simmer 3 minutes longer or until tender.

YIELD: 2 SERVINGS.

TIP

To keep fresh parsley in the refrigerator for several weeks, wash the entire bunch in warm water, shake off all excess moisture, wrap in a paper towel and seal in a plastic bag. If you need longer storage time, remove the paper towel and place the sealed bag in the freezer. Then simply break off and crumble the amount of parsley you need for soups, stews and other cooked dishes.

cranberry-apple sweet potatoes

PREP/TOTAL TIME: 30 MIN.

A few convenience items hurry along prep of this speedy casserole. A sweet-and-tangy fruit glaze tops canned sweet potatoes and apple pie filling with delicious results. Serve it alongside roasted meats or take it to a potluck.

Nella Parker, Hersey, Michigan

- 1 can (21 ounces) apple pie filling
- 1 can (2 pounds 8 ounces) cut sweet potatoes, drained and sliced
- 3/4 cup whole-berry cranberry sauce
- 2 tablespoons apricot preserves
- 2 tablespoons orange marmalade

1 Spread apple pie filling into a greased 8-in. square baking dish. Top with sweet potato slices. In a small bowl, combine the cranberry sauce, preserves and marmalade; spread over potatoes. Cover and bake at 350° for 20-25 minutes or until heated through.

YIELD: 6-8 SERVINGS.

This refreshing salad is perfect for Fourth of July celebrations—or any time at all. The blend of flavors is wonderful. I use this recipe as often as I can...it's just simply the best!

Bonnie Hawkins, Elkhorn, Wisconsin

creamed spinach

PREP/TOTAL TIME: 30 MIN.

This yummy recipe is a lifesaver during the holidays, when time is short. With only three ingredients, it's also super easy to double.

Sherri Hoover, Perth Road, Ontario

- 2 packages (10 ounces each) frozen chopped spinach, thawed and well drained
- 2 cups (16 ounces) sour cream
- 1 envelope onion soup mix

1 In a large bowl, combine all the ingredients. Spoon into a greased 1-qt. baking dish. Cover and bake at 350° for 25-30 minutes or until heated through.

YIELD: 4 SERVINGS.

red, white and bleu slaw

PREP/TOTAL TIME: 15 MIN.

- 6 cups angel hair coleslaw mix
- 12 cherry tomatoes, halved
- 3/4 cup coleslaw salad dressing
- 3/4 cup crumbled blue cheese, divided
- 1/2 cup real bacon bits

1 In a bowl, combine the coleslaw mix, tomatoes, salad dressing and 1/2 cup blue cheese. Cover and refrigerate until serving. Just before serving, sprinkle with bacon bits and remaining cheese.

YIELD: 6 SERVINGS.

mexican zucchini casserole

PREP: 15 MIN. BAKE: 20 MIN. + STANDING

1 egg
1 tablespoon canola oil
1/8 teaspoon salt
1/8 teaspoon pepper
1 cup shredded zucchini
1 tablespoon chopped seeded jalapeno pepper
1 tablespoon finely chopped onion
1/3 cup biscuit/baking mix
2 tablespoons shredded cheddar cheese

1 In a small bowl, beat the egg, oil, salt and pepper. Add the zucchini, jalapeno and onion; stir to coat. Stir in biscuit mix and cheese.

2 Pour into a 15-oz. baking dish coated with cooking spray. Bake at 375° for 18-20 minutes or until a toothpick comes out clean. Let stand for 10 minutes before serving.

YIELD: 2 SERVINGS.

EDITOR'S NOTE: When cutting hot peppers, disposable gloves are recommended. Avoid touching your face.

soups

Count on this pleasingly seasoned, hearty soup to satisfy the whole family. My husband and kids say brimming bowls of it are flavorful and filling. I also love the fact that I can make a big pot from a handy bean mix.

Laura Prokash
Algoma, Wisconsin

sixteen-bean soup

PREP: 10 MIN. + STANDING COOK: 2-3/4 HOURS

1 package (12 ounces) 16-bean soup mix
1 large onion, chopped
2 garlic cloves, minced
1 teaspoon salt
1 teaspoon chili powder
1/4 teaspoon pepper
1/8 teaspoon hot pepper sauce
1 bay leaf
8 cups water
1 can (14-1/2 ounces) stewed tomatoes
1 tablespoon lemon juice

1 Set aside seasoning packet from beans. Sort beans and rinse with cold water. Place beans in a Dutch oven; add water to cover by 2 in. Bring to a boil; boil for 2 minutes. Remove from the heat; cover and let stand for 1 to 4 hours or until beans are softened. Drain and rinse beans, discarding liquid.

2 Return beans to the pan. Add contents of bean seasoning packet, onion, garlic, salt, chili powder, pepper, pepper sauce, bay leaf and water. Bring to a boil. Reduce heat; cover and simmer for 2-1/2 to 3 hours or until beans are tender.

3 Add tomatoes and lemon juice. Simmer, uncovered, until heated through. Discard bay leaf.

YIELD: **10 SERVINGS (2-1/2 QUARTS).**

vegetable beef soup

PREP: 5 MIN. COOK: 30 MIN.

Your crew will chase away winter's chill with this robust soup. It's so rich...and it's full of nutritious vegetables and chunks of tender steak.

Brigitte Schultz, Barstow, California

1 pound beef top sirloin steak, cut into
    1/2-inch cubes
1/4 teaspoon pepper, divided
2 teaspoons olive oil
2 cans (14-1/2 ounces each) beef broth
2 cups cubed peeled potatoes
1-1/4 cups water
2 medium carrots, sliced
1 tablespoon onion soup mix
1 tablespoon dried basil
1/2 teaspoon dried tarragon
2 tablespoons cornstarch
1/2 cup white wine or additional beef broth

1 Sprinkle steak with 1/8 teaspoon pepper. In a Dutch oven, brown steak in batches in oil over medium heat. Add the broth, potatoes, water, carrots, onion soup mix, basil, tarragon and remaining pepper; bring to a boil. Reduce heat; cover and simmer for 20-25 minutes or until vegetables are tender.

2 In a small bowl, combine the cornstarch and wine until smooth; stir into soup. Bring to a boil; cook and stir for 2 minutes or until thickened.

YIELD: 7 SERVINGS.

farmhouse ham chowder

PREP: 10 MIN. COOK: 30 MIN.

1/2 cup finely chopped onion
1/2 cup finely chopped celery
1/2 cup chopped sweet red pepper
2 tablespoons butter
1/4 cup all-purpose flour
1 envelope ranch salad dressing mix
4-1/4 cups milk

This chowder is delicious and so comforting. Leftover ham and veggies add body, while Gouda cheese brings a special touch.

Lisa Renshaw, Kansas City, Missouri

2 cups frozen cubed hash brown
    potatoes, thawed
2 cups frozen corn, thawed
2 cups cubed fully cooked ham
1 teaspoon minced fresh thyme or
    1/4 teaspoon dried thyme
2 ounces smoked Gouda cheese, shredded

1 In a large saucepan, saute the onion, celery and red pepper in butter until vegetables are crisp-tender. Stir in flour and dressing mix until smooth; gradually stir in milk. Bring to a boil; cook and stir for 2 minutes or until thickened.

2 Add the potatoes, corn, ham and thyme. Bring to a boil. Reduce heat; simmer, uncovered, for 8-10 minutes or until heated through. Sprinkle with cheese before serving.

YIELD: 8 SERVINGS (2 QUARTS).

pizza soup

PREP: 5 MIN. COOK: 40 MIN.

This hearty soup is a hit with my gang and with my canasta group as well. I top each bowl with a slice of toasted bread and cheese, but you can have fun incorporating other pizza toppings.

Jackie Brossard, Kitchener, Ontario

- 2 cans (14-1/2 ounces each) diced tomatoes
- 2 cans (10-3/4 ounces each) condensed tomato soup, undiluted
- 2-1/2 cups water
- 1 package (3-1/2 ounces) sliced pepperoni, quartered
- 1 medium sweet red pepper, chopped
- 1 medium green pepper, chopped
- 1 cup sliced fresh mushrooms
- 2 garlic cloves, minced
- 1/2 teaspoon rubbed sage
- 1/2 teaspoon dried basil
- 1/2 teaspoon dried oregano
- Salt and pepper to taste
- 10 slices French bread, toasted
- 1-1/2 cups (6 ounces) shredded part-skim mozzarella cheese

1 In a Dutch oven, bring the tomatoes, soup and water to a boil. Reduce heat; cover and simmer for 15 minutes.

2 Mash with a potato masher. Add the pepperoni, red and green peppers, mushrooms, garlic, sage, basil, oregano, salt and pepper. Cover and simmer for 10 minutes or until vegetables are tender.

3 Ladle into ovenproof bowls. Top each with a slice of bread and sprinkle with cheese. Broil 4 in. from the heat until cheese is melted and bubbly.

YIELD: 10 SERVINGS (ABOUT 2-1/2 QUARTS).

Nothing beats a warm bowl of soup! This recipe is simple to make and leaves you feeling satisfied. Plus, it makes enough so you can enjoy leftovers later in the week.

Janelle Moore, Federal Way, Washington

zucchini sausage soup

PREP/TOTAL TIME: 30 MIN.

- 1 pound bulk Italian sausage
- 2/3 cup chopped onion
- 5 cups water
- 2 medium zucchini, sliced
- 1 can (14-1/2 ounces) diced tomatoes, undrained
- 1 jar (14 ounces) pizza sauce
- 3/4 cup uncooked orzo pasta
- 1 envelope au jus gravy mix
- 1 tablespoon dried basil
- 2 teaspoons dried oregano

1 In a Dutch oven, cook sausage and onion over medium heat until meat is no longer pink; drain. Stir in all the remaining ingredients. Bring to a boil. Reduce heat; cover and simmer for 10-15 minutes or until pasta is tender.

YIELD: 11 SERVINGS (2-3/4 QUARTS).

halibut chowder

PREP/TOTAL TIME: 20 MIN.

This rich, creamy chowder is so good you won't believe it starts with canned soup and frozen vegetables. It showcases tender chunks of halibut, but salmon or most any type of whitefish will do. I double this for large gatherings, and guests make sure they get every last drop.

Mary Davis, Palmer, Alaska

8 to 10 green onions, thinly sliced
2 tablespoons butter
2 garlic cloves, minced
4 cans (10-3/4 ounces each) condensed cream of potato soup, undiluted
2 cans (10-3/4 ounces each) condensed cream of mushroom soup, undiluted
4 cups 2% milk
2 packages (8 ounces each) cream cheese, cubed
1-1/2 pounds halibut or salmon fillets, cubed
1-1/2 cups frozen sliced carrots
1-1/2 cups frozen corn
1/8 to 1/4 teaspoon cayenne pepper, optional

1 In a Dutch oven, saute onions in butter until tender. Add garlic; cook 1 minute longer. Add the soups, milk and cream cheese; cook and stir until cheese is melted.

2 Bring to a boil. Stir in the fish, carrots and corn. Reduce heat; simmer, uncovered, for 5-10 minutes or until fish flakes easily with a fork and vegetables are tender. Add cayenne pepper if desired.

YIELD: 16 SERVINGS (ABOUT 4 QUARTS).

My husband is diabetic, and I'm watching my weight. This soup fits our diets perfectly. Friends and family will never guess it takes just a mere 15 minutes to make.

Carol Colvin, Derby, New York

broccoli cheese soup

PREP/TOTAL TIME: 15 MIN.

1 can (10-3/4 ounces) reduced-fat reduced-sodium condensed cream of celery soup, undiluted
1 can (10-3/4 ounces) reduced-fat reduced-sodium condensed cream of chicken soup, undiluted
3 cups fat-free milk
1 tablespoon dried minced onion
1 teaspoon dried parsley flakes
1/2 teaspoon garlic powder
1/4 teaspoon pepper
3 cups frozen chopped broccoli, thawed
1 can (14-1/2 ounces) sliced potatoes, drained
1/2 cup shredded reduced-fat cheddar cheese

1 In a large saucepan, combine the soups, milk, onion, parsley, garlic powder and pepper. Stir in broccoli and potatoes; heat through. Just before serving, sprinkle with cheese.

YIELD: 8 SERVINGS (ABOUT 2 QUARTS).

1 package (8 ounces) imitation crabmeat, chopped or 2 cans (6 ounces each) crabmeat, drained, flaked and cartilage removed

1 can (6-1/2 ounces) minced clams, undrained

1 In a Dutch oven, saute onion and green pepper in oil until onion is tender. Add garlic; stir 1 minute longer. Stir in the tomatoes, spaghetti sauce, salsa, broth, wine and seasonings. Bring to a boil. Reduce heat; cover and simmer for 20 minutes.

2 Add the shrimp, crab and clams. Cover and simmer for 5-7 minutes or until shrimp turn pink.

YIELD: 8 SERVINGS (2 QUARTS).

kielbasa with veggies

PREP/TOTAL TIME: 30 MIN.

This comforting combination takes advantage of time-saving frozen vegetables and fully cooked sausage. A little soup mix lends a mild onion flavor.

Taste of Home Test Kitchen

1 pound smoked kielbasa or Polish sausage, cut into 1/4-inch slices

1 tablespoon canola oil

1 package (16 ounces) frozen vegetables for beef stew

1 cup beef broth

1 tablespoon onion soup mix

1 tablespoon cornstarch

1 tablespoon cold water

1 In a large skillet, brown sausage in oil over medium-high heat. Remove with a slotted spoon and keep warm. Add the vegetables, broth and soup mix to skillet. Bring to a boil. Reduce heat; cover and simmer for 10-12 minutes or until vegetables are tender.

2 Return sausage to the pan. Combine cornstarch and water until smooth; stir into sausage mixture. Bring to a boil; cook and stir for 1 minute or until soup is thickened.

YIELD: 4 SERVINGS.

We love this filling soup on Sundays during football season. For a little extra zip to rally spirits, we sometimes add red pepper flakes or use jalapeno-flavored tomatoes. It's also delicious with real crabmeat.

Mary Adams, Fairport, New York

tomato seafood soup

PREP: 10 MIN. COOK: 35 MIN.

1/2 cup chopped onion

1/2 cup chopped green pepper

1 tablespoon olive oil

1/2 teaspoon minced garlic

1 can (14 ounces) diced tomatoes, undrained

1 jar (14 ounces) spaghetti sauce

1 cup salsa

3/4 cup chicken broth

1/2 cup white wine or additional chicken broth

3 teaspoons dried parsley flakes

1/4 teaspoon dried oregano

1/4 teaspoon dried basil

1/8 to 1/4 teaspoon pepper

1 package (12 ounces) frozen uncooked shrimp, thawed, peeled and deveined

chili with barley

PREP/TOTAL TIME: 30 MIN.

- 1 pound ground beef
- 1 medium onion, chopped
- 2 garlic cloves, minced
- 4 cups water
- 1 cup quick-cooking barley
- 1 can (16 ounces) chili beans, undrained
- 1 can (14-1/2 ounces) diced tomatoes, undrained
- 1 can (6 ounces) tomato paste
- 1 envelope chili seasoning

1 In a large saucepan, cook beef and onion over medium heat until meat is no longer pink. Add garlic; cook 1 minute longer. Drain.

2 Add water; bring to a boil. Stir in barley. Reduce heat; cover and simmer for 10 minutes or until barley is tender. Stir in the beans, tomatoes, tomato paste and chili seasoning; heat through.

YIELD: 6-8 SERVINGS (ABOUT 2 QUARTS).

TIP

Here are some fun toppings to sprinkle over chili: shredded cheese, such as cheddar, taco or pepper Jack; sour cream; chopped avocado; sliced jalapeno peppers; hot pepper sauce; chopped onions or green onions; or crushed tortilla chips.

This chowder is comfort food at its finest and perfect for a cold winter day.

Taste of Home Test Kitchen

chicken wild rice chowder

PREP/TOTAL TIME: 25 MIN.

2 cups sliced fresh carrots

1/2 cup chopped onion

1/2 cup chopped celery

2 tablespoons butter

3 tablespoons all-purpose flour

2 cans (14-1/2 ounces each) chicken broth

2-2/3 cups cubed cooked chicken breast

1 package (8.8 ounces) ready-to-serve long grain and wild rice

1/4 cup half-and-half cream

1/8 teaspoon pepper

1 In a large saucepan, saute the carrots, onion and celery in butter until tender. Stir in flour until blended; gradually add broth. Bring to a boil; cook and stir for 2 minutes or until thickened. Stir in the chicken, rice, cream and pepper; heat through (do not boil).

YIELD: 4 SERVINGS.

TIP

If you don't have cooked chicken that is readily available for Chicken Wild Rice Chowder, consider purchasing a package of convenient ready-to-serve chicken breast strips. They are preseasoned and completely cooked. All you would need to do is cut the strips into cubes.

cauliflower tomato soup

PREP/TOTAL TIME: 30 MIN.

We usually have tomato soup at least once a week, so I've tried to find ways to dress it up. This is one of my favorites.

Katherine Stallwood, Kennewick, Washington

- 1/4 cup sliced leek (white portion only)
- 1/4 cup chopped celery
- 1 tablespoon butter
- 1 can (10-3/4 ounces) condensed tomato soup, undiluted
- 1-1/4 cups water
- 1 cup fresh cauliflowerets
- 1/2 cup frozen peas
- 1/4 to 1/2 teaspoon dill weed
- 1/4 teaspoon salt

1 In a large saucepan, saute leek and celery in butter until tender. Stir in the remaining ingredients. Bring to a boil; reduce heat. Cover and simmer for 12-16 minutes or until the vegetables are tender.

YIELD: 3 SERVINGS.

We live on the Gulf Coast, where fresh seafood is plentiful. I adapted several recipes to come up with this rich bisque. It's fabulous as a first course or an entree. You can make it with shrimp or crabmeat alone if you'd like.

Pat Edwards, Dauphin Island, Alabama

seafood bisque

PREP/TOTAL TIME: 30 MIN.

- 2 cans (10-3/4 ounces each) condensed cream of mushroom soup, undiluted
- 1 can (10-3/4 ounces) condensed cream of celery soup, undiluted
- 2-2/3 cups 2% milk
- 4 green onions, chopped
- 1/2 cup finely chopped celery
- 1 garlic clove, minced
- 1 teaspoon Worcestershire sauce
- 1/4 teaspoon hot pepper sauce
- 1-1/2 pounds uncooked medium shrimp, peeled and deveined
- 1 can (6 ounces) crabmeat, drained, flaked and cartilage removed
- 1 jar (4-1/2 ounces) whole mushrooms, drained
- 3 tablespoons Madeira wine or chicken broth
- 1/2 teaspoon salt
- 1/2 teaspoon pepper
- Minced fresh parsley

1 In a Dutch oven, combine the soups, milk, green onions, celery, garlic, Worcestershire sauce and pepper sauce. Bring to a boil. Reduce heat; add the shrimp, crab and mushrooms. Simmer, uncovered, for 10 minutes.

2 Stir in the wine, salt and pepper; cook 2-3 minutes longer. Garnish with parsley.

YIELD: 10 SERVINGS (2-1/2 QUARTS).

veggie meatball soup

PREP: 20 MIN. COOK: 6 HOURS

- 1 package (12 ounces) frozen fully cooked Italian meatballs
- 1 can (28 ounces) diced tomatoes, undrained
- 3 cups beef broth
- 2 cups shredded cabbage
- 1 can (16 ounces) kidney beans, rinsed and drained
- 1 medium zucchini, sliced
- 1 cup fresh green beans, cut into 1-inch pieces
- 1 cup water
- 2 medium carrots, sliced
- 1 teaspoon dried basil
- 1/2 teaspoon minced garlic
- 1/4 teaspoon salt
- 1/8 teaspoon dried oregano
- 1/8 teaspoon pepper
- 1 cup uncooked elbow macaroni
- 1/4 cup minced fresh parsley
- Grated Parmesan cheese, optional

1 In a 5-qt. slow cooker, combine the meatballs, tomatoes, broth, cabbage, beans, zucchini, green beans, water, carrots, basil, garlic, salt, oregano and pepper. Cover and cook on low for 5-1/2 to 6 hours or until vegetables are almost tender.

2 Stir in the macaroni and parsley; cook 30 minutes longer or until macaroni is tender. Serve with cheese if desired.

YIELD: 6 SERVINGS (2-1/2 QUARTS).

almost
homemade

pantry chili

PREP: 10 MIN. COOK: 25 MIN.

I love a steaming hot bowl of this flavorful chili. It's conveniently made with items I keep in my pantry.

Dorothy Russell, Portage, Wisconsin

- 1 pound ground beef
- 1 small onion, chopped
- 1 can (16 ounces) chili beans, undrained
- 1 can (14-3/4 ounces) cream-style corn
- 1 can (14-1/2 ounces) whole peeled tomatoes, undrained and cut up
- 1 jar (14 ounces) spaghetti sauce
- 1 envelope taco seasoning
- 1/4 teaspoon pepper

1 In a large saucepan, cook beef and onion over medium heat until meat is no longer pink; drain. Stir in the chili beans, corn, tomatoes, spaghetti sauce, taco seasoning and pepper. Bring to a boil. Reduce heat; simmer, uncovered, for 10 minutes.

YIELD: 6-8 SERVINGS.

This delicious one-dish meal has a stew-like consistency and a peppy Tex-Mex flavor.

Agnes Hamilton, Scott Depot, West Virginia

zippy three-bean chili

PREP: 10 MIN. COOK: 1 HOUR 20 MIN.

- 1 pound lean ground beef (90% lean)
- 1/2 cup chopped onion
- 1 cup chopped fresh mushrooms
- 1/2 cup chopped green pepper
- 1/2 cup chopped sweet red pepper
- 1 garlic clove, minced
- 2 cups water
- 1 can (14-1/2 ounces) diced tomatoes and green chilies, undrained
- 1 envelope reduced-sodium taco seasoning
- 1 can (15-1/2 ounces) great northern beans, rinsed and drained
- 1 can (15 ounces) black beans, rinsed and drained
- 1 can (15 ounces) pinto beans, rinsed and drained
- 8 tablespoons shredded reduced-fat cheddar cheese, divided

1 In a large saucepan, cook beef and onion over medium heat until meat is no longer pink; drain. Add mushrooms and peppers; cook and stir 3 minutes longer or until vegetables are almost tender. Add garlic; cook 1 minute longer. Stir in the water, tomatoes and taco seasoning.

2 Bring to boil. Reduce heat; simmer, uncovered, for 30 minutes. Add beans; simmer 30 minutes longer. Sprinkle each serving with 1 tablespoon cheese.

YIELD: 8 SERVINGS (2 QUARTS).

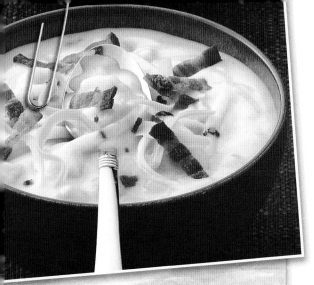

pumpkin corn soup

PREP: 20 MIN. COOK: 25 MIN.

My family loves this soup. With all the spices and color, it is perfect on a drab winter day. It's definitely not your normal pumpkin soup. I frequently garnish this with fresh cilantro.

Melissa Every, Austin, Texas

1 large onion, chopped
1 medium sweet red pepper, chopped
2 tablespoons butter
2 cups fresh or frozen corn, thawed
1 jalapeno pepper, seeded and chopped
2 garlic cloves, minced
2 teaspoons chili powder
2 cans (14-1/2 ounces each) vegetable broth
1 can (15 ounces) solid-pack pumpkin
1/2 teaspoon salt
Dash cayenne pepper
2 tablespoons lime juice

1 In a large saucepan, saute onion and red pepper in butter until almost tender. Add the corn, jalapeno, garlic and chili powder; saute 2 minutes longer.

2 Stir in the broth, pumpkin, salt and cayenne until blended. Bring to a boil. Reduce heat; cover and simmer for 10 minutes. Stir in lime juice.

YIELD: 7 SERVINGS.

EDITOR'S NOTE: When cutting hot peppers, disposable gloves are recommended. Avoid touching your face.

Tasty toppings jazz up this no-fuss soup with Mexican flair. The recipe was given to me by a friend. I make it often for company, and everyone asks for the directions. You can substitute pinto beans in red chili sauce for the regular pinto beans and cumin called for in the recipe.

Michelle Larson, Greentown, Indiana

tortilla soup

PREP/TOTAL TIME: 10 MIN.

1 can (10-1/2 ounces) condensed chicken with rice soup, undiluted
1-1/3 cups water
1 cup salsa
1 cup canned pinto beans, rinsed and drained
1 cup canned black beans, rinsed and drained
1 cup frozen corn
1 cup frozen diced cooked chicken
1 teaspoon ground cumin
Crushed tortilla chips, shredded cheddar cheese and sour cream

1 In a large saucepan, combine the soup, water, salsa, beans, corn, chicken and cumin. Cook over medium-high heat for 5-7 minutes or until heated through. Serve with the tortilla chips, cheese and sour cream.

YIELD: 5 SERVINGS.

Here's a surefire chill chaser. Even those who don't like tomato soup love this treat. It's awesome with the seasoned homemade oyster crackers.

Linda Parkhurst
Brooklyn, Michigan

cream of tomato soup

PREP/TOTAL TIME: 30 MIN.

1 can (14-1/2 ounces) stewed tomatoes
4 ounces cream cheese, cubed
1 medium onion, chopped
2 garlic cloves, minced
1/4 cup butter
3 cans (10-3/4 ounces each) condensed tomato soup, undiluted
2 cans (11-1/2 ounces each) V8 juice
1 cup half-and-half cream
1/2 teaspoon dried basil
SEASONED OYSTER CRACKERS:
3 cups oyster crackers
1/3 cup canola oil
1 tablespoon ranch salad dressing mix
1/2 teaspoon garlic powder
1/2 teaspoon dill weed
9 tablespoons shredded part-skim mozzarella cheese

1 In a food processor, combine the stewed tomatoes and cream cheese; cover and process until smooth. Set aside.

2 In a large saucepan, saute onion and garlic in butter. Whisk in tomato soup and V8 until blended. Gradually stir in the cream cheese mixture, cream and basil. Cook and stir until heated through (do not boil).

3 In a large bowl, combine the crackers, oil, dressing mix, garlic powder and dill; toss to coat. Ladle the soup into bowls; sprinkle with the crackers and mozzarella cheese.

YIELD: 9 SERVINGS (3 CUPS CRACKERS).

tortellini soup

PREP/TOTAL TIME: 30 MIN.

This soup is delicious, pretty and unbelievably fast to make. For a creamy variation, I sometimes substitute cream of mushroom soup for the French onion soup. If there are any leftovers, they taste even better the next day.

Marsha Farley, Bangor, Maine

- 1 pound ground beef
- 3-1/2 cups water
- 1 can (28 ounces) diced tomatoes, undrained
- 1 can (10-1/2 ounces) condensed French onion soup, undiluted
- 1 package (9 ounces) frozen cut green beans
- 1 package (9 ounces) refrigerated cheese tortellini
- 1 medium zucchini, chopped
- 1 teaspoon dried basil

1 In a large saucepan, cook beef over medium heat until no longer pink; drain. Add all the remaining ingredients; bring to a boil. Cook, uncovered, for 7-9 minutes or until tortellini is tender.

YIELD: 6-8 SERVINGS (ABOUT 2 QUARTS).

EDITOR'S NOTE: Alongside Tortellini Soup, serve refrigerated crescent rolls. Before baking, sprinkle dough with Parmesan cheese.

The ladies of a church I attended years ago served this hearty crowd-pleaser on many occasions. It's a very satisfying soup! It also makes a family-pleasing main dish for a weeknight meal.

Sara Nelson, Freeport, Michigan

chick-n-rice soup

PREP/TOTAL TIME: 30 MIN.

- 8 cups water
- 1-1/2 cups sliced celery
- 1 cup thinly sliced fresh carrots
- 4 cups cubed cooked chicken
- 1 package (6.9 ounces) chicken-flavored rice and vermicelli mix
- 4 teaspoons chicken bouillon granules

1 In a large saucepan, bring water, celery and carrots to a boil. Stir in the chicken, rice mix and bouillon. Return to a boil. Reduce heat; cover and simmer for 15-20 minutes or until rice is tender.

YIELD: 10 SERVINGS (ABOUT 2-1/2 QUARTS).

nacho chili

PREP: 15 MIN. BAKE: 1 HOUR

My husband and I work together and arrive home at the same time. So I appreciate quick and easy dishes like this. The nacho cheese topping is a great addition.

Sally Roos, Osakis, Minnesota

2 cans (14-1/2 ounces each) stewed tomatoes

2 cups chopped celery

1 jar (16 ounces) salsa

1 can (16 ounces) kidney beans, rinsed and drained

1 can (16 ounces) refried beans

1 medium onion, chopped

1 cup water

1 envelope taco seasoning

1/2 teaspoon pepper

1 can (11 ounces) condensed nacho cheese soup, undiluted

2 pounds extra-lean ground beef (95% lean)

1 In a large bowl, combine the tomatoes, celery, salsa, beans, refried beans, onion, water, taco seasoning, pepper and soup; crumble beef over mixture and mix well. Transfer to a greased ovenproof Dutch oven.

2 Cover and bake at 350° for 1 hour or until the meat is no longer pink, stirring once. Let stand for 5 minutes.

YIELD: 14 SERVINGS (3-1/2 QUARTS).

EDITOR'S NOTE: Serve warmed tortillas or corn chips with Nacho Chili. Or use some of the chili as a topping for baked potatoes or cooked pasta.

cream of crab soup

PREP: 20 MIN. COOK: 20 MIN.

1 large onion, finely chopped

1 medium green pepper, finely chopped

2 tablespoons butter

2 garlic cloves, minced

3 pints half-and-half cream

2 cups frozen shredded hash brown potatoes, thawed

A friend brought this soup to a potluck and I had to have the recipe. I love how delicious it is.

Marilyn Shaw, Middletown, Delaware

1 can (10-3/4 ounces) condensed cream of mushroom soup, undiluted

1 can (10-3/4 ounces) condensed cream of asparagus soup, undiluted

2 cans (6 ounces each) lump crabmeat, drained

1 package (8 ounces) imitation crabmeat, chopped

1-1/2 cups frozen corn, thawed

1 tablespoon dried parsley flakes

1-1/2 teaspoons dill weed

1-1/2 teaspoons seafood seasoning

1 teaspoon pepper

1 In a Dutch oven, saute onion and green pepper in butter until tender. Add garlic; saute 1 minute longer. Stir in all the remaining ingredients. Cook and stir over medium-low heat until heated through (do not boil).

YIELD: 14 SERVINGS (3-1/2 QUARTS).

1 tablespoon butter

1-1/2 cups reduced-sodium chicken broth

3/4 cup Alfredo sauce

3 tablespoons prepared pesto

2 tablespoons pine nuts, toasted

1 tablespoon shredded Parmesan cheese

1 Cook pasta according to package directions. Meanwhile, in a large saucepan, saute the chicken, spinach, red peppers, rosemary, garlic powder and pepper in butter until spinach is wilted. Stir in the broth, Alfredo sauce and pesto; cook for 4-5 minutes or until heated through. Drain the pasta and add to the soup. Sprinkle with the pine nuts and cheese.

YIELD: 5 CUPS.

My husband loves Alfredo sauce, so I'm always looking for new variations. This easy-to-make soup is wonderful with crusty Italian bread and a tomato-mozzarella-basil salad. Best of all, it's the perfect amount for two of us.

Cindie Henf, Sebastian, Florida

florentine chicken soup

PREP/TOTAL TIME: 30 MIN.

1 cup uncooked penne pasta

1 package (6 ounces) ready-to-use chicken breast cuts

4 cups chopped fresh spinach

1 jar (7 ounces) roasted sweet red peppers, drained and sliced

3 fresh rosemary sprigs, chopped

1/2 teaspoon garlic powder

1/4 teaspoon pepper

ramen corn chowder

PREP/TOTAL TIME: 15 MIN.

This chowder tastes as good as if it simmered for hours, but it's ready in 15 minutes. I thought the original recipe was lacking in flavor, so I jazzed it up with extra corn and crumbled bacon.

Darlene Brenden, Salem, Oregon

2 cups water

1 package (3 ounces) chicken ramen noodles

1 can (15-1/4 ounces) whole kernel corn, drained

1 can (14-3/4 ounces) cream-style corn

1 cup 2% milk

1 teaspoon dried minced onion

1/4 teaspoon curry powder

3/4 cup shredded cheddar cheese

1 tablespoon crumbled cooked bacon

1 tablespoon minced fresh parsley

1 In a small saucepan, bring water to a boil. Break noodles into large pieces. Add noodles and contents of seasoning packet to water. Reduce heat to medium. Cook, uncovered, for 2-3 minutes or until noodles are tender.

2 Stir in the corn, cream-style corn, milk, onion and curry; heat through. Stir in the cheese, bacon and parsley until blended.

YIELD: 4 SERVINGS.

almost homemade

four-bean taco chili

PREP: 15 MIN. COOK: 30 MIN.

Heat up the dinner table on a cold night with this zesty chili. It's chock-full of ground beef, beans, green chilies and taco seasoning.

Amy Martell, Canton, Pennsylvania

2 pounds ground beef

3 cups tomato juice

1 jar (16 ounces) salsa

1 can (16 ounces) kidney beans, rinsed and drained

1 can (16 ounces) butter beans, rinsed and drained

1 can (15-1/2 ounces) great northern beans, rinsed and drained

1 can (15 ounces) black beans, rinsed and drained

1 can (8 ounces) tomato sauce

1 can (6 ounces) tomato paste

1 can (4 ounces) chopped green chilies

1 envelope taco seasoning

1 In a Dutch oven, cook beef over medium heat until no longer pink; drain. Stir in all the remaining ingredients. Bring to a boil. Reduce heat; simmer, uncovered, for 15 minutes, stirring occasionally.

YIELD: 12 CUPS.

Since I make this rich and creamy creation in my slow cooker, the recipe is almost effortless. Because the chowder is ready in less than 4 hours, it can be prepared in the afternoon and served to dinner guests that night.

Will Zunio, Gretna, Louisiana

shrimp chowder

PREP: 15 MIN. BAKE: 3-1/2 HOURS

1/2 cup chopped onion

2 teaspoons butter

2 cans (12 ounces each) evaporated milk

2 cans (10-3/4 ounces each) condensed cream of potato soup, undiluted

2 cans (10-3/4 ounces each) condensed cream of chicken soup, undiluted

1 can (11 ounces) white or shoepeg corn, drained

1 teaspoon Creole seasoning

1/2 teaspoon garlic powder

2 pounds cooked small shrimp, peeled and deveined

1 package (3 ounces) cream cheese, cubed

1 In a small skillet, saute onion in butter until tender. In a 5-qt. slow cooker, combine the onion mixture, milk, soups, corn, Creole seasoning and garlic powder. Cover and cook on low for 3 hours.

2 Stir in shrimp and cream cheese. Cook 30 minutes longer or until shrimp are heated through and cheese is melted. Stir to blend.

YIELD: 12 SERVINGS (3 QUARTS).

EDITOR'S NOTE: The following spices may be substituted for 1 teaspoon Creole seasoning: 1/4 teaspoon each salt, garlic powder and paprika; and a pinch each of dried thyme, ground cumin and cayenne pepper.

1 Prepare soup mix according to package directions, adding zucchini and mushrooms. Meanwhile, in a large skillet, cook chicken in oil for 10-12 minutes or until juices run clear. Stir into soup.

2 For croutons, in a large bowl, combine butter and parsley. Add bread cubes and toss to coat. Arrange in a single layer on an ungreased baking sheet. Sprinkle with cheese.

3 Bake at 400° for 7-8 minutes or until golden brown, stirring occasionally. Serve with soup.

YIELD: 5 SERVINGS.

creamy potato soup

PREP/TOTAL TIME: 25 MIN.

A friend brought me this soup when I was sick. It tastes like it simmered for hours, but basic ingredients make it a snap to prepare any night of the week.

Pat Maruca, Philippi, West Virginia

1 package (30 ounces) frozen shredded hash brown potatoes
6 cups water
1/3 cup chopped onion
2 cans (10-3/4 ounces each) condensed cream of celery soup, undiluted
4 ounces process cheese (Velveeta), cubed
1 cup (8 ounces) sour cream
1/2 teaspoon salt
1/4 teaspoon pepper

1 In a large saucepan, combine the potatoes, water and onion. Bring to a boil. Reduce heat; stir in soup and cheese. Cook and stir until cheese is melted.

2 Stir in the sour cream, salt and pepper. Cook and stir until heated through (do not boil).

YIELD: 13 SERVINGS (ABOUT 3 QUARTS).

A packaged minestrone soup mix is dressed up with cubed chicken, fresh zucchini, portobello mushrooms and crunchy croutons for this satisfying main course. It's easy to make, yet seems like you fussed.

Taste of Home Test Kitchen

chicken minestrone

PREP/TOTAL TIME: 30 MIN.

1 package (9.3 ounces) minestrone soup mix
1 medium zucchini, quartered lengthwise and sliced
1 cup chopped baby portobello mushrooms
1 pound boneless skinless chicken breasts, cubed
1 tablespoon olive oil
1/4 cup butter, melted
1 teaspoon dried parsley flakes
6 slices day-old French bread (1 inch thick), cubed
2 tablespoons grated Parmesan cheese

A package of store-bought ramen noodles speeds up assembly of this colorful broth with shrimp and carrots. My mother passed the recipe on to me. It's delicious and so quick to fix.

Donna Hellinger
Lorain, Ohio

asian shrimp soup

PREP/TOTAL TIME: 15 MIN.

3-1/2 cups water
1 package (3 ounces) Oriental ramen noodles
1 cup frozen cooked small shrimp
1/2 cup chopped green onions
1 medium carrot, julienned
2 tablespoons soy sauce

1 In a large saucepan, bring water to a boil. Set aside seasoning packet from noodles. Add the noodles to boiling water; cook and stir for 3 minutes.

2 Add the shrimp, onions, carrot, soy sauce and contents of seasoning packet. Cook 3-4 minutes longer or until heated through.

YIELD: 4 SERVINGS.

TIP

To save a few minutes when you make Asian Shrimp Soup, buy a package of ready-to-use shredded carrots. You'll need 1/2 to 3/4 cup for the soup. Use the leftover carrots in a salad or stir-fry.

I entered the recipe for this satisfying soup in a contest sponsored by my hometown newspaper. I won first place and contributed the prize money to the area shelter for women and children.

Beth Jenkins-Horsley
Belmont, North Carolina

fiesta chicken chowder

PREP: 30 MIN. COOK: 15 MIN.

3 tablespoons all-purpose flour

1 envelope fajita seasoning, divided

1 pound boneless skinless chicken breasts, cut into 1-inch cubes

3 tablespoons canola oil

1 medium onion, chopped

2 garlic cloves, minced

3 cups water

1 can (15 ounces) black beans, rinsed and drained

1 can (14-1/2 ounces) Mexican stewed tomatoes, undrained

1 can (11 ounces) Mexicorn, drained

1 cup uncooked instant brown rice

1 can (4 ounces) chopped green chilies

1 can (11 ounces) condensed nacho cheese soup, undiluted

3 tablespoons minced fresh cilantro

1 tablespoon lime juice

1 In a large resealable plastic bag, combine flour and 2 tablespoons fajita seasoning; add chicken. Seal bag and shake to coat. In a large saucepan, saute chicken in oil until no longer pink. Remove and keep warm.

2 In the same pan, saute onion until onion is tender; add garlic and cook 1 minute longer. Stir in the water, beans, tomatoes, corn, rice, chilies and remaining fajita seasoning. Bring to a boil. Reduce heat; cover and simmer for 5 minutes or until rice is tender.

3 Stir in the soup, cilantro, lime juice and chicken; heat through.

YIELD: 10 SERVINGS (2-1/2 QUARTS).

chili macaroni soup

PREP/TOTAL TIME: 30 MIN.

Turn a boxed macaroni dinner into a thick, zesty soup with this recipe. Each helping is chock-full of ground beef, tomatoes, corn and more.

Flo Burtnett, Gage, Oklahoma

1 pound ground beef
1 medium onion, chopped
1/4 cup chopped green pepper
5 cups water
1 can (14-1/2 ounces) diced tomatoes, undrained
1 package (7-1/2 ounces) chili macaroni dinner mix
1 teaspoon chili powder
1/2 teaspoon garlic salt
1/4 teaspoon salt
1 can (8-3/4 ounces) whole kernel corn, drained
2 tablespoons sliced ripe olives

1 In a large saucepan, cook the beef, onion and green pepper over medium heat until meat is no longer pink; drain. Add the water, tomatoes, contents of sauce mix from the dinner mix, chili powder, garlic salt and salt. Simmer, uncovered, for 10 minutes.

2 Add macaroni from the dinner mix, corn and olives. Cover and simmer for 10 minutes or until macaroni is tender, stirring occasionally.

YIELD: 9 SERVINGS (ABOUT 2 QUARTS).

Busy cooks don't have time to simmer chili for hours on the stovetop. So we developed a speedy version using store-bought barbecued pork as well as canned tomatoes, beans and broth. Every spoonful is hearty and delicious.

Taste of Home Test Kitchen

cowboy chili

PREP/TOTAL TIME: 20 MIN.

1-1/2 cups refrigerated fully cooked barbecued shredded pork
1 can (14-1/2 ounces) diced tomatoes, undrained
1 cup canned black beans, rinsed and drained
3/4 cup beef broth
3/4 cup chopped green pepper
1/2 teaspoon minced garlic

1 In a large saucepan, combine all the ingredients. Bring to a boil. Reduce heat; simmer, uncovered, for 10-15 minutes or until heated through.

YIELD: 4 SERVINGS.

vegetable cheese soup

PREP: 15 MIN. COOK: 25 MIN.

1 medium potato, peeled and diced

1/4 cup each chopped onion, celery and carrot

1 teaspoon chicken bouillon granules

2-1/2 cups water

1-1/3 cups frozen mixed vegetables

1 can (10-3/4 ounces) condensed cream
of chicken soup, undiluted

1/2 pound process cheese (Velveeta), cubed

1 In a large saucepan, combine the potato, onion,
celery, carrot, bouillon and water. Bring to a boil.
Reduce heat; cover and simmer for 10-15 minutes
or until potatoes are almost tender.

2 Stir in mixed vegetables and chicken soup.
Bring to a boil. Reduce heat; cover and simmer
for 5-10 minutes or until vegetables are tender.
Stir in cheese just until melted (do not boil).

YIELD: 5 CUPS.

TIP

If you don't have chicken bouillon granules, you may
substitute a chicken bouillon cube. One bouillon
cube is the equivalent of 1 teaspoon of granules.

cream of spinach soup

PREP/TOTAL TIME: 15 MIN.

This rich and velvety soup tastes like it's made by a professional chef. You can also use drained canned spinach in the recipe, too.

Patricia Bradley, Rohnert Park, California

1 package (1.8 ounces) leek soup and dip mix
1 package (10 ounces) frozen chopped spinach, thawed and squeezed dry
1 cup (8 ounces) sour cream
1/4 teaspoon ground nutmeg
Lemon slices

1 Prepare soup mix according to package directions. Stir in spinach. Cover and simmer for 2 minutes. Remove from the heat; stir in sour cream and nutmeg. Garnish with lemon slices.

YIELD: 4 SERVINGS.

hominy taco chili

PREP: 15 MIN. COOK: 30 MIN.

1 pound ground beef
1 large onion, chopped
2 cans (15-1/2 ounces each) hominy, drained
2 cans (14-1/2 ounces each) stewed tomatoes, undrained
1 can (15-1/4 ounces) whole kernel corn, drained
1 can (15 ounces) pinto beans, rinsed and drained
1 can (15 ounces) black beans, rinsed and drained
1 cup water
1 envelope taco seasoning
1 envelope ranch salad dressing mix
2 teaspoons ground cumin
1/2 teaspoon garlic salt
1/2 teaspoon pepper
Corn chips, optional

1 In a Dutch oven, cook beef and onion over medium heat until meat is no longer pink; drain.

This savory chili is simple to prepare with canned items and receives rave reviews. The recipe makes enough for dinner with leftovers to freeze.

Barbara Wheless, Sheldon, South Carolina

Stir in the hominy, tomatoes, corn, beans, water, seasoning, salad dressing mix, cumin, garlic salt and pepper. Bring to a boil. Reduce heat; cover and simmer for 30 minutes.

2 Serve half of the chili with corn chips if desired. Freeze remaining chili in a freezer container for up to 3 months.

3 To use frozen chili: Thaw in the refrigerator. Transfer to a large saucepan; heat through, adding water if desired.

YIELD: 2 BATCHES (5 SERVINGS EACH).

stuffed pepper soup

PREP/TOTAL TIME: 30 MIN.

- 1 package (8.8 ounces) ready-to-serve long grain and wild rice
- 1 pound ground beef
- 2 cups frozen chopped green peppers, thawed
- 1 cup chopped onion
- 1 jar (26 ounces) chunky tomato pasta sauce
- 1 can (14-1/2 ounces) Italian diced tomatoes, undrained
- 1 can (14 ounces) beef broth

1 Prepare rice according to package directions. Meanwhile, in a large saucepan, cook the beef, green peppers and onion until meat is no longer pink; drain. Stir in the pasta sauce, tomatoes, broth and prepared rice; heat through.

YIELD: 6-8 SERVINGS (ABOUT 2 QUARTS).

TIP

To lighten up Stuffed Pepper Soup, use lean ground chicken or turkey breast in place of the ground beef. Replace the beef broth with a can of reduced-sodium chicken broth.

breads

Absolutely delicious describes this comforting coffee cake that features peaches and a delectable frosting. Serve it warm for an extra-special treat.

Virginia Krites
Cridersville, Ohio

peach cobbler coffee cake

PREP: 25 MIN. BAKE: 70 MIN. + COOLING

1 cup butter, softened
1 cup sugar
2 eggs
3 teaspoons vanilla extract
3 cups all-purpose flour
1 teaspoon baking powder
1 teaspoon baking soda
1/2 teaspoon salt
1-1/4 cups sour cream
1 can (21 ounces) peach pie filling
1 can (15-1/4 ounces) sliced peaches, drained
TOPPING:
1 cup packed brown sugar
1 cup all-purpose flour
1/2 cup quick-cooking oats
1/4 teaspoon ground cinnamon
1/2 cup cold butter, cubed

GLAZE:
1 cup confectioners' sugar
1 to 2 tablespoons 2% milk

1 In a bowl, cream butter and sugar. Add eggs, one at a time, beating well after each addition. Beat in vanilla. Combine flour, baking powder, baking soda and salt; add to creamed mixture alternately with sour cream. Beat just until combined.

2 Pour half of the batter into a greased 13-in. x 9-in. baking dish. Combine pie filling and peaches; spread over batter. Drop remaining batter by tablespoonfuls over filling.

3 In a bowl, combine the first four topping ingredients. Cut in butter until mixture is crumbly. Sprinkle over batter.

4 Bake at 350° for 70-75 minutes or until a toothpick inserted comes out clean. Cool on a wire rack.

5 In a small bowl, combine confectioner's sugar and enough milk to achieve desired consistency; drizzle over coffee cake.

YIELD: 12 SERVINGS.

honey chip muffins

PREP/TOTAL TIME: 30 MIN.

Packaged chocolate chip muffin mix gets a makeover with a few pantry staples. I love peanut butter, so I added it along with a little honey to this recipe.

Mary Young, Stroudsburg, Pennsylvania

1 package (17.8 ounces) chocolate chip
   muffin mix
1 tablespoon baking cocoa
2 tablespoons honey
1 tablespoon peanut butter
1 egg
3/4 cup water
1/4 cup semisweet chocolate chips

1 In a large bowl, combine the muffin mix and
cocoa. In a small bowl, combine honey and peanut
butter; add the egg and water. Stir into muffin mix
mixture with a spoon just until moistened, about
50 strokes (batter will be slightly lumpy). Stir in
chocolate chips.

2 Fill foil-or paper-lined muffin cups two-thirds full.
Bake at 400° for 17-20 minutes or until a toothpick
inserted near the center comes out clean. Cool for
5 minutes before removing from the pan to wire
rack. Serve warm.

YIELD: 1 DOZEN.

This recipe is really just a glorified Monkey Bread. I also make a savory version with garlic and cheese. When my neighbor has her Christmas brunch, she always requests I bring this.

Lois Rutherford, Elkton, Florida

surprise monkey bread

PREP: 25 MIN. BAKE: 40 MIN.

1 cup packed brown sugar
1/2 cup butter, cubed
2 tubes (12 ounces each) refrigerated
   flaky buttermilk biscuits
1/2 cup sugar
1 tablespoon ground cinnamon
1 package (8 ounces) cream cheese,
   cut into 20 cubes
1-1/2 cups chopped walnuts

1 In a small microwave-safe bowl, heat brown
sugar and butter on high for 1 minute or until
sugar is dissolved; set aside.

2 Flatten each biscuit into a 3-in. circle. Combine
sugar and cinnamon; sprinkle 1/2 teaspoon in the
center of each biscuit. Top with a cream cheese
cube. Fold dough over filling; pinch the edges
to seal tightly.

3 Sprinkle 1/2 cup walnuts into a 10-in. fluted tube
pan coated with cooking spray. Layer with half of
the biscuits, cinnamon-sugar and butter mixture
and 1/2 cup walnuts. Repeat layers.

4 Bake at 350° for 40-45 minutes or until golden
brown. Immediately invert onto a serving platter.
Serve warm. Refrigerate leftovers.

YIELD: 1 LOAF.

braided pizza loaf

PREP: 50 MIN. + RISING BAKE: 30 MIN.

Before you leave in the morning, take the frozen bread dough out of the freezer to thaw. That way you'll be ready to make this satisfying loaf when you get home.

Debbie Meduna, Plaza, North Dakota

- 1 loaf (1 pound) frozen bread dough, thawed
- 1 pound ground beef
- 1 medium onion, finely chopped
- 1 can (8 ounces) tomato sauce
- 1 teaspoon salt
- 1 teaspoon dried oregano
- 1 teaspoon paprika
- 1 teaspoon pepper
- 1/2 teaspoon garlic salt
- 1 cup (4 ounces) shredded cheddar cheese
- 1 cup (4 ounces) shredded part-skim mozzarella cheese
- Melted butter

1 Place dough in a greased bowl, turning once to grease top. Cover and let rise in a warm place until doubled, about 1 hour.

2 Meanwhile, in a large skillet, cook beef and onion over medium heat until meat is no longer pink; drain. Stir in tomato sauce and seasonings. Bring to a boil. Reduce heat; simmer, uncovered, for 30 minutes, stirring occasionally. Cool completely.

3 Punch dough down. Turn onto a lightly floured surface; roll into a 15-in. x 12-in. rectangle. Place on a greased baking sheet. Spread filling lengthwise down center third of rectangle. Sprinkle cheeses over filling.

4 On each long side, cut 1-1/2-in.-wide strips about 2-1/2 in. into center. Starting at one end, fold alternating strips at an angle across filling. Brush with butter.

5 Bake at 350° for 30-35 minutes or until golden brown. Serve warm. Refrigerate leftovers.

YIELD: 1 LOAF.

Here's a recipe that just couldn't be much quicker or easier and is sure to add a nice touch to any dinner. The garlic and Parmesan flavors really come through. Enjoy!

Lori Abad, East Haven, Connecticut

garlic-cheese crescent rolls

PREP/TOTAL TIME: 20 MIN.

- 1 tube (8 ounces) refrigerated crescent rolls
- 3 tablespoons butter, melted
- 1-1/2 teaspoons garlic powder
- 1 teaspoon dried oregano
- 2 tablespoons grated Parmesan cheese

1 Separate crescent dough into eight triangles. Roll up from the wide end and place point side down 2 in. apart on an ungreased baking sheet. Curve ends to form a crescent.

2 Combine the butter, garlic powder and oregano; brush over rolls. Sprinkle with cheese. Bake at 375° for 10-12 minutes or until golden brown. Serve the rolls warm.

YIELD: 8 SERVINGS.

rum sweet rolls

PREP: 25 MIN. + RISING BAKE: 20 MIN. + COOLING

1 package (16 ounces) hot roll mix
3 tablespoons butter, softened
2 cups confectioners' sugar
4-1/2 teaspoons water
3-1/2 teaspoons rum extract
1/2 teaspoon ground cinnamon

1 Prepare hot roll mix according to package directions. Turn dough onto a lightly floured surface; gently knead for 5 minutes. Cover with a bowl and let rest for 5 minutes. Roll into a 12-in. x 10-in. rectangle. Spread with butter to within 1/2 in. of edges.

2 In a large bowl, combine the confectioners' sugar, water and extract until smooth. Spread half of the mixture over butter. Sprinkle with cinnamon. Roll up jelly-roll style, starting with a long side; pinch seam to seal. Cut into 12 rolls. Place cut side up in a greased 11-in. x 7-in. baking dish. Cover and let rest until nearly doubled, about 25 minutes.

3 Bake at 375° for 20-25 minutes or until golden brown. Cool for 5 minutes before removing from pan to a wire rack. Cool for 15 minutes. Drizzle with the remaining confectioners' sugar mixture. Serve warm.

YIELD: 1 DOZEN.

caraway beer bread

PREP: 10 MIN. BAKE: 40 MIN. + COOLING

This moist and tender loaf boasts a mild beer and caraway flavor that can hold its own with hearty soups and chili. But surprise! It's also yummy spread with ham salad, cream cheese or assorted jams.

Janet Newmyer, Wilber, Nebraska

2-1/2 cups biscuit/baking mix
2 tablespoons sugar
1 teaspoon caraway seeds
2 eggs
1 cup beer or nonalcoholic beer
3 tablespoons butter, melted

1 In a large bowl, combine the biscuit mix, sugar and caraway seeds. In a small bowl, whisk the eggs, beer and butter until smooth. Stir into dry ingredients just until moistened.

2 Pour into a 9-in. x 5-in. loaf pan coated with cooking spray. Bake at 350° for 40-45 minutes or until a toothpick inserted near the center comes out clean. Cool for 10 minutes before removing to a wire rack.

YIELD: 1 LOAF (12 SLICES).

These savory biscuits couldn't be simpler to make. With from-scratch flavor and a golden cheese topping, they're sure to be a hit.

Lynn Tice, Osage City, Kansas

cheese biscuits

PREP/TOTAL TIME: 25 MIN.

1 tube (12 ounces) refrigerated buttermilk biscuits
1/4 cup prepared Italian salad dressing
1/3 cup grated Parmesan cheese
1/2 cup shredded part-skim mozzarella cheese

1 Separate biscuits; dip the top of each in salad dressing, then in Parmesan cheese. Place cheese side up on an ungreased baking sheet; sprinkle with mozzarella cheese. Bake at 400° for 9-11 minutes or until golden. Serve warm.

YIELD: 10 BISCUITS.

garlic cheese bubble bread

PREP: 15 MIN. + RISING BAKE: 20 MIN.

My daughter makes this easy bread when she serves spaghetti and lasagna. It's really delicious.

Evelyn Backhaus, Pollock, South Dakota

1 loaf (1 pound) frozen bread dough, thawed
2 pieces string cheese (1 ounce each)
1/4 cup butter, softened
2 tablespoons grated Parmesan cheese
1/2 teaspoon garlic salt

1 Divide dough into 10 portions. Cut each string cheese into 5 pieces. Wrap each portion of dough around a piece of cheese; shape into balls. Place in a greased 9-in. x 5-in. loaf pan.

2 In a large bowl, combine the butter, Parmesan cheese and garlic salt until blended; spread over top of dough. Cover and let rise in a warm place until doubled, about 1 hour.

3 Bake at 375° for 20-25 minutes or until golden brown. Cool for 10 minutes before removing from pan to a wire rack. Serve warm.

YIELD: 1 LOAF (16 SLICES).

Loaded with pizza flavor, these muffins are delectable! They're great for lunch but also make good appetizers when baked in mini muffin cups. For a change, add chopped mushrooms or green pepper to the batter.

Andra McGee, Port Alsworth, Alaska

pepperoni pizza muffins

PREP: 20 MIN. BAKE: 20 MIN.

3 cups biscuit/baking mix
1 can (10-3/4 ounces) condensed tomato soup, undiluted
3/4 cup water
1/2 cup shredded part-skim mozzarella cheese
1/2 cup shredded cheddar cheese
1/2 cup diced pepperoni
2 tablespoons chopped ripe olives
1 tablespoon dried minced onion
1 teaspoon Italian seasoning

1 Place biscuit mix in a bowl. Combine remaining ingredients; stir into biscuit mix just until moistened. Fill greased muffin cups three-fourths full.

2 Bake at 350° for 17-20 minutes or until a toothpick inserted near the center comes out clean. Cool for 5 minutes before removing from pans to wire racks. Serve warm. Refrigerate leftovers.

YIELD: 14 MUFFINS.

Convenient hot roll mix is the base for these pretty brown rolls. Parmesan cheese, pizza seasoning and garlic powder lend plenty of flavor when sprinkled over the top.

Taste of Home Test Kitchen

parmesan cloverleaf rolls

PREP: 15 MIN. + RISING BAKE: 15 MIN.

- 1 package (16 ounces) hot roll mix
- 2 tablespoons butter, melted
- 1/4 cup grated Parmesan cheese
- 2 teaspoons pizza seasoning or Italian seasoning
- 1/4 teaspoon garlic powder

1 Prepare roll mix according to package directions. Divide dough into 12 portions; divide each portion into three pieces. Shape each into a ball; place three balls each in 12 well-greased muffin cups. Brush with butter.

2 Combine the cheese, pizza seasoning and garlic powder; sprinkle over dough. Cover and let rise in a warm place for 10-15 minutes.

3 Bake at 375° for 15-20 minutes or until golden brown. Remove from the pan to a wire rack. Serve the rolls warm.

YIELD: 1 DOZEN.

cream cheese bran muffins

PREP: 15 MIN. + STANDING BAKE: 20 MIN.

These are really good and so moist. The cream cheese center eliminates the need to add butter to the muffin.

Jeannette Mack, Rushville, New York

- 1 cup All-Bran
- 1/2 cup 2% milk
- 1 cup (8 ounces) sour cream
- 1 egg, lightly beaten
- 1 package (16.6 ounces) date quick bread mix
- 1 package (3 ounces) cream cheese

1 In a large bowl, combine cereal and milk; let stand for 10 minutes. Stir in sour cream and egg. Stir in bread mix just until moistened.

2 Fill greased or paper-lined muffin cups about three-fourths full. Cut cream cheese into 12 cubes; gently press one cube into the center of each muffin cup just until covered with batter (cups will be full).

3 Bake at 400° for 18-20 minutes or until a toothpick inserted in the muffin comes out clean. Cool for 5 minutes before removing from pan to a wire rack. Serve warm. Refrigerate leftovers.

YIELD: 1 DOZEN.

TIP

To simplify the prep for the Parmesan Cloverleaf Rolls, you can also use 12 thawed frozen bread dough dinner rolls, which will eliminate the mixing and kneading step. Just divide each roll into three pieces and proceed as recipe directs.

I enjoy all kinds of breads and rolls, but this square loaf is a favorite of mine because it is so different. The bread is also great cooked on the grill. Simply cover and grill it over medium heat for about 30 minutes.

Charlotte Kidd
Lebanon, Indiana

fennel seed wheat bread

PREP: 15 MIN. + RISING BAKE: 30 MIN. + COOLING

1 package (16 ounces) hot roll mix
1 cup whole wheat flour
2 teaspoons fennel seed, crushed, divided
1-1/3 cups water
2 tablespoons butter
1 egg
3/4 cup shredded Swiss cheese
1 teaspoon 2% milk

1 In a large bowl, combine the contents of the roll mix and yeast packets with the whole wheat flour and 1-1/2 teaspoons fennel seed. In a small saucepan, heat water and butter to 120°-130°. Add to the flour mixture; beat just until moistened. Add egg; beat until blended.

2 Turn onto a floured surface. Knead in cheese until dough is smooth and elastic, about 4-6 minutes. Pat dough into a greased 9-in. square baking dish. Cover and let rise in a warm place until doubled, about 25 minutes.

3 Brush with milk and sprinkle with remaining fennel seed. Bake at 350° for 30-35 minutes or until golden brown. Cool for 15 minutes before removing from pan to a wire rack. Cut bread into four squares; cut each into three wedges.

YIELD: **1 LOAF (12 SLICES).**

apple pie coffee cake

PREP: 10 MIN. BAKE: 40 MIN. + COOLING

- 1 package (18-1/4 ounces) spice cake mix
- 1 can (21 ounces) apple pie filling
- 3 eggs
- 3/4 cup fat-free sour cream
- 1/4 cup water
- 2 tablespoons canola oil
- 1 teaspoon almond extract
- 2 tablespoons brown sugar
- 1-1/2 teaspoons ground cinnamon
- GLAZE:
- 2/3 cup confectioners' sugar
- 2 teaspoons fat-free milk

1 Set aside 1 tablespoon cake mix. Set aside 1-1/2 cups pie filling. In a large bowl, combine the eggs, sour cream, water, oil, extract and remaining cake mix and pie filling; beat on low speed for 30 seconds. Beat on medium for 2 minutes. Pour half of the batter into a 10-in. fluted tube pan coated with cooking spray.

2 In a small bowl, combine the brown sugar, cinnamon and reserved cake mix; sprinkle over batter. Spoon reserved pie filling over batter to within 3/4 in. of edges; top with remaining batter.

3 Bake at 350° for 40-45 minutes or until a toothpick inserted near the center comes out clean. Cool the cake for 10 minutes before removing from pan to a wire rack.

4 In a small bowl, combine glaze ingredients. Drizzle over cooled cake.

YIELD: 14 SERVINGS.

herbed bread twists

PREP: 30 MIN. + RISING BAKE: 10 MIN.

A blend of herbs and a special shape dress up ordinary frozen bread dough in this unbelievably easy treat.

Deb Stapert, Comstock Park, Michigan

1/4 cup butter, softened
1/4 teaspoon garlic powder
1/4 teaspoon each dried basil, marjoram
   and oregano
1 loaf (1 pound) frozen bread dough, thawed
3/4 cup shredded part-skim mozzarella cheese
1 egg
1 tablespoon water
4 teaspoons sesame seeds

1 In a small bowl, combine butter and seasonings.
On a lightly floured surface, roll dough into a
12-in. square. Spread with butter mixture to
within 1/2 in. of edges; sprinkle with cheese.

2 Fold dough into thirds. Cut widthwise into
24 strips. Twist each strip twice; pinch ends to
seal. Place 2 in. apart on greased baking sheets.
Cover and let rise in a warm place until doubled,
about 40 minutes.

3 Beat egg and water; brush over dough. Sprinkle
with sesame seeds. Bake at 375° for 10-12 minutes
or until light golden brown. Remove from pans
to wire racks.

YIELD: 2 DOZEN.

This recipe was created for Thanksgiving weekend with family members who were trying to be more health conscious. I wanted the flavor to still be there, and the candied ginger gives these scones a little zing!

Rebecca Guffey, Apex, North Carolina

spicy ginger scones

PREP/TOTAL TIME: 30 MIN.

2 cups biscuit/baking mix
2 tablespoons sugar
1 teaspoon ground cinnamon
1/4 teaspoon ground ginger
1/4 teaspoon ground nutmeg
2/3 cup half-and-half cream
1/2 cup golden raisins
2 tablespoons chopped crystallized ginger
Additional half-and-half cream and sugar

1 In a large bowl, combine the biscuit mix, sugar,
cinnamon, ginger and nutmeg. Stir in cream just
until moistened. Stir in raisins and ginger. Turn
onto a floured surface; knead 10 times.

2 Transfer dough to a greased baking sheet. Pat
into a 9-in. circle. Cut into eight wedges, but do
not separate. Brush tops lightly with additional
cream; sprinkle with additional sugar.

3 Bake at 425° for 12-15 minutes or until golden
brown. Serve warm.

YIELD: 8 SCONES.

Refrigerated rolls make this pretty braid both flaky and fuss-free while cinnamon and almond make it simply delicious! Try it with other types of refrigerated dough for a different texture. I've also made it with a crusty French loaf.

Nancy Gunn
Orem, Utah

cinnamon almond braid

PREP: 20 MIN. BAKE: 10 MIN. + COOLING

1 tube (8 ounces) refrigerated crescent rolls
2 tablespoons plus 1/4 cup sugar, divided
1 teaspoon ground cinnamon
1/2 cup finely chopped slivered almonds
1 tablespoon butter, melted
1/4 teaspoon almond extract
ICING:
1/2 cup confectioners' sugar
1/4 teaspoon almond extract
1-1/2 to 2 teaspoons milk
1/4 teaspoon ground cinnamon

1 Line a 15-in. x 10-in. x 1-in. baking pan with parchment paper. Unroll crescent dough into prepared pan; seal seams and perforations. Combine 2 tablespoons sugar and cinnamon; sprinkle over dough.

2 Combine the almonds, butter, extract and remaining sugar; spread lengthwise down the center of dough. On each long side, cut 1-in.-wide strips about 2-1/2 in. into center. Starting at one end, fold alternating strips at an angle across filling. Pinch ends to seal.

3 Bake at 375° for 10-15 minutes or until golden brown. Cool for 10 minutes; remove to a wire rack.

4 For icing, in a bowl, combine the confectioners' sugar, extract and enough milk to achieve drizzling consistency. Drizzle over braid; sprinkle with cinnamon. Serve warm.

YIELD: 1 LOAF (10 SLICES).

parmesan herb loaves

PREP: 10 MIN. + RISING BAKE: 20 MIN.

With the help of frozen dough, savory home-baked loaves take only a few minutes of your time. Let them rise while you prepare the rest of the meal. The aroma of freshly baked bread will entice your family to the table.

Shirley Sibit Rudder, Burkeville, Texas

2 loaves (1 pound each) frozen bread dough
1/2 cup shredded Parmesan cheese
1 tablespoon dried parsley flakes
1 tablespoon dried minced garlic
1/2 teaspoon dill weed
1/2 teaspoon salt
2 tablespoons butter, melted

1 Place dough in two greased 8-in. x 4-in. loaf pans. Thaw according to package directions. In a small bowl, combine the cheese, parsley, garlic, dill and salt. Brush dough with butter; sprinkle with cheese mixture. Cover and let rise in a warm place until nearly doubled, about 2-1/2 hours.

2 Bake at 350° for 20-25 minutes or until golden brown. Remove from pans to wire racks to cool.

YIELD: 2 LOAVES (16 SLICES EACH).

Add chilies and cheese to a boxed mix and what do you get? Easy muffins with zip!

Taste of Home Test Kitchen

chili-cheese corn muffins

PREP/TOTAL TIME: 30 MIN.

1 package (8-1/2 ounces) corn bread/muffin mix
1 egg, lightly beaten
1/3 cup 2% milk
1/2 cup shredded Mexican cheese blend
1 can (4 ounces) chopped green chilies, drained

1 In a large bowl, combine the corn bread mix, egg and milk just until blended. Stir in cheese and chilies. Coat muffin cups with cooking spray or use paper liners; fill three-fourths full with batter.

2 Bake at 400° for 20-22 minutes or until a toothpick inserted near the center comes out clean. Cool for 5 minutes before removing from pan to a wire rack. Serve warm.

YIELD: 8 MUFFINS.

poppy seed blueberry bread

PREP: 15 MIN. BAKE: 40 MIN. + COOLING

Poppy seeds and lemon peel perk up the flavor of these moist mini loaves while drizzled glaze sweetens their tops.

Jennifer Miller, Avon, Indiana

1 package (18-1/4 ounces) blueberry muffin mix
1 egg
3/4 cup water
3 tablespoons canola oil
1 to 2 tablespoons poppy seeds
2 to 3 teaspoons grated lemon peel
GLAZE:
1/2 cup confectioners' sugar
1 to 2 tablespoons lemon juice

1 Drain and rinse blueberries from muffin mix; set aside. In a bowl, combine the muffin mix, egg, water, oil, poppy seeds and lemon peel just until blended. Fold in blueberries. Transfer into two greased 5-3/4-in. x 3-in. x 2-in. loaf pans.

2 Bake at 350° for 40-45 minutes or until a toothpick inserted comes out clean. Cool for 10 minutes before removing from pans to wire racks.

3 In a small bowl, combine confectioners' sugar and enough lemon juice to achieve desired consistency; drizzle over warm loaves.

YIELD: 2 MINI LOAVES (5 SLICES EACH).

With rosemary and lots of cheese, these bread squares will make an everyday dinner seem like a festive occasion.

Shelley Ross, Bow, Washington

rosemary focaccia

PREP/TOTAL TIME: 25 MIN.

1 loaf (1 pound) frozen bread dough, thawed
2 tablespoons olive oil
1/4 cup thinly sliced onion
1-1/2 teaspoons minced garlic
1 cup (4 ounces) shredded part-skim mozzarella cheese
2 tablespoons minced fresh rosemary

1 Roll the dough into an ungreased 15-in. x 10-in. x 1-in. baking pan; build up edges slightly. Brush with oil; top with onion, garlic, cheese and rosemary.

2 Bake at 400° for 15-20 minutes or until golden brown and cheese is melted. Let stand for 5 minutes before slicing.

YIELD: 15 SERVINGS.

almost homemade

sour cream & chive biscuits

PREP/TOTAL TIME: 20 MIN.

Chives give a nice, mild onion taste to just about any dish, whether it be a soup, dip, baked potato or buttery spread. They really are a nice touch in these biscuits.

Priscilla Gilbert, Inidan Harbour Beach, Florida

3 cups biscuit/baking mix
3 tablespoons minced chives
2/3 cup water
2/3 cup sour cream

1 In a large bowl, combine biscuit mix and chives. Stir in water and sour cream just until moistened.

2 Drop by heaping tablespoonfuls onto a baking sheet coated with cooking spray. Bake at 450° for 8-10 minutes or until lightly browned. Serve warm.

YIELD: 16 BISCUITS.

This tender bread is delicious alone and even better spread with cream cheese or butter. It will seem like you spent a lot of time fussing, but it's made with convenient refrigerated biscuits.

Debbie Purdue, Westland, Michigan

cinnamon nut loaf

PREP: 20 MIN. BAKE: 25 MIN. + COOLING

1/3 cup finely chopped pecans or walnuts
1/4 cup sugar
3 tablespoons butter, melted
2 teaspoons ground cinnamon
2 tubes (7-1/2 ounces each) refrigerated buttermilk biscuits
1/2 cup confectioners' sugar
1 tablespoon 2% milk

1 In a small bowl, combine the nuts, sugar, butter and cinnamon. Separate biscuits; flatten slightly. Place about 1/2 teaspoon of nut mixture on one side of each biscuit; fold other side over filling. Press edges with a fork to seal. Forming five rows, arrange the biscuits folded side down in a greased 8-in. x 4-in. loaf pan. Spoon the remaining nut mixture over top.

2 Bake at 350° for 25-30 minutes or until golden brown. Cool for 10 minutes before removing from pan to a wire rack. Meanwhile, in a small bowl, combine confectioners' sugar and milk; drizzle over warm bread. Cut into slices or pull apart.

YIELD: 8-10 SERVINGS.

1 On a lightly floured surface, roll dough into a 15-in. x 9-in. rectangle. Transfer to a lightly greased baking sheet.

2 In a small bowl, beat cream cheese and sugar until smooth. Add egg and extract; mix well (filling will be soft). Spread down center of rectangle; sprinkle with chips.

3 On each long side, cut 1-in.-wide strips, about 1/2 in. from filling. Starting at one end, fold alternating strips at an angle across filling. Seal ends. Cover and let the coffee cake rise in a warm place until doubled, about 1 hour.

4 Brush with milk. Bake at 350° for 20-30 minutes or until golden brown. Cool on a wire rack.

5 For glaze, in a small bowl, combine confectioners' sugar and extract. Stir in enough milk to achieve desired consistency. Drizzle over coffee cake. Sprinkle with almonds.

YIELD: 8-10 SERVINGS.

This coffee cake is doubly delicious due to the cream cheese and vanilla chip filling. One piece leads to another!

Mary Shivers, Ada, Oklahoma

almond coffee cake

PREP: 35 MIN. + RISING BAKE: 20 MIN. + COOLING

1 loaf (1 pound) frozen bread dough, thawed
1 package (8 ounces) cream cheese, softened
1/4 cup sugar
1 egg
1/2 teaspoon almond extract
3/4 cup vanilla or white chips
1 tablespoon 2% milk
GLAZE:
1 cup confectioners' sugar
1/4 teaspoon almond extract
1 to 2 tablespoons 2% milk
1/2 cup slivered almonds, toasted

fruit bread twists

PREP: 15 MIN. + RISING BAKE: 25 MIN.

My husband loves this fruit-filled bread, so I fix it for him often. It's easy to prepare with frozen white and wheat bread dough, yet it's lovely enough for a special occasion.

Sandra Hessler, Caro, Michigan

1 loaf (1 pound) frozen white bread dough, thawed
1 loaf (1 pound) frozen whole wheat bread dough, thawed
1/2 cup sugar
1 teaspoon ground cinnamon
1 package (8 ounces) mixed dried fruit, chopped
GLAZE:
1 cup confectioners' sugar
1 tablespoon water
1 teaspoon vanilla extract

1 Cut each loaf of bread dough in half lengthwise. Roll each portion into an 18-in. x 5-in. rectangle. Brush lightly with water. Combine sugar and cinnamon; sprinkle over dough. Sprinkle with fruit. Roll up each rectangle, jelly-roll style, starting with a long side.

2 For each loaf, twist one white and one wheat rope together, pinching ends to seal. Place on greased baking sheets. Cover with plastic wrap coated with cooking spray; let rise in a warm place until doubled, about 30 minutes.

3 Remove plastic wrap. Bake at 350° for 25-30 minutes or until golden brown. Remove from pans to cool on wire racks. Combine glaze ingredients; drizzle over loaves.

YIELD: 2 LOAVES.

walnut-rippled coffee cake

PREP: 15 MIN. BAKE: 40 MIN. + COOLING

1 package (18-1/4 ounces) yellow cake mix
1 cup (8 ounces) sour cream
4 eggs
1/3 cup canola oil
1/4 cup water
2 tablespoons sugar
1 cup chopped walnuts
2 tablespoons brown sugar
2 teaspoons ground cinnamon

1 Set aside 2 tablespoons cake mix. In a large bowl, combine the sour cream, eggs, oil, water, sugar and remaining cake mix; beat on low speed for 30 seconds. Beat on medium for 2 minutes.

2 Pour half the batter into a greased and floured fluted 10-in. tube pan. Combine the walnuts,

An ideal treat any time of the day, this moist yellow brunch cake offers a delightful surprise of cinnamon, nuts and brown sugar in every slice.

Nanetta Larson, Canton, South Dakota

brown sugar, cinnamon and reserved cake mix; sprinkle over batter. Top with the remaining batter.

3 Bake at 350° for 40-45 minutes or until a toothpick inserted near the center comes out clean. Cool the coffee cake for 10 minutes before removing from pan to a wire rack.

YIELD: 12 SERVINGS.

jumbo cinnamon rolls

PREP: 15 MIN. + RISING BAKE: 15 MIN.

4 frozen Texas-size dinner rolls
2 tablespoons butter, melted
1/4 cup coarsely chopped pecans
2 tablespoons sugar
3/4 teaspoon ground cinnamon
HONEY BUTTER:
2 tablespoons butter, softened
2 teaspoons honey

1 Let rolls rise in a warm place until doubled, about 45 minutes. Punch down. Roll each into a 12-in. rope; brush with butter. In a shallow bowl, combine the pecans, sugar and cinnamon; roll ropes in the nut mixture.

2 Twist two ropes together; pinch ends to seal. Place in a greased 10-oz. custard cup. Repeat with remaining ropes. Cover and let rise for 30 minutes or until doubled.

3 Bake at 375° for 15-20 minutes or until golden brown. Meanwhile, combine the honey butter ingredients. Serve with rolls.

YIELD: 2 SERVINGS.

cookies

↑ chocolate cake cookies

PREP: 30 MIN. BAKE: 10 MIN./BATCH

- 1 package (18-1/4 ounces) chocolate fudge cake mix
- 2 packages (3.9 ounces each) instant chocolate fudge pudding mix
- 1-1/2 cups mayonnaise
- 2 cups (12 ounces) semisweet chocolate chips
- 1/2 cup chopped walnuts

1 In a large bowl, combine cake mix, pudding mixes and mayonnaise; mix well. Stir in chocolate chips and walnuts.

2 Shape by teaspoonfuls into balls; place on greased baking sheets. Bake at 350° for 9-10 minutes or until cookies puff and surface cracks slightly. Cool for 5 minutes before removing the cookies from pans to wire racks.

YIELD: 7 DOZEN.

TIP

Store soft cookies and crisp cookies in separate airtight containers. If stored together, the moisture from the soft cookies will soften the crisp cookies, making them lose their crunch.

star sandwich cookies

PREP: 30 MIN. BAKE: 10 MIN. + COOLING

These dazzling treats are sure to be the star of your holiday dessert tray. A rich mixture of white chocolate and cream cheese forms the sweet yet simple filling.

Taste of Home Test Kitchen

1/2 tube refrigerated sugar cookie dough, softened
1/3 cup all-purpose flour
Red sugars, nonpareils or sprinkles
1 ounce white baking chocolate
2 tablespoons cream cheese, softened
1 tablespoon butter, softened
4 drops red food coloring
1/2 cup confectioners' sugar

1 In a small bowl, beat cookie dough and flour until combined. Roll out on a lightly floured surface to 1/8-in. thickness. Cut with a floured 2-3/4-in. star cookie cutter.

2 Place 2 in. apart on ungreased baking sheets. Decorate half of the cookies with sugars and nonpareils. Bake at 350° for 7-9 minutes or until edges are golden brown. Remove the cookies to wire racks to cool.

3 In a microwave, melt white chocolate; stir until smooth. Cool. In a small bowl, beat the cream cheese, butter and food coloring until fluffy. Gradually beat in confectioners' sugar and melted chocolate until smooth. Spread over the bottoms of plain cookies; top with decorated cookies. Store in the refrigerator.

YIELD: ABOUT 1 DOZEN.

macaroon bars

PREP: 10 MIN. BAKE: 30 MIN.

3-1/4 cups flaked coconut, divided
1 can (14 ounces) sweetened condensed milk
1 teaspoon almond extract
1 tube (8 ounces) refrigerated crescent rolls

Guests will never recognize the refrigerated crescent roll dough that goes into these almond-flavored bars. You can assemble these coconut nibbles in no time.

Carolyn Kyzer, Alexander, Arkansas

1 Sprinkle 1-1/2 cups coconut into a well-greased 13-in. x 9-in. baking pan. Combine milk and extract; drizzle half over the coconut. Unroll crescent dough; arrange in a single layer over coconut. Drizzle with remaining milk mixture; sprinkle with remaining coconut.

2 Bake at 350° for 30-35 minutes or until golden brown. Cool completely on a wire rack before cutting. Store in the refrigerator.

YIELD: 3 DOZEN.

3 Press three-fourths into a greased 13-in. x 9-in. baking pan. Bake at 350° for 15 minutes. Place on a wire rack for 10 minutes.

4 Pour caramel mixture over the crust. Drop remaining dough by spoonfuls onto caramel layer. Bake for 25-30 minutes longer or until edges are golden brown.

5 Cool on a wire rack for 10 minutes; run a knife around edges of pan. Cool the bars 40 minutes longer; cover and refrigerate for at least 1 hour before serving.

YIELD: 2 DOZEN.

strawberry banana squares

PREP: 15 MIN. BAKE: 40 MIN. + COOLING

The flavors of strawberry, banana and coconut make a winning combination in these delightful squares. This dessert really does have it all, and your kids will notice!

Lucille Mead, Ilion, New York

1 package (14 ounces) banana quick bread and muffin mix
1/2 cup chopped walnuts
1/3 cup butter, softened
1 egg
1 can (14 ounces) sweetened condensed milk
1 can (20 ounces) strawberry pie filling
1/2 cup flaked coconut

1 In a small bowl, combine the bread mix, walnuts, butter and egg until crumbly. Press onto the bottom of a 13-in. x 9-in. baking dish coated with cooking spray. Bake at 350° for 8-10 minutes or until lightly browned.

2 Spread milk over crust; spoon pie filling over milk. Sprinkle with coconut. Bake 30-40 minutes longer or until golden brown. Cool on a wire rack. Cut into squares. Store in the refrigerator.

YIELD: 2 DOZEN.

It's fun to take a yellow cake mix and create something that is this rich and wonderful. We like eating the bars when they are cold, right out of the refrigerator. They're ideal with a tall glass of milk.

LaDonna Reed, Ponca City, Oklahoma

caramel chip bars

PREP: 30 MIN. + CHILLING BAKE: 25 MIN. + COOLING

1/2 cup butter, cubed
32 caramels
1 can (14 ounces) sweetened condensed milk
1 package (18-1/4 ounces) yellow cake mix
1/2 cup canola oil
2 eggs
2 cups miniature semisweet chocolate chips
1 cup vanilla or white chips
1 Heath candy bar (1.4 ounces), chopped

1 In a large saucepan, combine the butter, caramels and milk; cook and stir over medium-low heat until smooth. Cool.

2 In a large bowl, beat the cake mix, oil and eggs until blended. Stir in chips and chopped candy bar (dough will be stiff).

chocolate toffee cookies

PREP/TOTAL TIME: 20 MIN.

After one bite of these decadent and gooey cookies, friends and family will be surprised to learn that they started from a boxed cookie mix.

Patricia Van Wyk, Newton, Iowa

1 package (17-1/2 ounces) chocolate chip cookie mix
1/4 cup canola oil
1 egg
2 tablespoons water
1/2 cup English toffee bits or almond brickle chips

1 In a large bowl, combine the cookie mix, oil, egg and water. Stir in toffee bits.

2 Drop by tablespoonfuls 2 in. apart onto parchment paper-lined baking sheets. Bake at 350° for 10-12 minutes or until set. Cool for 2 minutes before removing to wire racks.

YIELD: 2 DOZEN.

butter ball chiffons

PREP/TOTAL TIME: 30 MIN.

1 cup butter, softened
1/4 cup confectioners' sugar
1 package (3.4 ounces) instant lemon pudding mix
2 teaspoons water
1 teaspoon vanilla extract
2 cups all-purpose flour
1 cup chopped pecans or walnuts
2 Heath candy bars (1.4 ounces each), chopped

1 In a small bowl, cream butter and confectioners' sugar until light and fluffy. Beat in the pudding mix, water and vanilla. Gradually add flour. Stir in nuts and chopped candy bars.

The blend of lemon pudding and toffee candy bars sets these crisp cookies apart from all others. Keep the ingredients on hand for when you need a treat in a hurry.

Myla Harvey, Stanton, Michigan

2 Roll into 1-in. balls. Place 2 in. apart on ungreased baking sheets. Bake at 325° for 12-15 minutes or until lightly browned. Cool for 3 minutes before removing to wire racks.

YIELD: 5 DOZEN.

EDITOR'S NOTE: This recipe does not use eggs.

1 In a large bowl, beat the brownie mix, oil, eggs and extract on medium speed until blended (batter will be stiff). Set aside 1 cup for topping.

2 Spread the remaining batter into a greased 13-in. x 9-in. baking pan. Bake at 350° for 10-15 minutes or until edges crack.

3 For filling, in a large bowl, beat the cream cheese, eggs and extracts until smooth. Gradually add confectioners' sugar and mix well. Fold in coconut. Carefully spread over brownies.

4 Drop reserved batter by teaspoonfuls over filling. Bake for 45-50 minutes or until a toothpick inserted near the center comes out clean (do not overbake). Cool on a wire rack. Store brownies in the refrigerator.

YIELD: 3 DOZEN.

My family enjoys the combination of chocolate and coconut. So I stirred coconut extract into brownie batter and added flaked coconut to the cream cheese filling. These fudgy bars are the tasty result!

Phyllis Perry, Vassar, Kansas

cobblestone brownies

PREP: 15 MIN. BAKE: 45 MIN. + COOLING

1 package fudge brownie mix (13-inch x 9-inch pan size)

1/2 cup canola oil

2 eggs

1/2 teaspoon coconut extract

FILLING:

1 package (8 ounces) cream cheese, softened

2 eggs

1 teaspoon coconut extract

1 teaspoon vanilla extract

3-3/4 cups confectioners' sugar

1 cup flaked coconut

easy macaroons

PREP: 20 MIN. BAKE: 15 MIN.

My gang likes macaroons, so when they raved about this easy-to-make pastel version, I knew I had a keeper.

Judy Farlow, Boise, Idaho

1 pint lemon or orange sherbet

2 tablespoons almond extract

1 package (18-1/4 ounces) white cake mix

6 cups flaked coconut

1 In a large bowl, beat sherbet and almond extract until sherbet is slightly softened. Gradually add cake mix. Stir in coconut.

2 Drop by rounded teaspoonfuls 2 in. apart onto greased baking sheets. Bake at 350° for 12-15 minutes or until edges are lightly browned. Remove to wire racks.

YIELD: ABOUT 10-1/2 DOZEN.

A hint of orange and a sprinkling of spices lend old-fashioned goodness to these delightful treats. The logs are dipped in melted chocolate and sprinkled with nuts for a special look.

Taste of Home
Test Kitchen

dipped spice cookies

PREP: 25 MIN. BAKE: 10 MIN./BATCH + STANDING

1/2 tube refrigerated sugar cookie dough, softened
1/2 cup all-purpose flour
1/4 cup packed brown sugar
1 tablespoon orange juice
3/4 teaspoon ground cinnamon
1/2 teaspoon ground ginger
1/2 teaspoon grated orange peel
1/2 cup semisweet chocolate chips
4 teaspoons shortening
1/4 cup finely chopped walnuts

1 In a large bowl, beat the cookie dough, flour, brown sugar, orange juice, cinnamon, ginger and orange peel until combined. Shape teaspoonfuls of dough into 2-in. logs. Place 2 in. apart on ungreased baking sheets.

2 Bake at 350° for 8-10 minutes or until edges are golden brown. Remove to wire racks to cool.

3 In a microwave-safe bowl, melt chocolate chips and shortening; stir until smooth. Dip one end of each cookie into melted chocolate, allowing excess to drip off. Place on waxed paper; sprinkle with walnuts. Let stand until set.

YIELD: ABOUT 3-1/2 DOZEN.

triple-tier brownies

PREP: 15 MIN. BAKE: 30 MIN. + CHILLING

1 package fudge brownie mix (13-inch x 9-inch
pan size)
1 package (11-1/2 ounces) milk chocolate chips
1 cup peanut butter
3 cups crisp rice cereal
1 can (16 ounces) cream cheese frosting
1 cup salted peanuts, chopped

1 Prepare and bake brownie mix according to
package directions, using a greased 13-in.
x 9-in. baking pan. Cool on a wire rack.

2 In a large saucepan, combine chocolate chips
and peanut butter. Cook over low heat for
4-5 minutes or until blended, stirring occasionally.
Stir in cereal; set aside.

3 Spread frosting over brownies. Sprinkle with
peanuts. Spread with peanut butter mixture.
Chill for 30 minutes or until set before cutting.
Store in the refrigerator.

YIELD: ABOUT 5 DOZEN.

cranberry crispies

PREP: 10 MIN. BAKE: 10 MIN./BATCH

At holiday rush time, you can't go wrong with these simple cookies. They're a snap to stir up with a boxed quick bread mix, and they bake up crisp and delicious.

LaVern Kraft, Lytton, Iowa

1 package (15.6 ounces) cranberry-orange quick bread mix
1/2 cup butter, melted
1/2 cup finely chopped walnuts
1 egg
1/2 cup dried cranberries

1 In a large bowl, combine the bread mix, butter, walnuts and egg. Stir in cranberries. Roll into 1-1/4-in. balls.

2 Place 3 in. apart on ungreased baking sheets. Flatten to 1/8-in. thickness with a glass dipped in sugar. Bake at 350° for 10-12 minutes or until light golden brown. Remove to wire racks to cool.

YIELD: 2-1/2 DOZEN.

These cookies are always a hit. One family even said they became a new staple in their home after I'd shared some with them.

Terri Keeney, Greeley, Colorado

chocolate peanut butter bites

PREP: 20 MIN. + COOLING

2/3 cup sweetened condensed milk
1/3 cup creamy peanut butter
1/2 teaspoon vanilla extract
1 cup biscuit/baking mix
1/3 cup semisweet chocolate chips

1 In a small bowl, beat the milk, peanut butter and vanilla until smooth. Add biscuit mix just until blended. Fold in chocolate chips.

2 Drop by rounded tablespoonfuls 2 in. apart onto ungreased baking sheets. Bake at 375° for 10-12 minutes or until edges are lightly browned. Cool for 2 minutes before removing to wire racks.

YIELD: 14 COOKIES.

EDITOR'S NOTE: Reduced-fat or generic brands of peanut butter are not recommended for this recipe.

TIP

For even baking, it's important that you make cookies the same size. For drop cookies, use a teaspoon or tablespoon from your flatware set or a small ice cream scoop.

mint-topped chocolate cookies

PREP: 20 MIN. BAKE: 10 MIN./BATCH + COOLING

1 package (18-1/4 ounces) devil's food cake mix
1/2 cup shortening
2 eggs
1 tablespoon water
Confectioners' sugar
40 chocolate-covered thin mints

1 In a large bowl, combine the cake mix, shortening, eggs and water. Shape into 1-in. balls; roll in confectioners' sugar.

2 Place 2 in. apart on ungreased baking sheets. Bake at 350° for 8-10 minutes or until slightly firm to the touch. Place a mint on each cookie; remove to wire racks to cool.

YIELD: 40 COOKIES.

EDITOR'S NOTE: These cookies were tested with Necco Thin Mints. They can be found at Walgreens stores.

TIP

Let baking sheets cool before placing the next batch of cookie dough on them; otherwise, the heat from the baking sheet will soften the dough causing the cookies to spread.

caramel pecan brownies

PREP: 25 MIN. BAKE: 20 MIN. + COOLING

A dressed-up cake mix turns into a pan of delightful brownies in no time!

Char Letavish, Woodhaven, Michigan

- 1 package (18-1/4 ounces) German chocolate cake mix
- 3/4 cup butter, melted
- 1 can (5 ounces) evaporated milk, divided
- 75 caramels
- 1 cup chopped pecans
- 1 cup (6 ounces) semisweet chocolate chips

1 In a large bowl, combine the cake mix, butter and 1/3 cup milk. Spread half of the mixture into a greased 13-in. x 9-in. baking pan. Bake at 350° for 15 minutes.

2 Meanwhile, in a microwave, heat caramels and remaining milk, uncovered, on high for 2-3 minutes or until caramels are melted; stir until smooth. Pour over crust. Sprinkle with pecans and chocolate chips. Drop reserved cake mixture by tablespoonfuls over the top.

3 Bake for 10 minutes; remove from the oven and smooth top. Bake 10-15 minutes longer or until top appears dry and is lightly browned. Cool on a wire rack. Cut into bars.

YIELD: 4 DOZEN.

EDITOR'S NOTE: This recipe was tested in a 1,100-watt microwave.

For a dessert or bake sale contribution, this recipe is ideal. A packaged brownie mix is jazzed up with two kinds of frosting, creating a two-toned treat with a luscious look and sweet taste.

Jean Kolessar, Orland Park, Illinois

double frosted brownies

PREP: 15 MIN. + CHILLING BAKE: 25 MIN. + COOLING

- 1 package fudge brownie mix (13-inch x 9-inch pan size)
- 1/2 cup butter, softened
- 1-1/2 cups confectioners' sugar
- 2 tablespoons instant vanilla pudding mix
- 2 to 3 tablespoons 2% milk
- 1 can (16 ounces) chocolate fudge frosting

1 Prepare brownie mix according to package directions. Spread the batter into a greased 13-in. x 9-in. baking pan. Bake at 350° for 25-30 minutes or until a toothpick inserted 2 in. from side of pan comes out clean. Cool completely on a wire rack.

2 In a large bowl, beat the butter, sugar and pudding mix until blended. Add enough milk to achieve spreading consistency. Frost brownies. Cover and refrigerate for 30 minutes.

3 Spread with fudge frosting. Cut into bars. Store in the refrigerator.

YIELD: 3 DOZEN.

peanut butter fudge bars

PREP: 20 MIN. BAKE: 20 MIN.

I rely on a cake mix and other pantry staples to make these rich crumb-topped treats.

Peggy Murray, Enfield, Maine

1 package (18-1/4 ounces) yellow cake mix
1 cup creamy peanut butter
1/2 cup canola oil
1 egg
1 can (14 ounces) sweetened condensed milk
1 cup (6 ounces) semisweet chocolate chips
2 tablespoons butter

1 In a large bowl, combine the cake mix, peanut butter, oil and egg until well blended. Press two-thirds of the mixture into a greased 13-in. x 9-in. baking pan. Bake at 350° for 10 minutes. Cool on a wire rack for 5 minutes.

2 In a heavy saucepan, heat the milk, chocolate chips and butter over low heat; stir until smooth. Pour over crust. Sprinkle with remaining crumb mixture.

3 Bake for 20-25 minutes longer or until golden brown. Cool on a wire rack. Cut into bars.

YIELD: 2-1/2 DOZEN.

EDITOR'S NOTE: Reduced-fat or generic brands of peanut butter are not recommended for this recipe.

Oatmeal and cherries add extra flavor and a special touch to this one-of-a-kind chocolate-chip cookie dessert. My kids help me create this, and it's so good.

Richelle White, Adair, Oklahoma

cherry oatmeal wedges

PREP/TOTAL TIME: 25 MIN.

1 tube (16-1/2 ounces) refrigerated chocolate chip cookie dough
3/4 cup old-fashioned oats
1 can (21 ounces) cherry pie filling

1 In a large bowl, combine cookie dough and oats. Press onto an ungreased 12-in. pizza pan.

2 Bake at 350° for 14-16 minutes or until golden brown. Cool on a wire rack for 5 minutes. Cut into wedges; top with pie filling.

YIELD: 12 SERVINGS.

grandma's oatmeal cookies

PREP: 15 MIN. BAKE: 15 MIN./BATCH

For a large batch of cookies that don't require much time in the kitchen, consider these down-home snacks. Ever since my husband's grandmother gave me the unique recipe, it's the only one I use when baking cookies. The pudding mix makes them particularly chewy.

Donna Trumbauer, Coopersburg, Pennsylvania

2 cups butter, softened
1-1/2 cups packed brown sugar
1/2 cup sugar
4 eggs
7 cups quick-cooking oats
2-1/2 cups all-purpose flour
1 package (5.1 ounces) instant vanilla
    pudding mix
2 teaspoons baking soda

1 In a large bowl, cream butter and sugars until light and fluffy. Add eggs, one at a time, beating well after each addition. Combine the oats, flour, pudding mix and baking soda; gradually add to the cream mixture and mix well.

2 Drop by heaping tablespoonfuls 2 in. apart onto lightly greased baking sheets. Bake at 375° for 12-14 minutes or until golden brown. Remove to wire racks to cool.

YIELD: 7 DOZEN.

Get ready to pour yourself a cup of tea, because you won't be able to resist sampling one of these cookies. Almonds add flavor and crunch to the simple strips that are dressed up with raspberry pie filling.

Taste of Home Test Kitchen

raspberry almond strips

PREP/TOTAL TIME: 30 MIN.

1/2 tube refrigerated sugar cookie
    dough, softened
1/3 cup all-purpose flour
1/4 cup finely chopped almonds
3 tablespoons raspberry filling
1/4 cup confectioners' sugar
1-1/2 teaspoons 2% milk
1/8 teaspoon almond extract

1 In a small bowl, beat the cookie dough, flour and almonds until combined. Roll into a 13-1/2-in. x 2-in. rectangle on an ungreased baking sheet.

2 Using the end of a wooden spoon handle, make a 1/4-in.-deep indentation lengthwise down the center of rectangle. Bake at 350° for 5 minutes.

3 Spoon raspberry filling into indentation. Bake 8-10 minutes longer or until lightly browned. Cool for 2 minutes. Remove to a cutting board; cut into 3/4-in. slices. Place on a wire rack.

4 In a small bowl, combine the confectioners' sugar, milk and extract until smooth. Drizzle over warm cookies.

YIELD: 16 COOKIES.

toffee-almond cookie slices

PREP: 15 MIN. BAKE: 40 MIN. + COOLING

1 package (17-1/2 ounces) sugar cookie mix
1/2 cup all-purpose flour
1/2 cup butter, softened
1 egg
1/3 cup slivered almonds, toasted
1/3 cup miniature semisweet chocolate chips
1/3 cup English toffee bits or almond
    brickle chips

1 In a large bowl, combine the sugar cookie mix, flour, butter and egg. Stir in the almonds, chocolate chips and toffee bits.

2 Divide dough in half. On an ungreased baking sheet, shape each portion into a 10-in. x 2-1/2-in. rectangle. Bake at 350° for 25-30 minutes or until lightly browned.

3 Carefully remove to wire racks; cool for 10 minutes. Transfer to a cutting board; with a serrated knife, cut each rectangle diagonally into 15 slices.

4 Place cookies cut side down on ungreased baking sheets. Bake for 15-20 minutes or until cookies are golden brown. Remove to wire racks to cool. Store the cookies in an airtight container.

YIELD: 2-1/2 DOZEN.

desserts

1. In a large bowl, combine the cake mix, eggs, orange juice and oil; beat on low speed for 30 seconds. Beat on medium for 2 minutes. Fold in blueberries and peels. Pour into two greased and floured 9-in. round baking pans.

2. Bake at 350° for 20-25 minutes or until a toothpick inserted near the center comes out clean. Cool for 10 minutes before removing from pans to wire racks to cool completely.

3. For frosting, in a small bowl, beat cream cheese and butter until fluffy. Add confectioners' sugar, orange juice and peels; beat until blended. Fold in whipped topping.

4. Spread frosting between layers and over the top and sides of cake. Refrigerate until serving.

YIELD: 12 SERVINGS.

My husband and I grow blueberries, and this cake is my favorite way to use them. Our fresh berries are enhanced by the light, citrusy cream cheese frosting.

Shirley Cooper, Salemburg, North Carolina

blueberry citrus cake

PREP: 40 MIN. BAKE: 20 MIN. + COOLING

1 package (18-1/4 ounces) yellow cake mix
3 eggs
1 cup orange juice
1/3 cup canola oil
1-1/2 cups fresh blueberries
1 tablespoon grated lemon peel
1 tablespoon grated orange peel
CITRUS FROSTING:
1 package (3 ounces) cream cheese, softened
1/4 cup butter, softened
3 cups confectioners' sugar
2 tablespoons orange juice
2 teaspoons grated orange peel
1 teaspoon grated lemon peel
2 cups whipped topping

coconut creme brulee

PREP/TOTAL TIME: 10 MIN.

There's always time for dessert, and this elegant, quick-to-fix treat is one I turn to regularly. After one bite, you may deem it a winner.

Gloria Jabaut, Red Bluff, California

2 refrigerated vanilla pudding snack cups (4 ounces each)
1 tablespoon sugar
2 tablespoons brown sugar
2 tablespoons flaked coconut
2 teaspoons butter, melted

1. Spoon pudding into two 6-oz. ramekins or custard cups. If broiling the custards, place ramekins on a baking sheet; let stand at room temperature for 15 minutes.

2. In a small bowl, combine the sugars, coconut and butter; sprinkle over pudding. Broil 8 in. from the heat for 2-3 minutes or until sugar is bubbly and golden brown. Serve warm.

3. If using a creme brulee torch, sprinkle custard with sugar mixture. Heat sugar with the torch until caramelized. Serve immediately.

YIELD: 2 SERVINGS.

almost homemade

peach-filled pastries

PREP: 20 MIN. + COOLING

1 sheet frozen puff pastry, thawed
1 egg white
1 tablespoon water
1-1/2 teaspoons sugar
1 can (21 ounces) peach or cherry pie filling
1/4 teaspoon almond extract
2 cups whipped topping

1 On a lightly floured surface, unfold pastry and roll to 3/8-in. thickness. Cut along fold seams into three pieces. Cut each piece in half widthwise; place on an ungreased baking sheet.

2 Beat egg white and water; brush over pastry. Sprinkle with sugar. Bake at 400° for 9-11 minutes or until golden brown. Cool on a wire rack.

3 Split each pastry in half horizontally. Combine pie filling and extract; spoon over bottom halves of pastries. Top with whipped topping and pastry tops.

YIELD: 6 SERVINGS.

banana split cheesecake

PREP: 35 MIN. + FREEZING

1 can (8 ounces) unsweetened crushed pineapple, divided
2 medium firm bananas, sliced
1 reduced-fat graham cracker crust (8 inches)
1 package (8 ounces) fat-free cream cheese
1-1/2 cups pineapple sherbet, softened
1 package (1 ounce) sugar-free instant vanilla pudding mix
1 carton (8 ounces) frozen reduced-fat whipped topping, thawed, divided
4 maraschino cherries, divided
1 tablespoon chocolate syrup
1 tablespoon caramel ice cream topping
1 tablespoon chopped pecans

1 Drain pineapple, reserving juice. In a small bowl, combine bananas and 2 tablespoons reserved juice; let stand for 5 minutes. Drain bananas, discarding juice. Arrange bananas over bottom of crust; set aside.

2 In a large bowl, beat the cream cheese and 2 tablespoons reserved pineapple juice. Gradually beat in sherbet. Gradually beat in pudding mix; beat 2 minutes longer. Refrigerate 1/3 cup pineapple until serving; fold remaining pineapple into cream cheese mixture. Fold in 2 cups whipped topping; spread evenly over banana slices. Cover and freeze until firm.

3 Remove from the freezer 10-15 minutes before serving. Chop three maraschino cherries and pat dry; arrange cherries and reserved pineapple around edge of pie. Drizzle with chocolate syrup and caramel topping. Dollop remaining whipped topping onto center of pie. Sprinkle with pecans; top with remaining cherry.

YIELD: 10 SERVINGS.

cranberry peach cobbler

PREP: 15 MIN. BAKE: 45 MIN.

This cobbler is nontraditional, but it will soon be at the front of your recipe list because it's an easy and tasty dessert. I like to serve it warm with ice cream.

Graciela Sandvigen, Rochester, New York

- 1/2 cup butter, melted
- 2 cans (29 ounces each) sliced peaches
- 1 package (15.6 ounces) cranberry-orange quick bread mix
- 1 egg
- 2 tablespoons grated orange peel, divided
- 1/3 cup dried cranberries
- 1/3 cup sugar

1 Pour butter into a 13-in. x 9-in. baking dish. Drain peaches, reserving 1 cup juice. Pat peaches dry. In a bowl, combine quick bread mix, egg, 1 tablespoon orange peel and reserved peach juice.

2 Drop batter by tablespoonfuls over butter; spread slightly. Arrange peaches over the top; sprinkle with cranberries. Combine sugar and remaining orange peel; sprinkle over peaches. Bake at 375° for 45-50 minutes or until golden brown.

YIELD: 12-15 SERVINGS.

Drizzled with melted chocolate, this frosty family favorite couldn't be much simpler to prepare.

Carol Marnach, Sioux Falls, South Dakota

chocolate chip cookie dessert

PREP: 25 MIN. BAKE: 15 MIN. + FREEZING

- 1 tube (16-1/2 ounces) refrigerated chocolate chip cookie dough
- 1/2 cup caramel ice cream topping
- 1/2 cup cold 2% milk
- 1 package (3.4 ounces) instant vanilla pudding mix
- 1 carton (8 ounces) frozen whipped topping, thawed
- 3/4 cup chopped nuts
- 3/4 cup English toffee bits or almond brickle chips
- 3 ounces semisweet chocolate, chopped
- 3 tablespoons butter

1 Let dough stand at room temperature for 5-10 minutes to soften. Press into an ungreased 13-in. x 9-in. baking pan. Bake at 350° for 14-16 minutes or until golden brown. Cool completely on a wire rack.

2 Spread caramel topping over crust. In a bowl, whisk milk and pudding mix for 2 minutes. Let stand for 2 minutes or until soft-set. Fold in whipped topping, nuts and toffee bits. Spread over caramel layer. Cover and freeze until firm.

3 In a microwave, melt chocolate and butter; stir until smooth. Drizzle over the pudding layer. Cut into squares.

YIELD: 16 SERVINGS.

No one will ever guess that I've cut some of the fat and calories in this smooth and creamy mint treat. For the holidays, it's fun to substitute 2 cups of crushed peppermint candy canes for the chocolate chunks.

Nancy Quelle, Cedar Rapids, Iowa

skinny mint-chip ice cream

PREP: 15 MIN. PROCESS: 20 MIN. + FREEZING

4 cups fat-free half-and-half
1 package (3.4 ounces) instant vanilla pudding mix
1 can (14 ounces) fat-free sweetened condensed milk
2 teaspoons mint extract
3 to 4 drops green food coloring, optional
1-1/2 cups semisweet chocolate chunks

1 In a large bowl, beat half-and-half and pudding mix on low speed for 2 minutes. Beat in the condensed milk, extract and food coloring if desired.

2 Fill cylinder of ice cream freezer; freeze according to manufacturer's directions. Coarsely chop

chocolate chunks if desired; stir into ice cream. Transfer to freezer containers. Freeze for 2-4 hours before serving.

YIELD: 1-1/2 QUARTS.

peanut butter cupcakes

PREP: 15 MIN. BAKE: 20 MIN. + COOLING

My family just loves these cupcakes, especially the subtle taste of peanut butter in the frosting. Chocolate frosting is an equally delicious option.

Alyce Wyman, Pembina, North Dakota

1 package (18-1/4 ounces) white cake mix
18 miniature peanut butter cups
1-1/3 cups prepared vanilla frosting
2 tablespoons creamy peanut butter

1 Prepare cake mix according to package directions. Spoon about 2 tablespoons of batter into each paper-lined muffin cup. Place a peanut butter cup in each; fill two-thirds full with remaining batter.

2 Bake at 350° for 20-25 minutes or until lightly browned and a toothpick inserted in cupcake comes out clean. Cool for 10 minutes before removing to wire racks to cool completely.

3 In a small bowl, combine frosting and peanut butter until smooth. Frost cupcakes.

YIELD: 1-1/2 DOZEN.

icy summer treats dessert

PREP/TOTAL TIME: 10 MIN.

Kids will just love these cool and refreshing snacks on hot summer days.

Darlene Brenden, Salem, Oregon

1 cup sugar

1 package (3 ounces) berry blue gelatin

1 package (.13 ounce) unsweetened berry blue soft drink mix

2 cups boiling water

2 cups cold water

10 disposable plastic cups (5 ounces)

Heavy-duty aluminum foil

10 Popsicle sticks

1 In a large bowl, combine the sugar, gelatin and drink mix in boiling water until dissolved. Add cold water. Pour into cups. Cover each cup with foil; insert sticks through foil (foil will hold sticks upright). Place in a 13-in. x 9-in. pan; freeze. To serve, remove foil and plastic cups.

YIELD: 10 SERVINGS.

The fantastic flavor from this pie comes from butterscotch pudding and canned pumpkin, which work surprisingly well together. Kids will go wild over the cream cheese layer!

Liz Raisig, New York, New York

gingersnap pumpkin pie

PREP: 30 MIN. + CHILLING

1-1/2 cups finely crushed gingersnaps (about 32 cookies)

1/4 cup butter, melted

4 ounces cream cheese, softened

1 tablespoon sugar

1-1/2 cups whipped topping

1 cup cold milk

2 packages (3.4 ounces each) instant butterscotch pudding mix

1/2 cup canned pumpkin

1/2 teaspoon pumpkin pie spice

1/2 teaspoon vanilla extract

1/4 teaspoon ground cinnamon

Additional whipped topping, optional

1 In a small bowl, combine cookie crumbs and butter. Press onto the bottom and up the sides of an ungreased 9-in. pie plate. Bake at 375° for 8-10 minutes or until crust is lightly browned. Cool on a wire rack.

2 For filling, in a small bowl, beat cream cheese and sugar until smooth. Fold in whipped topping. Spread over crust.

3 In a small bowl, beat milk and pudding mixes for 1 minute. Stir in the pumpkin, pie spice, vanilla and cinnamon. Spread over cream cheese layer. Cover and refrigerate overnight. Garnish with additional whipped topping if desired.

YIELD: 6-8 SERVINGS.

white chocolate mousse cherry pie

PREP: 1 HOUR BAKE: 15 MIN. + CHILLING

14 cream-filled chocolate sandwich cookies
3/4 cup chopped macadamia nuts
2 tablespoons butter, melted
FILLING:
1 tablespoon cornstarch
2 tablespoons water
1 can (21 ounces) cherry pie filling
1/2 teaspoon almond extract
WHITE CHOCOLATE MOUSSE:
1 cup cold 2% milk
1 package (3.3 ounces) instant white chocolate pudding mix
1 envelope unflavored gelatin
3 cups heavy whipping cream, divided
1/4 cup sugar
1/4 teaspoon almond extract
Chocolate curls, optional

1 In a food processor, process cookies and nuts until cookies are finely chopped. Add butter; cover and pulse until mixture resembles coarse crumbs. Press onto bottom and up sides of an ungreased 9-in. deep-dish pie plate. Bake at 350° for 8-10 minutes or until set. Cool on a wire rack.

2 For filling, mix cornstarch and water in a saucepan until smooth. Stir in pie filling. Bring to a boil; cook and stir for 1 minute or until slightly thickened. Remove from heat; stir in extract. Cool completely.

3 For mousse, in a large bowl, whisk milk and pudding mix for 2 minutes; set aside. In a small saucepan, sprinkle gelatin over 1/2 cup cream; let stand for 1 minute. Heat over low heat, stirring until gelatin is completely dissolved. Remove from the heat.

4 In a large bowl, beat remaining cream until it begins to thicken. Add sugar and extract; beat until soft peaks form. Gradually beat in gelatin mixture. Fold into pudding. Chill until slightly firm, about 30 minutes. Spread cooled filling into crust; top with mousse. Refrigerate for 2 hours or until firm. Garnish with chocolate curls if desired.

YIELD: 8-10 SERVINGS.

almost homemade

lemon-lime poppy seed cake

PREP: 20 MIN. BAKE: 40 MIN. + COOLING

There's plenty of lemon-lime flavor in this tender cake to please any citrus lover. Plus, it's a breeze to prepare.

Victoria Zmarzley-Hahn, Northhampton, Pennsylvania

1 package (18-1/4 ounces) yellow cake mix

1 package (3.4 ounces) instant vanilla pudding mix

1/4 cup poppy seeds

4 eggs

1/2 cup water

1/2 cup canola oil

1/4 cup lemon juice

1/4 cup lime juice

GLAZE:

1-3/4 cups confectioners' sugar

2 tablespoons lemon juice

2 tablespoons lime juice

1 In a large bowl, beat the first eight ingredients on low speed for 30 seconds; beat on medium for 2 minutes. Pour into a greased and floured 10-in. fluted tube pan.

2 Bake at 350° for 40-45 minutes or until a toothpick comes out clean. Cool for 10 minutes; remove from pan to a wire rack to cool completely.

3 In a small bowl, combine glaze ingredients until smooth; drizzle over cake.

YIELD: 12 SERVINGS.

mud pie

PREP: 15 MIN. + CHILLING

3 ounces semisweet chocolate, chopped

1/4 cup sweetened condensed milk

1 chocolate crumb crust (8 inches)

1/2 cup chopped pecans

2 cups cold 2% milk

2 packages (3.9 ounces each) instant chocolate pudding mix

1 carton (8 ounces) frozen whipped topping, thawed, divided

Coming from the South, we fell in love with chocolate pies filled with pecans. It could take all day to put together such a treat, but my version takes just 15 minutes of preparation before it's stored in the refrigerator until you're ready to serve.

Deboraha Woolard, Las Vegas, Nevada

1 In a microwave, melt chocolate; stir in condensed milk until smooth. Pour into the crust; sprinkle with the pecans.

2 In a small bowl, whisk milk and pudding mixes for 2 minutes. Let stand for 2 minutes or until soft-set. Carefully spread 1-1/2 cups of pudding mixture over pecans.

3 Fold 1/2 cup whipped topping into the remaining pudding mixture; spoon over pudding layer. Top with remaining whipped topping. Chill until set. Refrigerate leftovers.

YIELD: 8 SERVINGS.

special pleasure chocolate cheesecake

PREP: 20 MIN. BAKE: 40 MIN. + CHILLING

- 1 package (18 ounces) ready-to-bake refrigerated triple-chocolate cookie dough
- 1 package (8 ounces) milk chocolate toffee bits
- 1 package (9-1/2 ounces) Dove dark chocolate candies
- 3 packages (8 ounces each) cream cheese, softened
- 1 can (14 ounces) sweetened condensed milk
- 3/4 cup (6 ounces) vanilla yogurt
- 4 eggs, lightly beaten
- 1 teaspoon vanilla extract
- Whipped cream

1 Let dough stand at room temperature for 5-10 minutes to soften. Press nine portions of dough into an ungreased 13-in. x 9-in. baking dish (save remaining dough for another use). Set aside 2 tablespoons toffee bits for garnish; sprinkle remaining toffee bits over dough.

2 In a small microwave-safe bowl, heat chocolate candies at 70% power for 15 seconds; stir. Microwave in 5-second intervals until melted; stir until smooth.

3 In a large bowl, beat the cream cheese, milk and yogurt until smooth. Add eggs; beat on low speed just until combined. Fold in vanilla and melted chocolate. Pour over crust.

4 Bake at 350° for 40-45 minutes or until center is almost set. Cool on a wire rack. Refrigerate for 4 hours or overnight. Garnish with whipped cream and reserved toffee bits. Refrigerate leftovers.

YIELD: 24 SERVINGS.

strawberry trifle

PREP/TOTAL TIME: 30 MIN.

As pretty as a picture, this quick-and-easy trifle makes any gathering seem special. Busy cooks will appreciate the make-ahead convenience and the use of purchased pound cake.

Crystal Edwards, Van Alstyne, Texas

2 cups cold 2% milk

1 package (3.4 ounces) instant cheesecake or vanilla pudding mix

1 package (8 ounces) cream cheese, softened

2 teaspoons almond extract

1 carton (8 ounces) frozen whipped topping, thawed, divided

2 cups sliced fresh strawberries

1 carton (13-1/2 ounces) strawberry glaze

1 loaf (10-3/4 ounces) frozen pound cake, thawed and cubed

1/4 cup slivered almonds, toasted

1 In a large bowl, whisk milk and pudding mix for 2 minutes. Let stand for 2 minutes or until soft-set. Beat in cream cheese and extract until smooth. Fold in 2 cups whipped topping.

2 In a small bowl, gently combine strawberries and glaze. In a 3-qt. trifle bowl, layer with half the cake cubes, pudding mixture and strawberry mixture. Repeat layers. Garnish with remaining whipped topping. Refrigerate until serving. Sprinkle with almonds just before serving.

YIELD: 12 SERVINGS.

A pantry staple—biscuit mix—is the starting point for this classic dessert. Liven it up with miniature chocolate chips and the summer's freshest berries and fruits.

Taste of Home Test Kitchen

three-fruit shortcakes

PREP/TOTAL TIME: 30 MIN.

1 cup biscuit/baking mix

1/4 cup miniature semisweet chocolate chips

1/3 cup 2% milk

1/2 teaspoon sugar

1 cup sliced fresh strawberries

1 cup sliced peeled peaches

1 cup fresh blueberries

1 teaspoon lemon juice

1 tablespoon confectioners' sugar

Whipped topping, optional

1 In a small bowl, combine baking mix and chocolate chips; stir in milk until a soft dough forms. Drop by tablespoonfuls 2 in. apart onto a baking sheet coated with cooking spray. Sprinkle with sugar.

2 Bake at 425° for 12-14 minutes or until golden brown. Remove to a wire rack to cool.

3 In another large bowl, combine fruits and lemon juice. Add confectioners' sugar; toss to coat. Split shortcakes horizontally in half; spoon fruit over bottom halves. Replace tops. Serve with whipped topping if desired.

YIELD: 4 SERVINGS.

2 Stir in glaze mixture; fold in whipped topping and strawberries. Cover and refrigerate overnight. Garnish with additional strawberries if desired.

YIELD: 80 SERVINGS.

orange bundt cake

PREP: 15 MIN. BAKE: 40 MIN. + COOLING

This pretty cake comes together quickly with a boxed mix. Fat-free mayonnaise replaces the heavy oils, and the citrus glaze is a tasty touch.

Deborah Williams, Peoria, Arizona

1 package (18-1/4 ounces) yellow cake mix
1 envelope whipped topping mix (Dream Whip)
3/4 cup orange juice
3/4 cup fat-free mayonnaise
3 eggs
1 tablespoon grated orange peel
GLAZE:
1-1/2 cups confectioners' sugar
2 tablespoons orange juice

1 In a large bowl, combine the cake mix, whipped topping mix, orange juice, mayonnaise, eggs and orange peel; beat on low speed for 30 seconds. Beat on medium for 2 minutes. Coat a 10-in. fluted tube pan with cooking spray and dust with flour. Pour batter into pan.

2 Bake at 350° for 40-45 minutes or until a toothpick inserted near the center comes out clean. Cool for 10 minutes before removing from pan to a wire rack to cool completely. Combine the glaze ingredients; drizzle over cake.

YIELD: 14 SERVINGS.

This recipe from my sister-in-law was a big hit at our parents' 50th wedding anniversary. Guests always seem to enjoy the fluffy texture and the tangy flavor from the sliced berries.

Cindy Borg, Newfolden, Minnesota

strawberry fluff

PREP: 20 MIN. + CHILLING

1 package (3 ounces) strawberry gelatin
2 cartons (13-1/2 ounces each) strawberry glaze
2 quarts buttermilk
4 packages (5.1 ounces each) instant vanilla pudding mix
4 cartons (16 ounces each) frozen whipped topping, thawed
4 quarts fresh strawberries, sliced
Additional fresh strawberries, optional

1 In a small bowl, combine gelatin and glaze; set aside. In two large bowls, whisk buttermilk and pudding mixes for 2 minutes. Let stand for 2 minutes or until soft set.

TIP

To serve Strawberry Fluff to a crowd, use inexpensive small, clear plastic disposable drinking cups as individual serving dishes.

I love the combination of berries and lemon, and wanted to come up with a light, refreshing and tasty dessert that used them both. This yummy treat does the trick.

Anna Ginsberg
Austin, Texas

breezy lemon-berry dessert

PREP: 30 MIN. + CHILLING

- 2 envelopes unflavored gelatin
- 1/2 cup cold water
- 1 package (3 ounces) ladyfingers, split
- 1-1/2 cups fat-free milk
- 1/2 cup refrigerated French vanilla nondairy creamer
- 1 package (3.4 ounces) instant lemon pudding mix
- 1 carton (12 ounces) frozen reduced-fat whipped topping, thawed, divided
- 3 cups mixed fresh berries
- 2 cups sliced fresh strawberries

1 In a small saucepan, sprinkle gelatin over cold water; let stand for 1 minute. Cook over low heat, stirring until gelatin is completely dissolved. Remove from the heat and set aside.

2 Cut the ladyfingers in half widthwise; arrange cut side down around the sides of an ungreased 9-in. springform pan. Place the remaining ladyfingers in the bottom of the pan (the bottom will not be completely covered).

3 In a large bowl, whisk the milk, creamer and pudding mix for 2 minutes. Let stand for 2 minutes or until soft-set. Stir in gelatin mixture. Fold in 3 cups whipped topping.

4 Spread 2 cups of filling evenly into prepared pan; top with mixed berries. Spread with remaining filling (filling will be higher than ladyfinger border). Cover and refrigerate for 5 hours or until set. Garnish with remaining whipped topping and the strawberries.

YIELD: 12 SERVINGS.

2 Bake at 350° for 35-40 minutes or until a toothpick inserted near the center comes out clean. Cool on a wire rack.

3 With a meat fork or wooden skewer, poke holes about 2 in. apart into cake. Slowly pour condensed milk and caramel topping over cake; sprinkle with two-thirds of the crushed candy bars. Spread with whipped topping; sprinkle with remaining candy bars. Refrigerate until serving.

YIELD: 18 SERVINGS.

blueberry swirl cheesecake

PREP: 15 MIN. BAKE: 35 MIN. + CHILLING

Convenient canned blueberry pie filling and a prepared graham cracker crust make this dessert extra easy.

Suzanne McKinley, Lyons, Georgia

- 2 packages (8 ounces each) cream cheese, softened
- 1/2 cup sugar
- 1/4 teaspoon vanilla extract
- 2 eggs, lightly beaten
- 1 graham cracker crust (9 inches)
- 1 can (21 ounces) blueberry pie filling, divided

1 In a large bowl, beat the cream cheese, sugar and vanilla until smooth. Add eggs, beating just until combined. Pour into crust. Drop 1/2 cup of pie filling by heaping teaspoonfuls onto the cream cheese mixture; cut through with a knife to swirl the pie filling.

2 Bake at 350° for 35-40 minutes or until center is almost set. Cool on a wire rack for 1 hour. Refrigerate for 2 hours. Top with remaining pie filling. Refrigerate leftovers.

YIELD: 8 SERVINGS.

I love how this cake comes together with a boxed mix, water and egg whites. The candy bars are a fun and decadent touch in a light cake.

Heather Dollins, Poplar Bluff, Missouri

caramel crunch cake

PREP: 15 MIN. BAKE: 35 MIN. + COOLING

- 1 package (18-1/4 ounces) devil's food cake mix
- 1-1/3 cups water
- 5 egg whites
- 1 can (14 ounces) fat-free sweetened condensed milk
- 1/2 cup fat-free caramel ice cream topping
- 5 fun-size Butterfinger candy bars, crushed
- 1 carton (8 ounces) frozen fat-free whipped topping, thawed

1 In a large bowl, combine the cake mix, water and egg whites; beat on low speed for 30 seconds. Beat on medium for 2 minutes. Pour into a 13-in. x 9-in. baking pan coated with cooking spray.

raspberry angel cake

PREP: 15 MIN. BAKE: 45 MIN. + COOLING

Not only is this a refreshing treat, but it's virtually fat-free and has no cholesterol.

Sheri Erickson, Montrose, Iowa

- 1 package (16 ounces) angel food cake mix
- 1/2 teaspoon almond extract
- 1/2 teaspoon vanilla extract
- 1 package (.3 ounce) sugar-free raspberry gelatin
- 1 package (12 ounces) frozen unsweetened raspberries, thawed
- 1 tablespoon sugar

1 Prepare cake batter according to package directions. Fold in extracts. Spoon two-thirds of the batter into an ungreased 10-in. tube pan. Add gelatin powder to remaining batter; drop by tablespoonfuls over batter in pan. Cut through with a knife to swirl.

2 Bake according to package directions. Immediately invert pan onto a wire rack; cool completely, about 1 hour. Carefully run a knife around sides of pan to remove cake. Cut into slices.

3 Combine raspberries and sugar; serve over cake.

YIELD: 12 SERVINGS.

This scrumptious pie is sprinkled with a crunchy streusel topping.

Billie Moss, Walnut Creek, California

peanut butter crumb apple pie

PREP: 10 MIN. BAKE: 20 MIN. + COOLING

- 1 can (21 ounces) apple pie filling
- 1 teaspoon lemon juice
- 1 pastry shell (9 inches), baked
- 1/2 cup all-purpose flour
- 1/3 cup packed brown sugar
- 1 to 3 teaspoons grated lemon peel
- 1/2 teaspoon ground cinnamon
- 1/4 teaspoon ground nutmeg
- 6 tablespoons chunky peanut butter
- 2 tablespoons cold butter

1 In a bowl, combine pie filling and juice; spoon into pastry shell. In a bowl, combine the next five ingredients; cut in peanut butter and butter until crumbly. Sprinkle over filling.

2 Bake at 400° for 20-22 minutes or until topping is lightly browned. Cool on a wire rack.

YIELD: 6-8 SERVINGS.

Lemonade concentrate and lemon juice give this special pie an excellent citrus flavor. I also like to add some lemon zest on top of the meringue.

Kay Seiler
Grennville, Ohio

lemonade meringue pie

PREP: 30 MIN. + STANDING BAKE: 15 MIN. + CHILLING

- 3 eggs, separated
- 1 package (4.6 ounces) cook-and-serve vanilla pudding mix
- 1-1/4 cups 2% milk
- 1 cup (8 ounces) sour cream
- 1/3 cup thawed lemonade concentrate
- 1 teaspoon lemon juice
- 1/4 teaspoon cream of tartar
- 6 tablespoons sugar
- 1 pastry shell (9 inches), baked

1 Place egg whites in a small bowl; let stand at room temperature for 30 minutes.

2 Meanwhile, in a large saucepan, combine the pudding mix, milk and sour cream until smooth.

Cook and stir over medium heat until thickened and bubbly, about 5 minutes. Reduce heat; cook and stir 2 minutes longer. Remove from the heat. Gradually whisk 1 cup hot filling into egg yolks; return all to the pan. Bring to a gentle boil; cook and stir for 2 minutes. Remove from the heat. Gently stir in lemonade concentrate; keep warm.

3 Add lemon juice and cream of tartar to egg whites; beat on medium speed until soft peaks form. Gradually beat in sugar, 1 tablespoon at a time, on high until stiff glossy peaks form and sugar is dissolved.

4 Pour warm filling into pastry shell. Spread meringue over filling, sealing edges to pastry. Bake at 350° for 15-20 minutes or until meringue is golden brown. Cool on a wire rack for 1 hour. Refrigerate for at least 3 hours before serving.

YIELD: 6-8 SERVINGS.

almost homemade

frosty pistachio delight

PREP: 25 MIN. + FREEZING

I love the simple make-ahead convenience of this refreshing dessert drizzled with fudge topping. Since I can make this the night before and then freeze it, it gives me time to work on all those last-minute dinner details!

Sandie Davenport, Farmer City, Illinois

2-1/2 cups chocolate graham cracker crumbs

2/3 cup butter, melted

1 carton (1-3/4 quarts) vanilla ice cream, softened

2 packages (3.4 ounces each) instant pistachio pudding mix

1 cup plus 2 tablespoons pistachios, chopped, divided

3 drops green food coloring, optional

1 carton (8 ounces) frozen whipped topping, thawed

1 jar (11-3/4 ounces) hot fudge ice cream topping, warmed

1 In a small bowl, combine cracker crumbs and butter. Press into a greased 13-in. x 9-in. baking dish. Bake at 350° for 7-9 minutes or until set. Cool on a wire rack.

2 In a large bowl, combine the ice cream, pudding mixes, 1 cup pistachios and food coloring if desired. Fold in whipped topping. Spread over crust. Cover and freeze for at least 4 hours.

3 Remove from the freezer 10 minutes before serving. Drizzle with fudge topping; sprinkle with remaining pistachios.

YIELD: 15 SERVINGS.

This is one of my favorite treats. I took it to a family reunion, and everyone couldn't stop talking about how much they loved it.

Jessie Bradley, Bella Vista, Arkansas

delicious angel food dessert

PREP: 20 MIN. + CHILLING

2 cans (20 ounces each) unsweetened crushed pineapple, drained

4 medium firm bananas, sliced

1 loaf-shaped angel food cake (10-1/2 ounces), cut into 1-inch cubes

3 cups cold fat-free milk

2 packages (1 ounce each) sugar-free instant vanilla pudding mix

1 carton (8 ounces) frozen reduced-fat whipped topping, thawed

1/3 cup chopped pecans, toasted

1 Place the pineapple in a large bowl; gently fold in bananas. Place cake cubes in a 13-in. x 9-in. dish. Spoon fruit over cake.

2 In another large bowl, whisk milk and pudding mixes for 2 minutes. Let stand for 2 minutes or until soft-set. Spread over fruit. Carefully spread whipped topping over pudding. Sprinkle with pecans. Cover and refrigerate for at least 2 hours before serving.

YIELD: 15 SERVINGS.

Everyone will love finding the delicious goodie inside these tender treats! I tried this recipe at our teenager's New Year's Eve party—it was a hit.

Joyce Platfoot, Wapakoneta, Ohio

crescent bundle surprises

PREP/TOTAL TIME: 30 MIN.

1 tube (8 ounces) refrigerated crescent rolls
8 fun-size Snickers candy bars, halved
1/4 cup cream cheese frosting

1 Separate crescent dough into eight triangles; cut each in half, forming two triangles. Place a candy bar half on each triangle. Fold dough over candy and pinch corners together to seal. Place on an ungreased baking sheet.

2 Bake at 375° for 15-18 minutes or until golden. Remove to a wire rack. Cut a small hole in the corner of a resealable plastic bag. Fill bag with frosting; pipe over rolls.

YIELD: 16 SERVINGS.

apple turnovers

PREP: 25 MIN. BAKE: 15 MIN.

I had a package of puff pastry in my freezer and mentioned to a friend that I'd like to make apple turnovers. She shared a recipe that I adapted for the puff pastry. These turnovers were fabulous on my first try!

Coleen Cavallaro, Oak Hill, New York

1/3 cup sugar
1 tablespoon all-purpose flour
1/2 teaspoon ground cinnamon
4 cups chopped peeled apples
1 package (17.3 ounces) frozen puff pastry, thawed
TOPPING:
3 tablespoons butter, melted
2 tablespoons sugar
1/4 teaspoon ground cinnamon
Vanilla ice cream, optional

1 In a large bowl, combine the sugar, flour and cinnamon; add apples and toss to coat. On a lightly floured surface, roll out each pastry sheet into a 12-in. square. Cut each into four squares.

2 Spoon 1/2 cup apple mixture into the center of each square; fold diagonally in half and press edges to seal. Place on a parchment paper-lined baking sheet.

3 In a small bowl, combine the butter, sugar and cinnamon; brush over pastry. Bake at 400° for 12-16 minutes or until golden brown. Serve warm with ice cream if desired.

YIELD: 8 SERVINGS.

tiramisu parfaits

PREP: 40 MIN. + CHILLING

4-1/2 teaspoons instant coffee granules

1/3 cup boiling water

2 cups cold fat-free milk

2 packages (1 ounce each) sugar-free instant vanilla pudding mix

4 ounces fat-free cream cheese

1 package (3 ounces) ladyfingers, split and cubed

2 cups fat-free whipped topping

2 tablespoons miniature chocolate chips

1 teaspoon baking cocoa

1 Dissolve coffee in boiling water; cool to room temperature. In a large bowl, whisk milk and pudding mixes for 2 minutes. Let stand for 2 minutes or until soft-set. In another large bowl, beat cream cheese until smooth. Gradually fold in pudding.

2 Place ladyfinger cubes in a bowl. Add coffee; toss to coat. Let stand for 5 minutes.

3 Divide half of the ladyfinger cubes among six parfait glasses or serving dishes. Top with half of the pudding mixture, 1 cup whipped topping and 1 tablespoon chocolate chips. Repeat layers. Cover and refrigerate for 8 hours or overnight. Just before serving, dust with cocoa.

YIELD: 6 SERVINGS.

raspberry apple cake

PREP: 15 MIN. BAKE: 30 MIN. + CHILLING

1/3 cup butter, softened
1/3 cup packed brown sugar
1 egg
1 cup all-purpose flour
1/2 teaspoon baking powder
1/4 teaspoon salt
1/4 cup seedless raspberry jam
1 can (21 ounces) apple pie filling
4 tablespoons sugar, divided
1/2 teaspoon ground cinnamon
1 cup (8 ounces) sour cream
1 teaspoon vanilla extract

1 In a small bowl, cream butter and brown sugar until light and fluffy. Beat in egg. Combine the flour, baking powder and salt; gradually add to creamed mixture and mix well.

2 Spread the batter into a greased 9-in. square baking pan. Bake at 350° for 20-25 minutes or until lightly browned.

3 Remove cake. Spread with jam and top with pie filling. Combine 1 tablespoon sugar and cinnamon; sprinkle over filling. Combine the sour cream, vanilla and remaining sugar; spread over top. Bake 10 minutes longer or until topping is set. Cool on a wire rack for 1 hour. Refrigerate for 3 hours or until chilled.

YIELD: 6 SERVINGS.

nutty chocolate cake

PREP: 30 MIN. BAKE: 25 MIN. + COOLING

I got the idea for this incredibly easy, yet impressive holiday dessert from a magazine. It's been a family favorite for several years. It is absolutely gorgeous on my buffet.

Linda DuVal, Colorado Springs, Colorado

1 package (18-1/4 ounces) chocolate cake mix
1 can (8 ounces) almond paste
1/2 cup butter, softened
1/2 cup heavy whipping cream
2 cups (12 ounces) semisweet chocolate chips
1 cup (8 ounces) sour cream
Dash salt
1/2 cup sliced almonds, toasted

1 Prepare and bake cakes according to package directions, using two greased 9-in. round baking pans. Cool for 10 minutes before removing from pans to wire racks to cool completely.

2 For filling, in a small bowl, beat almond paste and butter until smooth. Gradually beat in cream until fluffy. Cut each cake layer horizontally in half; spread filling over bottom layers. Replace top layers.

3 In a microwave, melt chocolate chips; stir until smooth. Stir in sour cream and salt. Spread over the top of each cake. Sprinkle with almonds. Refrigerate leftovers.

YIELD: 2 CAKES (8 SERVINGS EACH).

Cherries and chocolate just naturally taste great together, but the combination is even better when enhanced by tender crepes and a creamy filling.

Mary Relyea, Canastota, New York

black forest crepes

PREP/TOTAL TIME: 20 MIN.

1 package (8 ounces) reduced-fat cream cheese, softened
1/2 cup reduced-fat sour cream
1/2 teaspoon vanilla extract
2/3 cup confectioners' sugar
8 prepared crepes (9 inches)
1 can (20 ounces) reduced-sugar cherry pie filling, warmed
1/4 cup chocolate syrup

1 In a bowl, beat the cream cheese, sour cream and vanilla until smooth. Gradually beat in confectioners' sugar. Spread about 3 tablespoons over each crepe to within 1/2 in. of edges and roll up.

2 Arrange the crepes in an ungreased 13-in. x 9-in. baking dish. Bake, uncovered, at 350° for 5-7 minutes or until crepes are warm. To serve, top each crepe with 1/4 cup pie filling and drizzle with 1-1/2 teaspoons chocolate syrup.

YIELD: 8 SERVINGS.

strawberry sorbet sensation

PREP: 20 MIN. + FREEZING

2 cups strawberry sorbet, softened

1 cup cold fat-free milk

1 package (1 ounce) sugar-free instant vanilla pudding mix

1 carton (8 ounces) frozen reduced-fat whipped topping, thawed

1 cup sliced fresh strawberries

1 Line an 8-in. x 4-in. loaf pan with heavy-duty foil. Spoon sorbet into pan; freeze for 15 minutes.

2 In a small bowl, whisk milk and pudding mix for 2 minutes. Let stand for 2 minutes or until soft-set. Set aside 1/2 cup whipped topping for garnish; refrigerate until serving. Fold remaining whipped topping into pudding; spoon over sorbet. Cover and freeze for 4 hours or overnight.

3 Remove the dessert from the freezer 10-15 minutes before serving; unmold onto a serving plate and remove the foil. Serve with the strawberries and reserved whipped topping.

YIELD: 8 SERVINGS.

fluffy lemon squares

PREP: 25 MIN. + CHILLING

These rich bars with a vanilla wafer crust get their sweet-tart flavor from lemon gelatin, sherbet and pudding mix. They're fun to make with my grandchildren, and they're delicious, too.

Joyce Speerbrecher, Grafton, Wisconsin

1-1/2 cups crushed vanilla wafers
    (about 45 wafers)
1/3 cup chopped pecans
6 tablespoons butter, melted
1/2 cup heavy whipping cream
2 packages (3 ounces each) lemon gelatin
1-1/4 cups boiling water
1 package (3.4 ounces) instant lemon
    pudding mix
1 pint lemon sherbet, softened

1 In a small bowl, combine the wafer crumbs, pecans and butter; set aside 1/4 cup for topping. Press remaining crumb mixture into an ungreased 11-in. x 7-in. dish. Cover and refrigerate for 30 minutes.

2 Meanwhile, in a small bowl, beat cream until stiff peaks form; set aside. In a large bowl, dissolve gelatin in boiling water. Add pudding mix; beat on low speed for 2 minutes. Add sherbet; beat on low for 1 minute or until soft-set. Gently fold in whipped cream.

3 Spread over crust; sprinkle with reserved crumb mixture. Refrigerate for 1 hour or until set.

YIELD: 12 SERVINGS.

raspberry swirl cupcakes

PREP: 20 MIN. BAKE: 20 MIN.

1 package (18-1/4 ounces) white cake mix
1/4 cup raspberry pie filling
1/2 cup shortening
1/3 cup 2% milk
1 teaspoon vanilla extract
1/4 teaspoon salt

I live on a farm and enjoy cooking and baking. These cupcakes are a favorite of mine because they taste great and they're so easy to do.

Christine Sohm, Newton, Ontario

3 cups confectioners' sugar
Fresh raspberries and coarse sugar, optional

1 Prepare and bake cake mix according to package directions. Fill paper-lined muffin cups two-thirds full. Drop 1/2 teaspoon of pie filling in the center of each; cut through batter with a knife to swirl.

2 Bake at 350° for 20-25 minutes or until a toothpick inserted in the cupcake comes out clean. Cool for 10 minutes before removing from pans to wire racks to cool completely.

3 In a large bowl, beat shortening until fluffy. Add the milk, vanilla, salt and confectioners' sugar; beat until smooth. Frost cupcakes. Garnish with raspberries and coarse sugar if desired.

YIELD: ABOUT 2 DOZEN.

ALPHABETICAL INDEX

This handy index lists every recipe in alphabetical order, so you can easily find your favorite recipe.

GENERAL INDEX

This index lists recipes by food category and major ingredient, so you can easily locate recipes that suit your needs.

almost homemade

almost
homemade